Political Institutions and Lesbian and Gay Rights in the United States and Canada

Lesbian and gay citizens today enjoy a much broader array of rights and obligations and a greater ability to live their lives openly in both the U.S. and Canada. However, while human rights protections have been exponentially expanded in Canada over the last twenty years, even basic protections in areas such as employment discrimination are still unavailable to many in the United States. This book examines why these similar societies have produced such divergent policy outcomes, focusing on how differences between the political institutions of the U.S. and Canada have shaped the terrain of social movement and counter-movement mobilization. It analyzes cross-national variance in public policies toward lesbians and gay men, especially in the areas of the decriminalization of sodomy, the passage of anti-discrimination laws, and the enactment of measures to recognize same-sex relationships. For political science, sociology, and queer studies alike, this book will prove vital as movements for lesbian and gay rights continue to recast the social landscape in North America and beyond.

Miriam Smith is Professor in the School of Public Policy and Administration at York University, Toronto, Canada. She is the author of *Lesbian and Gay Rights in Canada: Social Movements and Equality-Seeking, 1971–1995* (1999) and co-editor with Michael Orsini of *Critical Policy Studies* (2007).

Routledge Studies in North American Politics

Political Institutions and Lesbian and Gay Rights in the United States and Canada

Miriam Smith

Routledge
Taylor & Francis Group
New York London

First published 2008
by Routledge
270 Madison Ave, New York, NY 10016

Simultaneously published in the UK
by Routledge
2 Park Square, Milton Park, Abingdon, Oxon OX14 4RN

This edition first published in paperback in 2009.

Routledge is an imprint of the Taylor & Francis Group, an informa business

Typeset in Sabon by IBT Global.
Printed and bound in the United States of America on acid-free paper by IBT Global.

Library of Congress Cataloging in Publication Data
Smith, Miriam Catherine.
    Political institutions and lesbian and gay rights in the United States and Canada /
Miriam Smith.—1st ed.
        p. cm. — (Routledge studies in North American Politics ; 1)
    Includes bibliographical references and index.
    ISBN 978-0-415-98871-1
    1. Gay rights—United States. 2. Gay rights—Canada. 3. Gay men—Legal
status, laws, etc. 4. Lesbians—Legal status, laws, etc. 5. Same-sex marriage—
United States. 6. Same-sex marriage—Canada. 7. Sex discrimination—United
States. 8. Sex discrimination—Canada. 9. United States—Politics and
government. 10. United States—Politics and government. I. Title.
    HQ76.8.U5.S65 2008
    323.3'2640973—dc22
    2007051460

ISBN10: 0-415-98871-3 (hbk)
ISBN10: 0-415-80651-8 (pbk)
ISBN10: 0-203-89501-0 (ebk)

ISBN13: 978-0-415-98871-1 (hbk)
ISBN13: 978-0-415-80651-0 (pbk)
ISBN13: 978-0-203-89501-6 (ebk)

Contents

Preface

Over the last twenty years, scholars in the fields of American political development (APD) and historical institutionalism have introduced new ways of thinking about American politics. By asking the big questions about the historical trajectory of the U.S., scholars in these areas have deployed a macro-historical and macro-sociological lens, similar to that long used in studies of European political development or even in studies of development in the global south. Topics such as state-building (Skowronek 1982; Orren and Skowronek 2004), citizenship (R. Smith 1999), the development of the welfare state (Pierson 1994), the impact of business and labor organizing (Orren 1992), and, most recently, the gendered development of social policy (Mettler 1998) and the politics of race (Frymer 1999; Lieberman 2005; Lowndes, Novkov and Warren 2007) have taken the study of U.S. politics in new directions. The result has been the creation of a defined field of American political development, one that overlaps with historical institutionalism, which has also come into its own over the same period as an approach within the field of comparative politics. Historical institutionalism is distinguished by its attention to specific sets of propositions about the role of political institutions in structuring political life, the impact of institutional configurations and the legacies of previous policies on policy outcomes, and the role of time and timing in relation to long-term social and political processes (Pierson and Skocpol 2002).

This book draws on these approaches to explore the recent evolution of lesbian and gay politics and public policy, a topic that has not received a great deal of attention in either the APD or historical institutionalist literatures.[1] While recent scholarship has begun to incorporate gender and race into APD in a more structural and systematic way, the study of lesbian and gay politics in the U.S. has mainly been the province of sociologists studying social movements (Soule 2004; Kane 2003, 2007), political theorists considering queer exclusion (Phelan 2000, 2001), and literary theorists making gender trouble (Butler 1990). In political science, the empirical study of lesbian and gay politics has been dominated by studies of public opinion (e.g., Wilcox, Brewer, Shames and Lake 2007), legal and judicial behavior (Pinello 2003; Pierceson 2005) and interest group politics (Andersen 2005;

Engel 2007). Along with gun control and abortion, "gay rights" is often treated as a question of morality politics, that is, a question about which Americans have well-developed and seemingly immovable views of right and wrong, as a hot-button issue that is used by the Christian Right to mobilize its base, and as a public policy issue arena in which public opinion plays a key or even determinative part (Rom 2007; Lofton and Haider-Markel 2007).

In contrast, this study understands sexuality as a system of social power that structures gender relationships. States contribute very directly to the construction and production of this system by choosing to recognize (or not) specific gendered relationships and sexual preferences. While lesbian and gay rights might appear as a boutique issue that affects only a small group in society, a structural approach to gender and sexuality draws our attention to the fact that all public policies are gendered and sexed in particular ways. Heterosexuals and heterosexual relationships are part of the sex/gender system and benefit in specific material ways from the unequal power relationships that are encoded in public policy (Canaday 2003). Other topics in comparative public policy analysis such as health care or social policy may just as well be defined as issues of "morality politics" given that these topics concern fundamental questions of power, justice, and inequality. The tools of APD and historical institutionalism may be used to understand the development of the most recent period of U.S. public policy on lesbian and gay rights, just as they can be used to understand fiscal policy or welfare policy. States differ in the way they treat their lesbian and gay citizens and, like any other area of public policy, these differences can be described, understood, and explained as a task of critical comparative analysis. As this study will show, public opinion and political culture are important. However, a solid analysis of, and explanation of, lesbian and gay politics also requires that we pay attention to other factors. Notably, as historical institutionalists have suggested, public policies are shaped by the structure of political institutions and by the legacies of past policies; APD and historical institutionalist approaches also emphasize the importance of understanding the process of political change in terms of historical trajectories rather than through snapshots of the political world.

Building on these perspectives, I undertake a close comparison of lesbian and gay rights policies in the U.S. and Canada from 1969 to 2005, covering the period from the rise of the gay liberation movement through the *Lawrence* and *Goodridge* decisions in the U.S. in 2003 and the legalization of same-sex marriage in Canada in 2005. Historical institutionalist and APD scholarship emphasize the importance of critical junctures and turning points in which new policy pathways are set or new political orders are constituted. In Canada, in 1969, homosexual sodomy was removed from the Criminal Code while, in the U.S., an analogous development had to await the Supreme Court's ruling in *Lawrence*. Therefore, the starting point of the study is marked not only by the years of the emergence of the gay liberation and lesbian feminist movements but also by an important initial policy divergence between the two cases. This divergence persists over the entire time period covered in the study, which closes with the passage of statutory and constitutional bans on same-sex marriage in many states in the U.S. contrasted with the legalization of same-sex marriage in Canada in 2005. While public opinion and political cultural approaches have dominated the empirical study of lesbian and gay politics, the analysis here focuses on the role of political institutional structures and legacies of previous polities in shaping the policy trajectory on lesbian and gay rights over time. By using a macro-historical approach to exploring the shifts in these policies, the analysis highlights the extent to which institutional and policy legacies provide a context for political leadership and for social movement mobilization.

In comparing the two cases over time, I restrict the story to the key moments in policy development in the areas of the criminal regulation of homosexual sodomy, the development of anti-discrimination protections, and the emergence of same-sex marriage as dominant issues at the national level. The analysis moves between the federal and sub-state levels in explaining the trajectory of policy development. It is impossible to understand the evolution of lesbian and gay rights in these two federal systems without considering the role of the federal division of powers and the impact of judicial federalism in the U.S. (compared to its absence in Canada) in providing the vital background context for the agency of social movement organizations and political leaders, as well as for the decisions of judges and the process of legal mobilization. Because the study moves across the different scales of the political-institutional structure and because it emphasizes the importance of situating policy development in historical time, I do not necessarily provide detailed coverage of all aspects of these policy areas; rather, I look for the key developments and turning points that have dominated the evolution of lesbian and gay rights policy in national politics. There are other important areas of lesbian and gay policy that are not covered in this study including parenting, education, and hate crimes. These issues have not dominated political debates in the U.S. in the same way as sodomy laws or same-sex marriage. In order to cover a longer time period, the depth and breadth of coverage on each particular aspect of lesbian and gay rights have been curtailed.

Courts have played an important role in the evolution of lesbian and gay rights policies. Reading the role of courts through the lens of APD and historical institutionalism, I argue that, in order to understand the trajectory of policy development in this area, we need to step back from debates over judicial behavior and about why judges rule as they do. Rather, I build on recent developments in law and courts scholarship that have emphasized the political sources of judicial review and judicial supremacy and that have sought to understand the impact of courts from an inter-branch perspective, viewing the impact of courts in relation to other political institutions

(Hiebert 2002; Whittington 2007). The close comparison with Canada brings into stark relief the well-known features of the U.S. separation of powers system and the key role of inter-branch relationships in shaping public policy. In addition, the analysis highlights other aspects of U.S. political institutions that have received very little attention in the discussion of lesbian and gay rights, importantly, the impact of federalism, specifically, the relatively decentralized jurisdictions of key areas of lesbian and gay rights policy in the U.S. (compared to centralized jurisdictions in Canada); the impact of state constitutions (compared to their absence in Canada); and the role of judicial federalism (compared to its absence in Canada). By considering the separation of powers in the U.S. system vertically (the division between the federal government and the states) as well as horizontally (the separation of powers at both federal and state levels), the analysis situates courts at the vectors of these institutional structures and shows that these institutional structures help to determine the policy impact of court decisions. While my previous works explored how the judicialization of politics in Canada affected the development of the lesbian and gay movement (Smith 1999), the analysis of this volume focuses more specifically on the evolution of public policy, rather than on the evolution of social movement politics. Nonetheless, as I outline in the conclusion, this close comparison of these similar systems over a thirty-five-year time period suggests some further avenues for research with regard to how political institutions shape social movement strategies, organization, and claims-making.

In describing the evolution of these policies, I use the term "human rights" defined as both freedom from arbitrary interference by the state and freedom from discrimination by state or private actors based on race, national origin, ethnicity, citizenship status, religion, (dis)ability, sex, sexual orientation, gender identity, and other grounds. In the U.S., these rights are often referred to as "civil rights" while in Canada, the term "human rights" developed in the 1940s to distinguish the claims of minority groups from "civil liberties" groups, which were concerned with the liberal freedoms of speech, association and so forth (see Lambertson 2005). I prefer to use the term "human rights" in the very broadest sense because, for LGBT people, as for many other groups such as racialized minorities, discriminatory treatment spans the traditional civil liberties (e.g., freedom from arbitrary detention) and the traditional "civil rights" or "human rights" areas (non-discrimination in education, public accommodation and employment). Furthermore, a broad concept of "human rights" is used in other comparable jurisdictions such as the European Union (EU) and is often invoked in global politics and in the institutions of international law and practice (Lauren 1998). By using the term "human rights" in this broad sense, I wish to draw attention to the linkages among different forms of LGBT political struggle, to avoid artificial boundaries between public and private action, and to contest the boundary between "domestic" and "international" rights struggles.

In focusing on the evolution of human rights policies, this work is also based on the assumption that differences in law and policy at the level of the nation-state are important to the lives of lesbian, gay, bisexual, and transgender citizens and that understanding why some states embrace lesbians and gays as full citizens, as Canada is beginning to do, while other states deem lesbians and gays as "strangers" to citizenship, in Phelan's (2001) terms, is an important explanatory task. The incorporation of lesbians and gays into a normalized citizenship based on liberal equality has been critiqued by many activists in the LGBT communities in North America and the U.K. and by many scholars who have developed compelling analyses of the pitfalls of incorporation, particularly in terms of the relationship between policies such as same-sex marriage on one hand, and the neoliberal political project, on the other hand (Boyd and Young 2003; Richardson 2005; Shepard 2001). These critiques form a vital part of the democratic politics of LGBT communities, not to mention one of the most creative areas of LGBT scholarship; however, this book is not aimed at contributing directly to this debate. Rather, it is based on the assumption that it is important for LGBT (and allied) communities to understand and explain the origins and political effects of struggles over policies such as same-sex marriage or anti-discrimination laws, regardless of the legitimate debates within the community and among queer and queer-friendly scholars regarding the normative status of these goals (see also Egan and Sherrill 2005).

I hope that this work will contribute to the ongoing effort to bring the study of sexuality into the mainstream of APD and comparative politics so that we may better understand the complex relationships among race, class, gender, and sexuality in the trajectory of North American political development.

Acknowledgments

This book would not have been possible without the financial support of the standard research grant program of the Social Sciences and Humanities Research Council of Canada (SSHRC) and the teaching release time provided by SSHRC's 2006 Bora Laskin National Fellowship in Human Rights Research. SSHRC plays a very important role in the scholarly life of Canada (and beyond) and it is to be hoped that this collective commitment to independent, peer-reviewed research funding will be maintained. I would also like to acknowledge the support of the Canada–U.S. Fulbright Program during my period as Visiting Chair in Law and Society at New York University in the fall term, 2007. My exchanges with colleagues in New York were very helpful as I was putting the finishing touches on this manuscript.

I would like to acknowledge the diligent work of research assistants including Jennifer Dalton, Tammy Findlay, Mike Graydon, Piper Henderson, Sarah Lamble, and Kelly Pritchard. I appreciate the efforts of the lawyers and activists who took the time to share their views with me or with research assistants on this project and on my previous research dating back to 1995. The names of specific interview subjects are listed in the bibliography. Sage Publications gave permission to reprint from "Framing Same-Sex Marriage in Canada and the United States: *Goodridge, Halpern* and the National Boundaries of Political Discourse," *Social and Legal Studies* 16:1 (March 2007): 5–26 and from "Social Movements and Judicial Empowerment: Courts, Public Policy and Lesbian and Gay Organizing in Canada," *Politics & Society* 33: 2 (June 2005): 327–353. Cambridge University Press gave permission to reprint from "The Politics of Same-Sex Marriage in Canada and the United States," *PS: Political Science and Politics* XXXVIII: 2 (April 2005): 225–228.

A number of colleagues provided assistance with various aspects of the project including Sylvia Bashevkin, Jordi Díaz, Tina Fetner, and Lorna Weir. I owe a special debt of gratitude to Jacqueline Krikorian and Michael Orsini who provided invaluable comments on the draft manuscript and to Nancy Nicol with whom I have discussed many aspects of this material as part of our ongoing research collaboration. Ellen Andersen went above and beyond the call in providing comments on the final manuscript, and her assistance is very much appreciated. Conference papers based on this work were presented at the University of Kent's Research Centre on Law, Gender, and Sexuality, the Department of Political Science at the University of Victoria, the Canadian Studies Seminar at Harvard University, the Canadian Political Science Association, the American Sociological Association and the American Political Science Association and many colleagues provided useful reactions in those venues. The reviewers for Routledge provided excellent comments that challenged me to aim higher, and I thank them for their work. Ben Holtzman and the staff at Routledge were a pleasure to work with through each of the stages of bringing this book to fruition.

1 The Comparative Politics of Lesbian and Gay Rights

In February 2004, the newly elected mayor of San Francisco, Gavin New-som, surprised the city and the nation by announcing that he would autho-rize municipal authorities to issue marriage licenses to same-sex couples. Newsom decided to take the action after hearing President Bush oppose same-sex marriage during the January 2004 State of the Union address. On the first weekend, 2,000 couples lined up around the block at San Francisco City Hall to obtain a marriage license. Phyllis Lyon and Del Martin were the first to be married. The couple, who had been together for more than fifty years, led the fight for lesbian rights in the 1950s and 1960s, prior to the rise of the women's liberation and gay liberation movements, and had founded the lesbian organization Daughters of Bilitis in 1955 (National Organization of Women 2004). Of his decision to sanction same-sex marriage at San Francisco City Hall, Newsom commented, "While some may believe that separate and unequal institutions are acceptable, we will oppose intolerance and discrimination every step of the way. San Francisco is a city of tolerance and mutual respect and we will accept nothing less than full civil rights for all our residents" (San Francisco 2004). On August 12, 2004, the California Supreme Court invalidated Lyon and Martin's marriage, ruling that Newsom did not have the right to issue marriage licenses to same-sex couples. Of the Court's decision, Lyon remarked, "Del is 83 years old and I am 79. After being together for more than 50 years, it is a terrible blow to have the rights and protections of marriage taken away from us. At our age, we do not have the luxury of time" (cited in American Civil Liberties Union 2004).

At the same time, same-sex couples in Canada began challenging exclu-sionary marriage laws by applying for marriage licenses and by seeking alternative means of legalizing their unions. In January 2001, two same-sex couples were married at the Metropolitan Community Church Toronto (MCCT), a gay- and lesbian-friendly congregation, after the reading about banns of marriage. The weddings of Kevin Bourassa and Joe Varnell, and Elaine and Anne Vautour, were witnessed by a packed church and the nup-tials were reported in the Canadian and international media. The couples applied for the registration of their marriages and, when denied, filed a case against the federal government along with other same-sex couples, claiming that their equality rights had been violated. The MCCT also participated, arguing that its freedom of religion had been denied. In June 2003, the Ontario Court of Appeal ruled in favour of the couples and the church and ordered the issuing of marriage licenses to same-sex couples in Ontario and the registration of the weddings that had taken place at MCCT. These marriages provided the spark for the eventual passage of pan-Canadian legislation legalizing same-sex marriage in June 2005.[1]

The early 2000s were a critical juncture in lesbian and gay politics in the U.S. and Canada. In the 2004 U.S. elections, state constitutional amendments banning same-sex marriage in thirteen states were credited with having increased voter turnout among conservative Christians and with having helped to seal Republican electoral success.[2] The re-election of George W. Bush led to a new pessimism in national lesbian and gay organizing in the U.S., as national gay and lesbian groups such as the Human Rights Campaign and National Gay and Lesbian Task Force (Task Force) sought to regroup in the wake of the Bush victory and the passage of gay marriage bans. Despite the U.S. Supreme Court decision in *Lawrence v. Texas* in 2003, in which the court ruled that statutory bans on homosexual sexual behavior were unconstitutional, only 48% of Americans lived in jurisdictions with basic anti-discrimination protections for lesbian and gay men (Cahill and Tobias 2007: 44). In contrast, in Canada, by 2004, all jurisdictions prohibited discrimination based on sexual orientation, several prohibited gender identity discrimination,[3] and all provided clear procedures for bringing a claim of discrimination on these grounds against governments or in the private sector. Courts in the three most populous provinces had ruled in favour of same-sex marriage and the federal government had proposed legislation that would legalize same-sex civil marriage throughout Canada. While the rise of the Christian Right in the Bush era in the U.S. seemed to portend a return to traditional morality and a reassertion of the superiority of heterosexual family relationships, Canada was touted as a haven for gay "refugees" from the Bush administration and as a model of tolerance and diversity. While George W. Bush sought to reassert his opposition to same-sex marriage, especially after the victories for same-sex couples before state courts in Vermont and Massachusetts, politicians in the governing Liberal Party in Canada, regardless of their private doubts about same-sex marriage, were at pains to defer to the Supreme Court of Canada's view that lesbian and gay rights were protected in the Canadian Charter of Rights and Freedoms (Charter), Canada's constitutionally entrenched bill of rights. Even the leader of the opposition Conservative Party, Stephen Harper, who, in January 2006, became prime minister, was careful to couch his opposition to same-sex marriage in terms that were respectful of existing lesbian and gay rights protections in Canadian law. While Harper opposed same-sex marriage and indicated that he might reopen debate on the measure in

Parliament, he gave no indication that he opposed the existing recognition of same-sex relationships that had been previously implemented.

This book aims to explain the policy differences in human rights policies for lesbians and gays between the two countries. By international standards, the U.S. and Canada are similar systems, developed capitalist democracies and continental neighbours, sharing a common history and legal heritage. These societies have seen major changes in social, family and gender norms since the 1960s with the entry of women into the labour force, the advent of reproductive freedom for women, rising divorce rates and declining religiosity and church attendance. Both countries saw the rise of the gay liberation and lesbian feminist movements in the late 1960s and early 1970s, movements that challenged the patriarchal and heteronormative organization of gender, sexuality and the family. I ask why these two countries, which are similar in so many ways, at least compared to other countries and cultures around the world, have produced such different policy outcomes in the area of lesbian and gay rights protections. I outline the most important policy differences between the two countries, demonstrating the depths of the differences that currently divide policies and practices across the border and focusing on several centrally important areas of policy divergence: the criminal regulation of sodomy, anti-discrimination provisions, relationship recognition, and same-sex marriage. Inspired by studies of American political development and drawing specifically on historical institutionalist theory as well as on insights from sociolegal studies (especially, the legal mobilization literature), I argue that the legacies of previous policies as well as political institutional differences play a structuring role in this policy area, creating obstacles to policy change for the U.S. lesbian and gay movement while providing institutional opportunity for the gay and lesbian movement in Canada.

Political institutions do not create societal demands or social movements. However, institutions provide the strategic context for political actors, structuring the play of social forces in the policy process. Differences in core political institutions (federalism, separation of powers, and the role of courts) combined with differences in constitutional rules and practices between the two countries, have played a major role in facilitating very rapid policy change in Canada over the last decade while blocking policy change in the U.S. While courts have played a central role in policy changes in the U.S. and Canada, the impact of courts can only be assessed in relation to the larger political institutional structure of which they are a part. In Canada, since the entrenchment of a constitutional bill of rights (the Charter) in 1982, courts are uniquely powerful in part because they are not as hemmed in by institutional limits, as U.S. courts. The analysis shows how these limits and constraints play out over time in shaping the recent development of human rights policies in this area.

DIVERGING PATHS IN LESBIAN AND GAY RIGHTS

The U.S. and Canada increasingly demonstrate substantial differences in the extent to which lesbian and gay citizens are recognized in law and public policy. As Barry Adam has remarked, "legislation to bring gay and lesbian Americans full citizenship rights has been proceeding at a glacial pace," a situation he characterizes as yet another form of American exceptionalism (2003: 261). The most visible recent public issues—same-sex marriage—offer symbolic contrasts between the two countries. In the U.S., courts in Hawai'i (1993, 1996), Alaska (1998), Vermont (1999) and Massachusetts (2003, 2004) supported same-sex marriage, while, in Canada, court rulings in the three most populous provinces (Ontario, B.C. and Quebec) in 2002–2004 favoured same-sex marriage. Following these victories, especially the Ontario victory in the pivotal *Halpern v. Canada* (2003) case, in which the Ontario Court of Appeal ordered Toronto City Hall to issue marriage licenses to same-sex couples, the federal government crafted legislation to recognize same-sex marriage and referred the legislation to the Supreme Court of Canada for a ruling on its constitutionality. In 2004, the Court ruled that the legislation was constitutional and it was eventually passed during the minority Liberal government of Paul Martin in 2005, legalizing same-sex marriage throughout Canada.

In the U.S., reaction to court rulings led to a widespread movement to reassert the heterosexual nature of marriage. In 1996, Congress passed the Defense of Marriage Act (DOMA), which defines marriage as heterosexual for the purposes of federal law and policy[4] and which recognizes the right of states to deny the legality of marriages or civil unions between same-sex couples from other states.[5] Many states do not recognize same-sex marriages or civil unions performed in other states or jurisdictions. As of 2007, twenty-six states have passed constitutional amendments restricting marriage to opposite-sex couples while another nineteen states have passed legislation prohibiting same-sex marriage. Of these, seventeen states have laws or state constitutional amendments that might be interpreted to bar same-sex domestic partners (Human Rights Campaign 2007a). Only one state—Massachusetts—permits same-sex marriage. Four other states—Vermont, New Hampshire, New Jersey and Connecticut—recognize civil unions while other jurisdictions (Hawai'i, California, Maine, Washington) offer domestic partnership arrangements in which some rights are provided to same-sex couples (Lambda Legal 2006). Oregon is slated to institute the recognition of same-sex domestic partnerships in 2008. New York currently honors marriages contracted in other jurisdictions. However, as of 2007, legal challenges on same-sex marriage continue in California, Connecticut, and Iowa (Lambda Legal 2007).

Cross-national differences in human rights policies between the U.S. and Canada do not end on the same-sex marriage issue. In Canada, same-sex marriage is the culmination of a decade of legal and legislative change in the status of lesbian and gay citizens in Canadian society, changes that include broad measures recognizing same-sex relationships and parenting rights as well as systematic and constitutionally protected bans on public and private discrimination. In the United States, same-sex marriage is a potent issue for the lesbian and gay communities in part because, in many jurisdictions, it is legal to discriminate against lesbians and gays in areas such as employment and housing and, despite recognition of LGBT parenting rights in some states, the recognition of same-sex relationships is not nearly as widespread as it is in Canada. While anti-discrimination measures have been solidly in place for ten years in most Canadian jurisdictions, such measures are non-existent in many U.S. jurisdictions. In 2007, only eleven U.S. states prohibited employment discrimination against lesbians and gay men at the state level and anti-gay ordinances are often used to forestall discrimination protection in cities and states across the U.S. (Human Rights Campaign 2007b; see also Solokar 2001). Local and city level bans on sexual orientation discrimination are usually restricted to the public sector and often lack effective mechanisms for enforcement (Wald, Button and Rienzo 2000). Proposals at the federal level to add sexual orientation to the 1964 Civil Rights Act[6] have failed and, to date, the proposed federal Employment Non-Discrimination Act (ENDA) to ban discrimination in employment based on sexual orientation and gender identity has not been passed.[7] On the issue of relationship recognition for co-habiting same-sex couples, the Liberal government in Canada passed comprehensive federal legislation in 2000 to extend benefits and recognition to these couples, and this has been followed by many provinces and territories (Smith 2005a). In contrast, in the U.S., relationship recognition has developed piecemeal across public and private sector employers. In Canada, same-sex marriage is a final and to some extent symbolic step in a successful legal and political campaign for the recognition of same-sex partners in Canadian law and policy. In the U.S., same-sex marriage is seen as the means to the achievement of many of the parenting and relationship rights that are already available to lesbians and gay men in Canada (Moats 2004).

The U.S. and Canada also differ greatly with regard to the history of the criminalization of homosexual behavior. Until the U.S. Supreme Court's 2003 decision in *Lawrence*, sodomy laws prohibited a range of private sexual practices by heterosexuals and homosexuals, usually including oral and anal sex. In the modern era, such laws have been principally aimed at regulating same-sex sexual behavior. Prior to the *Lawrence* decision in 2003, four states—Texas, Kansas, Missouri, and Oklahoma—prohibited such consensual sexual behavior between same-sex couples while nine other states—Alabama, Florida, Idaho, Louisiana, Mississippi, North

Carolina, South Carolina, Virginia, and Utah (and Puerto Rico)—prohibited such behavior by opposite-sex or same-sex couples. In practice, such laws were rarely applied, although, when they were, they were applied almost solely to same-sex couples (Lambda Legal 2003). As I will discuss in detail later in the book, despite the lack of enforcement, sodomy laws in the U.S. had important effects on the overall shape of public policies toward lesbian and gay citizens. By stigmatizing lesbian and gay people as criminals, these laws impeded the passage and implementation of anti-discrimination laws and the extension of relationship recognition and parenting rights to lesbian and gay people in the U.S. In contrast, in Canada, homosexuality was "decriminalized" by the passage of an amendment of the criminal law in 1969. As part of a package of measures that loosened the divorce laws, homosexual sexual conduct between consenting adults twenty-one years of age or older was removed from the Criminal Code, the federal legislation that codifies most criminal law in Canada. The decriminalization measures followed British thinking about the regulation of homosexuality, stemming in particular from the findings of the U.K. Wolfenden Report (1957), which defined homosexuality as a private question that should not be regulated or criminalized by the state. The Canadian and British practice was not exactly liberatory for lesbian and gay people as it demarcated a realm of privacy that was not far removed from the realm of secrecy. Nonetheless, this change cleared the policy agenda in Canada for subsequent steps such as anti-discrimination measures and, eventually, relationship and parenting rights and same-sex marriage.

Therefore, in terms of same-sex marriage, relationship recognition, and the criminalization of homosexual sexual behavior, the U.S. and Canada present a very different picture of human rights for lesbian and gay citizens. No matter what point we choose in the timeline of policy change since 1969—the year in which homosexuality was decriminalized in Canada—Canada has provided more extensive recognition of lesbian and gay rights in law and policy than the United States. Explaining this consistent pattern of policy variation over almost forty years is the main aim of this book.

Some comparative analyses of this policy field have argued that lesbian and gay rights policies follow a predictable pattern, beginning with decriminalization, moving through anti-discrimination measures to protect lesbians and gay men based on their sexual orientation and, finally, the stage of relationship recognition (Merin 2002). Relationship recognition itself can be imagined on a continuum from recognition of same-sex partners by employers through to domestic partnership arrangements, recognition of same-sex relationships as equal to common law heterosexual relationships or through to same-sex marriage itself. Yet, there are a number of problems with positing such a clear teleology of the evolution of human rights policies. While Merin (2002) argues in favour of this pattern, his own analysis shows that the U.S. is far ahead of Europe in granting adoption and parenting rights to same-sex couples and to lesbian and gay parents despite the fact that, according to his linear view of the development of lesbian and gay rights, the U.S. should not grant more parenting rights than European countries, given that it introduced restrictive sodomy laws during the same period that these laws were eliminated in Europe. Merin argues that economic rights are easier to grant than family and domestic rights; yet, in the case of Canada, economic and family rights have been granted while certain rights regarding the equalization of the age of consent for sexual activity have not been changed. In fact, in Canada, following the recognition of same-sex marriage, new campaigns were underway to create a uniform age of consent and to oppose policy proposals from Canada's Conservative government, elected in 2006, for increasing the age of consent for heterosexual and homosexual sexual activity. Therefore, the argument that economic benefits are easier to grant than family benefits does not hold up to comparative analysis. Although the sodomy laws in the U.S. have had a shaping effect on lesbian and gay politics in the U.S., decriminalization is a complex policy issue and not a simple one-time policy change.

AMERICAN POLITICAL DEVELOPMENT AND HISTORICAL INSTITUTIONALISM

My approach to explaining and interpreting these profound policy differences draws on the developing theoretical traditions of American political development and historical institutionalism, which emphasize the evolution of large-scale political and social changes over longer historical periods. In contrast to political cultural and public opinion approaches, historical institutionalism specifically suggests that the organization of social forces is shaped by institutional factors and by the legacies of previous policies (Pierson and Skocpol 2002; see also Pierson 2004). In thinking about policy divergence in this area, historical institutionalists start with state structures, with the field of political institutions and the legacies of previous policies, to explain divergent policy outcomes, whether between countries or between jurisdictions. That is, rather than focusing on public opinion, political culture, or political economy, historical institutionalists treat the state in the Weberian tradition as an independent player and not simply as the passive reflection of the play of social forces, however conceived (Skocpol 1985; see also Graefe 2007). Despite recent debates on the decline of the state in the era of globalization, the rise of Foucauldian approaches to understanding power beyond formal political institutions and in using governmentality as a method of policy analysis (Murray 2007), and the turn to constructivist, discursive and cultural approaches to public policy (Fischer 2003), the analysis of the exercise of power through the formal institutions of the state is still central to the policy project of human rights. Even if shaped by international law and practice and by the pressures of a global civil society, in countries such as the U.S. and Canada, the state still holds a monopoly on the deployment of legitimate force and, hence, is the authoritative arena and fulcrum of human rights practices. Historical institutionalism has distinct advantages in providing explanatory leverage for this type of cross-national policy divergence in a specific policy sector and, as I will demonstrate at length, it has particular advantages in situating the role of courts in shaping policy outcomes.

In explaining Canada–U.S. policy divergence in the lesbian and gay rights area, the analysis will focus on the configuration of the executive, the legislature and the courts along with the meta-institutional rules or the constitutional rules that govern the interaction of these elements in shaping the terrain of political struggle. Policy legacies also exert important effects and recent historical institutionalist analyses emphasize the extent to which past policy choices in themselves constitute "institutions" (Pierson 2006). The legacies of previous policies exert influence on contemporary political battles by closing off certain policy choices or making them more difficult, less feasible, more expensive or difficult to envisage. Policy discussion never occurs on a blank slate; the terrain of policy discourse is shaped by the weight of current policies and by the political, bureaucratic, administrative, and legal apparatuses that have been created by them (Pierson and Skocpol 2002).

In this sense, historical institutionalism can be used to flesh out the concept of the political opportunity structure, a concept that was developed to explain the success and failure of social movements. While the political opportunity structure describes the obstacles and openings for social movement action that operate externally to the movement itself (Kitschelt 1986; Tarrow 1998; see also McCammon et al. 2001), historical institutionalism draws our attention to the role and impact of political institutional differences as a key aspect of opportunity for social movements (Smith 1999). Ellen Andersen (2005) has extended the concept of political opportunity to refer specifically to the range of legal opportunities that are open to social movement actors and, in her study of Lambda Legal, she argues that changes in the structure of legal opportunity help to explain the course of Lambda's evolving litigation. However, the concept of legal opportunity focuses principally on how the growth of the lesbian and gay community and changing public attitudes toward homosexuality influence the reactions of courts to lesbian and gay claims. A comparative analysis helps to sharpen our focus on the extent to which the growth of the lesbian and gay community or changes in public opinion are mediated by specific institutional structures. While Andersen's analysis points to the ways in which legal opportunities improved over time for Lambda Legal, in part because of Lambda's impact and agency as a political actor, the structure of legal opportunity cannot adequately explain cross-national differences. Legal opportunities expanded for the Canadian lesbian and gay movement over the same period and with very different policy results. A comparative perspective provides more explanatory leverage in understanding policy outcomes and, with very few exceptions (Merin 2002; Pierceson 2005) almost all of the scholarship on lesbian and gay litigation in the U.S. has taken the form of the single case study.

Studies of law and courts, especially in the legal mobilization tradition, have also explored the successes and failures of social movements (especially progressive social movements) in using the courts to achieve policy change. Work in this tradition has sought to understand the complex relationships between engagement with law as a political strategy and effective policy change, pointing to the potentially conservatizing effects of legal mobilization for social movement politics, as well as the institutional limits of legal change in the American political system (Scheingold 1974; Rosenberg 1991; McCann 1993; on Canada, see Mandel 1987 and Smith 1999). On one hand, claims for equal treatment under the law have a profound resonance in American politics because of the strength of rights-based liberalism and, as Stuart Scheingold (1974) pointed out in his classic work, the "myth of rights" can be usefully mobilized by progressive movements who may use the rights template to convert individual grievances into political mobilization and political action. At the same time, however, Scheingold cautioned the student of American politics that the quest for rights was a "myth" in part because of the many challenges and obstacles in making legal claims effective through the political system. Following on this, Gerald Rosenberg (1991) presented extensive evidence that the use of the courts by the civil rights movement had not led to social change. Importantly, Rosenberg emphasized the distance between court decisions (such as *Brown v. Board of Education*) and the implementation of judicial decisions and the achievement of social change and, in particular, the critically important distinction between judicial decisions—that is, decisions made by courts—and the actual implementation of judicial decisions.

Rosenberg's work implicitly casts a critical light on much of the dominant debate in law and courts scholarship in the U.S. that is concerned with explaining judicial decisions (e.g., Segal, Spaeth and Benesh 2005; see also Baum 2006). Such work has explained the decisions of judges using two dominant models—the attitudinal model and the strategic model, the latter based on rational choice theory. The attitudinal model explains the decisions of judges (especially at the Supreme Court level) with reference to their attitudes on policy issues, viewing judges as policy actors that seek to implement specific policy preferences. Strategic models explain decisions in terms of rational calculating by judges with a more diverse range of preferences, including the desire not to be overturned by higher courts or to see their decisions rolled back by legislatures (Epstein and Knight 1998). The strategic model introduces the notion of the judges' legitimacy as policy-makers into the equation; however, it defines and considers institutional legitimacy in terms of individual preferences rather than as a feature of institutional structures, in the historical institutionalist sense. Studies of attitudinal and strategic models have found that attitudes are a better predictor of Supreme Court decisions while strategic behavior better explains lower court decisions. Daniel Pinello has presented extensive evidence demonstrating the importance of judicial attitudes in lesbian and gay rights decisions, especially at the highest levels (Pinello 2003).

However, the comparison of lesbian and gay rights in the U.S. and Canada highlights the difficulties originally discussed by Rosenberg regarding the implementation of judicial decisions. While the explanation of judicial behavior is important and while attitudinal factors may greatly assist in explaining why a specific judge might rule in a specific way on a specific day, institutionalist analysis is better suited to the task of comparative policy analysis. Explaining judicial rulings in terms of judicial attitudes is a different task than explaining the overall impact of courts on the shape of public policy in a particular area. If our purpose is to explain policy outcomes rather than simply to explain specific court rulings, then historical institutionalism offers a powerful approach, one that allows us to embed judicial behavior within the larger structure of political institutions and to explore the extent to which contemporary policy and legal debates and discourse are shaped by past policies or policy legacies which have been institutionalized in ways that shape and structure the ongoing process of political conflict.

Recent historical work in "law and courts" scholarship draws on institutionalist approaches in understanding the relationship between courts and legislatures or the role of political parties in relation to key court judgments (Gillman and Clayton 1999). Further, like the analysis presented here, recent scholarship has emphasized the role of other political institutions in constitutional interpretation (Burgess 1992; Hiebert 2002) as well as the importance of political and even partisan support for judicial review and judicial supremacy (Whittington 2007). However, with few exceptions (e.g., Kahn 2006), this scholarship does not theorize institutions with the specific attention to institutional structures, policy legacies and historical timing in the sense that has been very specifically developed by scholars working especially in the area of comparative social policy and American political development (e.g., Pierson 1994; Maioni 1998; Skocpol 1992; see also Whittington 2000). Applied to the study of law and courts, historical institutionalism suggests that the role, power and impact of courts cannot be evaluated without reference to the institutional relationships within which courts function and to the historical pacing and timing of institutional and legal changes.

The structure of political institutions refers not only to the structure of the system of legal decision-making and the relationship between the different levels and jurisdictions of courts within a single country, but also to the structure of political institutions themselves, including the horizontal relationships among the judicial, legislative and executive branches and the vertical relationships among the three branches in a federal system of government. As Barnes (2007) has argued, inter-branch analysis of law and courts in relation to the broad field of American politics is relatively rare because of the complexities of the institutional system, including the role of judicial federalism and the separation of powers, which have led scholars to specialize in studies of particular levels of the judicial system, with much attention understandably focused on the U.S. Supreme Court. When inter-institutional and inter-branch relationships (especially between courts and legislatures) are assessed, this often occurs through the lens of rational choice theory and game theory models which analyze judicial behavior by assessing the decisions of judges in relation to other political actors such as legislatures or by evaluating the impact of judicial attitudes on court rulings. For example, a rational choice approach might stress that judges may forego their personal preferences and produce judicial decisions that are designed to prevent attacks from the legislature. Studies of the strategic decision-making of judges in a particular context have produced important analyses of particular cases (Epstein and Knight 1998; on attitudes, in general, see Segal, Spaeth and Benesh 2005).

This analysis shares with rational choice and game theory the assumption that courts are strategic actors. However, rather than conceptualizing individual judges as individual rational actors, the focus here is on the patterned interaction of courts as political institutions in relation to other political institutions. For historical institutionalists, institutions are structures of power, not simply the sum total of the preferences of individuals who hold roles in institutions, such as judges. Historical institutionalist approaches emphasize the importance of the long-term historical view in the evolution of policy outcomes, treating outcomes or policies as, in themselves, institutions that shape the behavior of political actors (Pierson 2006). Unlike Canadian dialogue or relational approaches (see Hiebert 2002) and unlike American proto-institutionalist approaches that exclude consideration of social forces (except in the highly partisan definition of social forces as "special interests" with the air of hangdog illegitimacy), historical institutionalism is precisely interested in the ways in which the interplay of social forces in political conflict over policy outcomes and policy stakes is itself mediated by political institutional factors.

Therefore, in discussing the evolution of lesbian and gay rights policies, it is centrally important to contextualize the decisions of courts in relation to other institutions and to temper our focus on the role of religion, public opinion and advocacy groups with a thorough historical understanding of the institutional structures within which political actors and social movements seek to influence public policy. In this context, it is striking that discussions of lesbian and gay rights are so strongly focused on the impact of public opinion and evangelical organizing on policy outcomes, as if the institutional structures of American politics do not exist in this policy sector, as they have been deemed to do in so many others. In a recent edited collection of essays on same-sex marriage (Rimmerman and Wilcox 2007), not a single author paid systematic attention to political institutional factors in explaining the push and pull of the debate over same-sex marriage in the U.S.; instead, the collection focuses overwhelmingly on the strategies of advocacy and litigation groups, the mobilization of the Christian Right, and the framing of gay rights and same-sex marriage in American public opinion. In contrast, a recent collection of essays on American political development (Pierson and Skocpol 2007) draws on historical institutionalist approaches to understanding policy choices, the turn to political conservativism in the U.S., and the ways in which the growth of the state in the post-war period spawned interest and advocacy organizations. The volume focuses overwhelmingly on the evolution of social and tax policy in the U.S. and, in doing so, it does not contain a single stand-alone study of U.S. public opinion or even general reference to raw public opinion numbers. Rather, chapters discuss the process of political mobilization through political parties, advocacy organizations, the media and other institutions, presenting data on topics such as government spending, taxes, legislative patterns, and advocacy organization. The differences between these two volumes exemplify the extent to which same-sex marriage and "gay rights" are clearly defined as "moral issues" in which religion and public opinion drive the agenda while social and economic policy are viewed through the lens of structural theories of political development. This book aims to correct the overemphasis on religion and opinion in the study of gay rights in the U.S. and Canada and to bring into focus the long-term and slow-moving historical processes (Pierson 2004) that are less clearly visible than the latest public opinion poll. The processes of opinion formation and political mobilization do not occur in a historical or institutional vacuum. Political institutions matter to the ways in which people think about politics and the ways in which they mobilize in the political process, whether the issue is tax policy or same-sex marriage.

The study also builds on the legal mobilization approaches that have been developed by Rosenberg (1991) and McCann (1993), which demonstrate that progressive social forces have deliberately used political litigation for the purposes of achieving specific policy outcomes. By reading the discussion of legal mobilization in light of the insights of historical institutionalism, we can develop explanations of cross-national policy divergence that explicitly include the role of law and courts in producing outcomes, but that view courts as structured political institutions in the sense suggested by historical institutionalist theory. By using a historical institutionalist approach, the role of courts and law is placed in a much broader, richer historical context, one that yields new insights on the relationships between courts and other political institutions and that allows us to specify the conditions under which courts will influence policy outcomes. In doing so, we strengthen our ability to explain the impact of courts on policy, rather than simply explaining judicial behavior. Scholars of social movements have long emphasized the role of the structure of political opportunity in facilitating success for social movements. Historical institutionalism complements these political process theories by highlighting two specific dimensions of political opportunity: the idea that political opportunity is dynamic and historically shaped and constructed and the idea that political institutions and legacies of previous policies form institutional structures that undergird the features identified in classic analyses of political opportunity by Kitchschelt (1986) and Tarrow (1998). Therefore, the openings provided by courts form one aspect of the political opportunity structure.

By using historical institutionalism to understand legal mobilization by social movements, I emphasize that we cannot discuss the impact and role of courts on policy outcomes in the abstract, without looking at the way in which courts are embedded in and influenced by the larger political institutional system of which they are a part. In order to evaluate the impact of courts on policy, we must explore how other political institutions interact with courts and how other political institutions react to and make judgments about court rulings, especially the legislature and the executive as well as examining the institutional and constitutional tools these other institutions can bring to bear on court decisions (e.g., constitutional amendment, direct democracy or the Canadian constitutional override). Differences in the separation of powers system and Westminster parliamentarism as well as the associated differences in the organization of political parties play an important role in cross-national policy variation. In addition to these factors, I highlight the differences in the division of powers in federal systems on issues related to lesbian and gay rights and the role of policy legacies in framing policy debates. The role of courts is of central importance in understanding the evolution of lesbian and gay rights policies in both countries over the period since the rise of the modern lesbian and gay rights movement in the early 1970s. However, my analysis of the role of courts emphasizes the place of court decisions relative to other institutional dimensions, especially the separation (or fusion) of powers, federalism and policy legacies. By reading courts as part of a set of structured relationships among institutions, the aim is to provide an explanation of *policy* differences rather than *judicial* outcomes (see Barclay and Birkland 1998).

In emphasizing the structuring role of specific features of American and Canadian political institutions, the analysis does not take up the question of the origins of these institutions or the role of social movement actors and other political actors in influencing the configuration of institutions. Further, the analysis does not explore the ways in which the agents of political action may internalize institutional norms and how these norms may shape their interpretation of the political world. These are critically important aspects of institutionalism and they have been explored at length in social movement theory (Clemens 1997) and in more sociological forms of institutionalism (Hall and Taylor 1996). Over the period considered here, the lesbian and gay movement did not play an important or influential role in shaping foundational political institutions such as the structure of the separation of powers, federalism (in both judicial and jurisdictional dimensions) or the role of courts. Even in the case of Canada, which underwent important political institutional change during this period, with the 1982 constitutional amendment and the entrenchment of a constitutional bill of rights, the lesbian and gay movement did not play any specific role in the social movement politics of Charter debates, especially compared to the role played by the women's movement, ethnocultural communities and First Nations (see Smith 1999: 41–110; James 2006). Therefore, the emphasis in this analysis is on political institutions as stable structures, often operating behind the scenes or without conscious reference by political actors. While this approach may seem overly structural, mechanical, and neglectful of the agency of actors, it is my view that a strong dose of institutional realism is badly needed in a field in which public policy has so often been read as the unmediated reflection of the moral and religious views of citizens.

CROSS-NATIONAL INSTITUTIONAL DIFFERENCES

There are four political institutional differences that play a role in explaining the pattern of policy variation between these two similar systems: separation of powers vs. Westminster parliamentarism and the attendant differences in the organization of political parties; jurisdictional differences in the structure of federalism; differences in the role of courts; and the impact of policy legacies. In exploring the role of these factors in the development of public policy over time in the two cases, we can trace the process of policy change through exploring how each change interacts with others to produce particular sequences and pathways that accelerate policy changes in particular directions at particular historical tipping points.

First, the separation of powers system creates obstacles to policy change as, indeed, it was designed to do. In contrast, the parliamentary system, especially when combined with the first-past-the-post electoral system and with a high level of party cohesion and discipline, as in the Canadian case, usually produces centralized authority. Legislative and executive power is fused, in that the prime minister and cabinet's tenure in office depends on the ability to command majority support in the legislature, at least on measures of confidence such as budgetary and spending measures. Even under conditions of minority government, the executive enjoys substantial power to pursue a legislative agenda unhindered by the necessity of compromise with any other party. While internal party dissension may provide a check on the power of the party leadership, the prime minister holds the levers of power and appointment and can use these carrots and sticks to ensure party loyalty. Comparative research has shown that Canadian party leaders—especially Liberal leaders—have been particularly skilled at managing their members in Parliament compared to the party leadership in other Westminster systems (Garner and Letki 2005).

At many of the key moments in the evolution of lesbian and gay human rights policy in Canada, important changes have been enacted on the initiative of the prime minister and cabinet. In the U.S., even a determined executive that wished to enact human rights measures would be faced with the task of building support for such measures in Congress. In both cases, the power of the federal executive is checked by the operation of the federal system, which divides sovereignty and authority between two levels of government and by the power of the courts, which may strike down laws as unconstitutional. However, even without the checks provided by courts and by federalism, the executive in Canada has greater power to enact policy change than does the executive in the American system. This greater power to shape the legislative agenda has sometimes been admired in the United States, especially by political scientists, who see the parliamentary system as one that provides for greater transparency and accountability and a higher level of more informed public debate. Because of the fusion of legislative and executive authority, the executive must answer to the legislative as both a practical political and a constitutional exercise. Moreover, the separation of powers system weakens political parties and lack of party discipline in the U.S. system means that well-organized groups can easily lobby legislators and bring pressure to bear, whereas, in the disciplined Canadian party system, it is more of a challenge for outside groups to influence caucus deliberations. In the Canadian system, the leadership of the government and the parties plays a much more important role in policy-making as do the bureaucrats in the centralized policy apparatuses of the government, all of which has been permeated by the practice of legally "proofing" policy in the Charter era, as the work of James Kelly (2005) has shown.

Political parties are, of course, critically important to making political institutions work and the partisan conflict between political parties is greatly exacerbated in the U.S. by the design of U.S. political institutions. Over the last decade, scholars have emphasized that the shift to the right in the U.S. is not the product of a more conservative U.S. electorate. Rather, the shift has been driven by neoconservative political elites and conservative movements such as the Christian Right that have used the multiple openings of the U.S. system to drive the Republican Party in a more radical direction (Hacker and Pierson 2005). Those who make this argument stress a number of features of U.S. political institutions that have created openings for this surge. In addition to longstanding features such as the design of the electoral college, which emphasizes campaigning in the vote-rich large states, the separation of powers also creates uniquely weak political parties in the U.S., parties that are de facto coalitions of professional fundraisers and increasingly independent candidates (Levinson 2006). Changes in institutional rules that were undertaken by reformers in the 1970s in order to prevent the abuses of the Watergate era ironically opened up the U.S. party system, ushered in the end of the era of party machines and transition to a party structure dominated by professional fundraisers and a mass mail order party base (Campbell 2007). The Republican Party has been permeable and vulnerable to an influx of evangelical grass roots activism and neoconservative elites, operating through a network of lobbyists and think tanks to influence the primary election process and threaten moderate candidates (Wilcox 2006; Hacker and Pierson 2005). While Canadian parties are also influenced by the impact of media on election campaigns (Carty, Cross and Young 2000), underlying institutional structures in Canada make it more difficult for outside movements to exercise influence within the parties. These vulnerabilities of political parties in the U.S. are not found in Canada because of the top-down control of the parties over nomination contests. It is difficult for the Christian Right in Canada to mount challenges to the nomination of candidates in the Canadian party system. The structure of the parties is in itself linked to the separation of powers in the U.S. system and the fusion of authority in the parliamentary system. There is no institutional reason for U.S. parties to be disciplined and, again, this opens up multiple opportunities for influence by those with the organization and resources.

A second major institutional difference that affects this policy area is the structuring of federalism. Most commonly, U.S./Canada differences in this area are discussed in terms of the centralization and decentralization of political power. Despite the fact that residual power is reserved to the federal level in Canada and to the states in the U.S. system, most observers emphasize that Canada is more decentralized than the U.S. (e.g., Watts 1987). In particular, provinces in Canada have freedom to deliver social policies such as education, health care (through the single payer Medicare system) and social assistance while education and social assistance policies in the U.S. are more strongly controlled through federal purse strings. Further, regional, provincial and sub-national political identities are stronger in Canada. Quebec nationalism has long been a decentralizing force in the Canadian federation as Quebec's leaders reject the assumption that Quebec is a province like the others and, rather, emphasize that the provincial state has an important role to play in protecting the interests of the francophone minority within Canada (Russell 2004). In contrast, in the U.S., although regional political cultures are important, there is a strong sense of U.S. nationalism that overrides the fissiparous centrifugal dynamic of regionalism and states' rights. With the exception of Native Americans, minority groups within the U.S. have not constituted themselves as nations that challenge the federal government, as have Quebec nationalists. American political development after World War II has been largely told as a story of the nationalization of rights, especially because of the strong federal action in the area of African American civil rights. For these reasons, the two federal systems are often seen as differing on the continuum of centralization/decentralization with the U.S. as a more centralized federal system than Canada.

However, in the area of lesbian and gay rights, the opposite holds true. The federal government in Canada has more power to effect change in the lesbian and gay rights policy area than does the federal government in the U.S. With respect to the division of powers, in the U.S., the states have jurisdiction over policy areas that have a substantial impact on lesbian and gay citizens, such as the criminal law and the right to marry. Criminal law is one of the most important areas for lesbian and gay rights, especially because the criminal law regulates sexual behavior in a number of areas that affect homosexuality. This ranges from the question of the legality of the practice of sodomy between consenting adults (whether in same-sex or opposite sex couples), the regulation of the age of consent for sexual activity, the regulation of sex in public spaces such as parks or public places, and the regulation of the sex trade. Because of federal jurisdiction in this area, in Canada, a determined federal government had the jurisdiction to change the criminal law in 1969. Similarly, on the issue of same-sex marriage, the federal government in Canada has jurisdiction over who can get married. In the U.S., the lesbian and gay movement requires vast resources of organization and coordination to compete on a state-by-state playing field in order to change policies that are within the jurisdiction (Kane 2007). This has meant that U.S. lesbian and gay organizations have required formidable financial and organizational resources in order to press legal and lobbying campaigns across the U.S., state-by-state. While there was a nationalization of civil rights during the 1960s in order to enact measures for racial equality and, later on, to some extent, to enact measures for women's equality, lesbian and gay rights in the U.S. remains remarkably local. Federal intervention in lesbian and gay rights policies in the U.S. is still pending, given the uncertain constitutional status of the 1996 Defense of Marriage Act.

Another dimension of federalism that affects the lesbian and gay rights conflict is that, in contrast to Canadian provinces, American states possess freestanding written constitutions while provinces in Canada do not.[8] Beginning in the 1970s, U.S. state courts began to play a more prominent role in interpreting the rights guarantees of their own constitutions in a more expansive way than the rights guarantees of the federal constitution. Some have argued that this "new judicial federalism" occurred as progressive state courts tried to evade the more conservative post-Warren period of the U.S. Supreme Court (see Tarr 1998: 161ff). Lesbian and gay plaintiffs—particularly, same-sex couples—have benefitted from the new judicial federalism as, in some states such as Hawai'i, Alaska, Vermont, and Massachusetts, state constitutions have provided scope for state courts to draw on variations in constitutional provisions to rule in favour of lesbian and gay rights (Andersen 2005; Pierceson 2005). In these states, state courts used equal protection and other provisions of state constitutions to legitimate gay and lesbian rights claims. However, at the same time, many state constitutions also provide mechanisms for ballot initiatives and referenda, mechanisms which are absent in Canada (Smith and Tolbert 2004).[9] These measures of direct democracy may be used to initiate ordinary legislation and, in eighteen states, citizens may initiate a constitutional amendment, either directly to the voters or to the legislature (Tarr 1998: 25). These states include Colorado where conservatives and the Christian Right used this mechanism to pass a state constitutional amendment prohibiting discrimination protections based on sexual orientation. State constitutions can also be amended and many of them have been amended to constitutionally preclude the recognition of same-sex marriage in law and policy. In Massachusetts, conservatives and the Christian Right have repeatedly pushed for an amendment to the state constitution to repeal same-sex marriage in that state. State constitutional amendments require popular ratification, which may subject minority rights to popular override by the majority. In general, it is much easier to amend a state constitution than to amend the U.S. constitution and state constitutions are amended and revised frequently (Tarr 1998; see also Dinan 2006). The use of constitutional amendment (initiated by citizens or by legislators) and the use of citizen ballot initiatives does not exist in Canada in the same form.

With regard to constitutional amendment at the federal level, in Canada, discussion of constitutional change—especially on the scale needed to entrench a "Defense of Marriage" Amendment—is currently unthinkable for reasons that have nothing to do with lesbian and gay rights. Even opponents of same-sex marriage have not argued—at least not with any credibility—that the constitution should be amended to ban same-sex marriage, mainly due to the unwillingness of political elites to open up the Pandora's Box of constitutional change, which might lead to further challenges from Quebec sovereignists or regionalist political leaders (Russell 2004). Nevertheless, in the U.S., there is discussion of a Federal Marriage Amendment (FMA)[10] to constitutionally prohibit same-sex marriage, in addition to the state measures to this effect that have already been passed. Even if it is unlikely that the FMA will pass, the proposal has been used to mobilize lesbian and gay rights opponents and to frame policy debates about the legitimacy of promoting the heterosexual family over families headed by same-sex couples (Human Rights Campaign 2007c). Thus, the process of constitutional amendment (which is more politically possible in the U.S. system) and the process of state constitutional amendment (which is institutionally easier in the U.S. and nonexistent in the same sense in Canada) create mechanisms through which court decisions can be directly blocked and through which the conservative movement can be mobilized against same-sex marriage and other areas of lesbian and gay rights.

By U.S. standards, Canadian conservatives and evangelicals lack institutional levers or pressure points to counter the decisions of courts except to win a majority government at the federal level. Even then, in order to counter court decisions in Canada, the government of the day would have to meet the fairly high bar of deploying the notwithstanding clause (the override clause) of the Charter of Rights, given the jurisprudential direction of the courts. The notwithstanding clause, section 33 of the Charter, permits federal and provincial governments to pass legislation notwithstanding sections 2 and 7–15 inclusive of the Charter, sections which include funda-mental legal rights and equality rights. The clause expires after five years, after which it must be renewed; the clause is very rarely used and, therefore, it has become something of a taboo, especially in federal politics. Techni-cally, the clause could be used to forestall lesbian and gay rights; how-ever, for other constitutional and political reasons, the clause has become politically costly or even impossible for the federal government to deploy (Hiebert 2002; Leeson 2000).

A third important institutional difference concerns the role of courts. Courts have played a key role in lesbian and gay rights in both the U.S. and Canada and, especially, have set the policy agenda on important issues such as same-sex marriage. In his classic (1991) study of the U.S. civil rights movement, Gerald Rosenberg asked whether courts produce social change. I cast the question somewhat differently to ask *how* and *under what cir-cumstances* the courts produce *policy* change. My work suggests that the answer to that question depends on the ways in which courts are situated within political institutional structures. In both the U.S. and Canada, courts have set the agenda on issues such as same-sex marriage. In fact, it was a U.S. court that first framed this policy area in the Hawai'i same-sex marriage case in 1993. Both Canadian and American courts have ruled in favour of same-sex marriage and the claims-making in these cases is simi-lar on the two sides of the border (Smith 2007). Nonetheless, U.S. courts have not had the same influence and policy impact as Canadian courts.

This book uses a comparative analysis to specify the conditions under which courts will influence policy in the area of lesbian and gay rights. In the U.S., there is much more room for pushback against court decisions than in the Canadian institutional structure. The desire to circumvent the decisions of judges was an important reason for the development of direct democracy in the American states, especially in the Progressive era, and, in general, while judicial review is accepted in the states, judicial supremacy is weaker in the states than at the national level. In the states, there is a long history of using ballot initiatives, recall, election of judges and other measures of popular democracy to counterbalance the rulings of the courts (Dinan 2006: 29–64; 97–136). In general, state courts in the U.S. are more independent of federal power than are provincial courts in Canada because the U.S. court structure is organized around the principle of judicial fed-eralism, in which there are separate and independent court systems. The federal courts were established after the state courts and were structured independently in their jurisdiction and administration (Abrahamson and Gutmann 1987).

In contrast, in Canada, the judicial system is relatively unified in compari-son to the U.S. model. In general, aside from certain specialized areas of tax and administrative law in which federal courts operate, most cases begin in lower provincial courts such as trial courts (depending on the issue) and wend their way through the superior courts of the province (superior trial courts and courts of appeal) and from there to the highest court of appeal, the Supreme Court of Canada. Superior courts in Canadian provinces have inherent jurisdiction to hear any case that is not specifically reserved to another court (Russell 1987; Greene 2006). While in the U.S., the states control the method of selection of the judges of their own state courts and many states rely on election of judges and even provide for the recall of judges, Canadian judges at the superior court level (trial and appeal) in the provinces as well as the judges of the federal courts and the Supreme Court of Canada are all appointed by the federal government acting alone with minimal provincial and parliamentary consultation (Greene 2006). Because of the unified executive and legislative powers of the parliamentary system, this means that the Canadian judicial system is highly centralized compared to the U.S. system and that it places a great deal of power in the hands of the prime minister in the appointment of judges while, in the U.S., the President's nominees for the justices of the Supreme Court must be ratified in the Senate.

In the U.S., civil rights have been nationalized through a long and sometimes painful process of bringing the states into line with federal standards as the Bill of Rights has been applied to the states over time and as the federal government has directly intervened in order to ensure that civil rights are protected (Abrahamson and Gutman 1987; Galie 1987). However, this process of nationalization has not yet occurred in the adjudication of lesbian and gay legal claims and the states continue to play a vital and important role in this area as the recent decisions by state courts on same-sex marriage have vividly shown. In contrast, in Canada, as we will see, the entrenchment of a constitutional bill of rights for the first time in the 1980s has ensured the development of federal and pan-Canadian human rights protections, a development from which lesbians and gays were the unintended beneficiaries. Therefore, in considering the impact of courts on social change and their role in influencing public policy, this analysis situates courts in relation to the broad institutional structure of which the courts are a part, specifically including the division of powers and judicial federalism.

In addition to these factors, the jurisprudential differences or differences in law (and its application and interpretation by judges) between the U.S. and Canada with respect to civil rights (U.S.) and equality rights (Canada) create openings for lesbian and gay litigation that do not exist in the U.S. constitution. While "law" has been out of vogue as an explanatory factor since the behavioral revolution, there are signs that the impact of law and jurisprudence in relation to public policy outcomes is in the process of being resuscitated from near-death by law and courts scholars (e.g., Kahn 2006). In this comparative analysis of lesbian and gay rights, it is evident that the jurisprudential structure of equal protection doctrine in the U.S. can be defined as a policy legacy, one that has created a multiple tier system of civil rights in U.S. constitutional law. These multiple tiers mitigate against lesbian and gay rights claims (Gerstmann 1999). The Canadian constitution provides openings for gay and lesbian litigants in part because it is a newer constitution and because the jurisprudential structure of rights in Canada does not create blockages as does American equal protection doctrine. In particular, the comparative analysis draws attention to the crucial role of slavery and the racialization of African Americans in American politics in creating a jurisprudential structure of equal protection that creates insuperable complications (legal and political) for lesbian and gay rights claims.

Specifically, the jurisprudential structure of the Fourteenth Amendment of the U.S. Constitution compared to section 15 of the Canadian Charter of Rights and Freedoms makes litigation much easier for Canadian lesbian and gay plaintiffs. The Bill of Rights was only gradually incorporated for application at the state level and the fact of judicial federalism means that the Bill of Rights has been interpreted as the constitutional floor for certain rights protections, which may be exceeded by states using their own constitutions. In contrast, the Canadian Charter is a frankly centralizing document that applies to all governments, federal and provincial (and *inter alia* to municipalities and local governments). The Fourteenth Amendment sets up a hierarchy of rights protections with strict scrutiny of government action for groups that are determined to hold suspect class status, mainly groups distinguished on the grounds of race. Heightened scrutiny is required for groups in the quasi-suspect class, such as sex, while rational basis review is the weakest level of protection and considered to be highly deferential to legislative and governmental objectives. In contrast, the Canadian Charter has a straightforward equality rights clause that prohibits discrimination by governments on a set of named grounds that are all accorded the same status within the clause. Although sexual orientation and gender identity are not explicitly included, sexual orientation has been read into the clause by the courts as an analogous ground to the others and there are signs that the same is in the process of occurring with gender identity. Once "read in" to section 15 of the Charter, a named ground of discrimination is "in" and there is no legal hierarchy or further distinction of legal principle within the wording of the clause or in the way that the courts have applied it. In addition, lesbian and gay rights in the U.S., in the areas of criminal law and marriage, have been litigated based on the doctrine of fundamental rights, including the right to privacy, the right to intimate association and the right to marry. These rights cannot be said to exist in the same form in Canada or to play the same role in relation to lesbian and gay rights policies, as we shall see.

While private discrimination is covered in the U.S. mainly through the use of the federal commerce power, under which the Civil Rights Act (1964) was passed, the federal and provincial governments in Canada must regulate private discrimination in a manner that is consistent with the Charter, which applies to all of their actions, including their policies on redress for private discrimination. Because of the long historical evolution of the U.S. Bill of Rights and the much earlier timing of its constitutional codification (almost two centuries prior to the Canadian Charter), it is not surprising that the jurisprudential legacies of rights protections in the U.S. reflect the historical struggles of other groups—especially African Americans—for full citizenship. By the standards of the U.S. Bill of Rights, the lesbian and gay movement is a latecomer to the jurisprudential and political discussion while, in Canada, the lesbian and gay movement arose almost contemporaneously with the entrenchment of the Charter of Rights.

A fourth important factor is the role of policy legacies and historical timing in generating and reinforcing policy divergence. The emergence of the lesbian and gay movement in the U.S. and Canada and, especially, the emergence of the gay liberation movement in the countries in the period 1969–1971, must be read in the context of the broad political and partisan context of the period. Over the period from the birth of gay liberation through to the reelection of George W. Bush in 2004 and the legalization of same-sex civil marriage in Canada in 2005, the political trajectories of the U.S. and Canada have differed in important respects. The opportunities and obstacles for social movement politics were shaped by the political landscape they faced at the movement of their historical arrival. Lesbian and gay movements in the U.S. and Canada were relatively similar in many important respects, especially in their commitment to a discourse of citizenship and rights. These similarities were particularly striking in English-speaking Canada and the U.S. because of the diffusion of templates of social movement activism from the U.S. to Canada (Adam 1995; Warner 2002). However, the fate of the two social movements and the evolution of lesbian and gay rights policies in Canada and the U.S. were also influenced by the overall shape of partisan party conflict during this period. As lesbian and gay rights came out of the closet and became defined as a public policy issue in American and Canadian politics, these were packaged along with other public policy issues and framed as part of a broader debate between a progressive and liberal politics on one hand and a neo-conservative and neo-liberal politics on the other hand. In this process of framing and policy positioning, "gay rights" in the U.S. became associated with another set of public policy issues including welfare reform, school prayer, and abortion while, in Canada, "gay rights" became defined and framed in policy debates as a human rights issue.

Very importantly, the Canadian lesbian and gay right movement came of age during a period of Liberal Party ascendance while the U.S. lesbian and gay rights movement came of age during a period of Democratic Party decline. However, the story is much more complicated than simply tallying up the effect of the partisan complexion of government on human rights policies and arguing that Canada's centrist Liberals have been supportive of human rights while the Republican ascendancy in U.S. politics has curtailed lesbian and gay rights' initiatives. While ideological differences between the political parties are important, what is more important is the

broad historical context in which policy debates have occurred, the historical pacing and sequencing of key events, and the ways in which, over time,
policy legacies have defined a broad discursive terrain of political debate.
This means that we must pay attention to the ways in which lesbian and
gay rights are tied to other political issues in policy debates and, critically,
to debates over gender and, especially, race.

While both countries have many sources of internal difference, historically, the most important internal division in the U.S. is race, specifically,
the racialized legacy of slavery while, in Canada, the most important internal division has concerned the place of Quebec in Canada. Whether or not
these differences are the most important source of sociological difference,
they have served to organize party competition and, therefore, they have
important effects on policy discourse. To put it another way, these particular divisions have been the most strongly mobilized into electoral and partisan party competition. Frymer's (1999) work on the U.S. and Brodie and
Jenson's (1988) analysis of Canadian parties offer complementary analyses
of the ways in which political parties mobilized race, ethnicity, national,
and linguistic differences in seeking to build a national electoral base. As
the South swung into the Republican column over the period covered in this
volume, the Democrats became identified with the big government of the
Great Society era, programs that were sometimes presented to white voters
as disproportionately benefitting minority groups. The explosive nature of
debates over affirmative action in the U.S. and the profound racialization
of debates on social policy (especially welfare reform) served to identify a
cluster of issues on the Democratic side of the ledger, which were discur-
sively defined and constructed as special interests. Gay rights was quickly
assimilated into the discourse of special interests and special rights as gays
were often depicted by the Christian Right as a group seeking special rights
and privileges (Goldberg-Hiller 2002).

The contrast with Canadian public discourse could not be greater. In
English-speaking Canada, the country's new constitutional Charter of
Rights was quickly adopted and popularized as a part of English-speaking
Canada's national identity. This allowed lesbian and gay rights claimants
to position their equality arguments as "Canadian values" or "Charter
values," values that assumed a quasi-sacred status in political debates in
English-speaking Canada during the 1990s and 2000s. The political order
encoded in the new Charter was constituted as a means of blocking the
Quebec sovereignty movement. The identification of the human rights
regime of the Charter with the Liberal Party and, in turn, with English
Canadian political nationalism created an important political opportunity
for lesbian and gay activists in Canada while the definition of gay rights as
just another in the grab bag of the Democratic Party's "special interests"
made an uphill battle for U.S. lesbian and gay activists (Smith 2007). These
differences in turn stem from the specific historical timing of the lesbian
and gay movement in the two countries and the relationship between the

legacies of other social movements such as the civil rights movement and the emerging claims of the lesbian and gay movement.

RELIGION, CULTURE, AND INSTITUTIONS

The most common explanation of policy difference between the U.S. and other countries on lesbian and gay rights is that Americans are simply more religious and more conservative than the citizens of other developed democratic capitalist societies (Rayside 2007). Analysis of Canadian politics and policy has long provided a useful comparative perspective for understanding U.S. politics because of the many historical similarities between the two North American neighbours. Generally, where differences are discovered, they have been overwhelmingly ascribed to differences in political culture.

Seymour Martin Lipset (1963, 1990) and Louis Hartz ([1955] 1991) both wrote about North American political development as a long-term historical process in which the formative events of early immigration and settlement set the stage for the development of liberal political culture. Lipset's formative events approach evolved from his interest in explaining the weakness of the left in U.S. politics compared to the stronger position of the left in Canadian politics, as evidenced by the emergence of a socialist/social democratic third party in Canadian politics in the 1930s and the greater strength of trade unionism in Canada than in the U.S. Lipset used public policy as an indicator of political cultural differences, pointing to Canadians' greater interest in statist and collectivist public policy solutions, such as publicly funded health care, as indicators of political cultural difference. According to Lipset (1990), because of the American Revolution, Canada was pushed in the direction of traditional values such as ascription, deference to authority, elitism, noblesse, collectivism and statism, while the U.S. took off in an entirely new direction in shaking off the fetters of European feudal values. Therefore, Lipset saw the U.S. and Canada as fundamentally different societies and would explain contemporary policy with reference to the impact of the American Revolution on North American political development. Similarly, Louis Hartz ([1955] 1991) also emphasized North American political development in historical terms, seeking explanations for contemporary differences in the origins of the two societies in the period of early European immigration and settlement. Hartz viewed English-speaking Canadians and Americans as representing liberal political fragments, espousing the values of democratic self-government, individualism and egalitarianism in contrast to Europe during the same period. Hartz argued that English-speaking Canada had a "Tory touch" resulting from the impact of the American Revolution and the longer exposure to the British connection (see also Horowitz 1968; Forbes 1987).

A contemporary restatement of the fundamental differences between the U.S. and Canada is found in the work of Michael Adams (2003), who argues that the U.S. and Canada have been heading in very different directions politically over the last decade. Adams argues that Canadians are becoming more tolerant and flexible while Americans are becoming authoritarian, intolerant and patriarchal. Therefore, human rights policies diverge between the U.S. and Canada because Canadians are more tolerant and flexible than Americans. In this view, public policy may be seen as conditioned at least in part by public opinion and political culture. Policy divergence on issues such as same-sex marriage can be explained by the fact that Canadians have more open views on homosexuality and other social issues than Americans do. Recent analyses of regional differences in political culture (Grabb and Curtis 2005) take issue with Adams's interpretation of public opinion data, arguing that they have slightly different views on "moral issues, religion, family values and crime," the political cultural distance is greatest when measured in terms of regional sub-variation (Grabb and Curtis 2005: 140–165), with Quebec by far the most liberal on these issues, followed by the rest of Canada, the northern U.S. and the South. The greatest gap is between Quebec and the South, not between Canadians and Americans as such. Further, on other political cultural measures such as individualism, collectivism and the role of the state—issues that are usually seen as differentiating Canada from the U.S.—there is very little difference between Canadians and Americans (Grabb and Curtis 2005: 183). Moreover, post-materialist approaches to political culture, as epitomized in the work of the World Values Survey, suggest that Canadians are becoming more like Americans, not less so (e.g., Nevitte 1996).

While political cultural explanations shed light on the general context of political change, they do not tell the whole story (see also Maioni 1998). From a conceptual standpoint, political culture is often defined as including the beliefs of citizens as evidenced in polling data, the success or failure of political parties, and the nature and extent of policy variance. However, if policy variation is an indicator of political cultural difference (e.g., Canadians are more politically tolerant than Americans are, as evidenced by the fact that Canada permits same-sex marriage), then political cultural difference cannot explain policy variation. If political culture is measured in polls, then the argument is reduced to the assertion that public opinion causes public policy. According to public opinion polls, Americans are far more politically moderate than are the policies pursued by the Republican political leadership in the George W. Bush era (Hacker and Pierson 2005). In addition, this restrictive or narrow view of political culture suggests that culture operates separately from other factors such as political institutions or political economy. Political institutions, especially the institutions of public law that will be the focus of analysis in this volume, exist in a cultural structure and only make sense and take on meaning within a specific discursive context. From this perspective, all of politics occurs within culture and it is not possible to separate political culture from the operation of political institutions or the choices made in public policy.

Political cultural approaches, especially as they have been used in American/Canadian comparison, tend to take the values and beliefs of citizens as given, rather than viewing the beliefs of citizens as themselves a dependent variable that are shaped by a broad range of structural influences (e.g., an unequal capitalist society media concentration that restricts the range of opinion available; the unequal structure of representation in political and social institutions) as well as the choices of political actors who mobilize some opinions rather than others. As Frymer (1999) has emphasized, party elites in the U.S. have chosen to mobilize race in American politics in particular ways. That is a choice that has shaped the values and beliefs of Americans about race. Frymer argues that Republican and Democratic Party elites were not compelled to play the race card but that the political mobilization of race in American politics was in part the result of choices made by parties and candidates. Frymer's analysis challenges the simple view of a generalizable national political culture that somehow determines or dictates policy choices.

Public opinion polling is a very blunt instrument while policymaking is a complex process with complicated outcomes that cannot always be defined in terms of simple binaries. While public opinion may provide a contextual background for the policy process and for policy decisions, it does not dictate the specific timing and content of complex policy outcomes and it could not possibly do so, even if we ignore the possibility that policy and legal change interact with public opinion and that policy and legal changes themselves have a shaping impact on public opinion. Even if polling data did correlate with public policies, we would still need an explanation of how differences in political beliefs and public opinion translate into policy differences.

This critique of political cultural arguments is further supported by a consideration of policy differences and public opinion studies in the two countries. On some policy issues, there is virtually no difference between Canadian and American public opinion. For example, public opinion in the U.S. overwhelmingly favours anti-discrimination measures in employment for lesbian and gay citizens and scholarly analysis of the recent evolution of public opinion shows dramatic change in favour of lesbian and gay rights in the U.S. over the course of the 1990s (Yang 1997; Lewis and Rogers 1999; Brewer 2003a). Yet, despite public support, even simple anti-discrimination measures are not in force in most U.S. states and federal anti-discrimination legislation, which was first proposed by Bella Abzug in 1974, has not yet been passed. While Canada legalized same-sex marriage in 2005, the U.S. is debating a constitutional amendment to ban same-sex marriage. Nonetheless, public opinion polls have reported a wide range of results on this issue in the two countries, ranging from a low of 28% support for same-sex marriage in Canada outside Quebec (putting English-speaking Canada

behind the U.S. in support for same-sex marriage) to a national high of
54% (Fournier et al. 2004; Ipsos Reid 2003). U.S. opinion has ranged as
high as 50% in support of same-sex marriage, depending on the wording
of the question (Grossman 2003). Furthermore, recent analyses of the evolution of public opinion in Canada on the issue of same-sex marriage over
the last ten years demonstrate that public opinion has been strongly cued
by policy decisions and, importantly, by decisions from the Supreme Court
of Canada (Matthews 2005). This analysis suggests that public opinion is
a background factor that provides a political context for policy discussion
and debate but that, at best, it is a rough guide to the politically possible,
one that is in itself vulnerable to the shaping and mobilizing influences of
political actors.

The idea that evangelical and Christian Right organizing in the U.S.
have driven public policy on lesbian and gay rights suffers from the same
problems as other political culture approaches. The presence of evangelicals is no guarantee that they will mobilize politically or that they will be
successful in influencing public policy. As Sam Reimer's (2003) study of
evangelical subcultures in Canada and the U.S. shows, evangelicals in the
two countries have similar beliefs and values and, in many ways, belong
to shared subcultures of religious community. However, Canadian evangelicals are less interested in influencing politics, despite the similarity of
their religious beliefs to American evangelicals. This suggests that political variables—such as the institutional factors that will be emphasized in
this volume—play an important role in mobilizing religious beliefs and
that sweeping generalizations about religion and conservatism in the U.S.
need to be tempered with careful empirical analysis of the circumstances in
which the Christian Right mobilizes and the factors that influence the process and outcome of such mobilization. Factors such as the extent of social
and political cultural support for lesbian and gay rights whether measured
in public opinion polls, (particular) religious beliefs, or in social movement
resources are important in providing context in this policy area. However,
on their own, they cannot account for the rapid and substantial pace of
policy change on lesbian and gay rights in Canada and the laggard status
of the U.S. in this policy area.

CHAPTER OUTLINE

In the next chapter, I provide a comparative analysis of the starting points
for the lesbian and gay movement in the two cases by explaining the Criminal Code revision of 1969 that "decriminalized" homosexuality in Canada
and comparing this to the state sodomy laws in the U.S. of the same period.
Federalism in the U.S. assigns criminal law to the states, forcing the lesbian
and gay movement to wage a state-by-state battle while, in Canada, the
criminal law power rests with the federal level. Action from the executive

or from courts in the U.S. has been rolled back or constrained by legislative responses and direct democracy, which are weak or nonexistent in
Canada's Westminster-style parliamentarism. The chapter also shows how
lesbian and gay rights were associated with liberalism in the U.S. at a period
in which liberalism was under political attack while, in Canada, lesbian
and gay rights were positively associated with the liberal nationalism of the
Liberal Party, situating the lesbian and gay movement in a more advanta-
geous position in the partisan conflict between political parties. This chapter shows how policy legacies and institutional differences played out in this
initial period from the rise of the gay liberation movement in 1969–1971
through to the initial impact of the AIDS crisis in 1980.

Chapter 3 focuses on the period of the AIDS crisis and explores the
process of mobilization and countermobilization between the lesbian and
gay movement and the Christian Right that occurred over this period in
the U.S. The chapter emphasizes the opening provided by U.S. political
institutions for Christian Right countermobilizing in the face of the initial
steps toward the implementation of anti-discrimination measures in the
U.S., specifically, the role of freestanding state constitutions in American
federalism, the role of ballot initiatives and state constitutional amendment
and the absence of all of these institutional tools in the Canadian system.
The second part of the chapter focuses on the impact of policy legacies and
partisan political conflict by contrasting the U.S. Supreme Court's decision
in the infamous *Bowers v. Hardwick* case in 1986 with the evolution of
Canada's constitutional discourse on rights during the same period. The
entrenchment of new constitutional rights provisions in Canada sparked
an important discussion of equality rights during the mid-1980s. Jurisprudential differences in the treatment of rights claims in the two legal systems
were shaped, in part, by the legacy of previous policies and by the constant "reply" to the courts from the American Christian Right and other
conservatives, a response that was made possible by the extensive political openings provided by decentralized and fragmented American political
institutions.

Chapter 4 contrasts the development of litigation on discrimination in
Canada and the U.S. over the decade after *Bowers* in the U.S. and after the
entrenchment of the Charter in Canada. In the U.S., progress on lesbian
and gay rights led to the passage of Amendment 2 in Colorado and, in
turn, to the *Romer v. Evans* (1996) decision in the Supreme Court. The
chapter compares *Romer* as well as some other U.S. cases of this period
on discrimination (*Boy Scouts v. Dale* and *Shahar v. Bowers*) to Canadian
jurisprudence (*Vriend v. Alberta*) , showing how Canada moved in a radi-
cally different direction than the U.S. in this period. Policy legacies played
a key role in reinforcing stigma for lesbian and gay political claims in the
U.S. while Canadian lesbian and gay rights claims were increasingly cast
in the shining symbolic light of the Charter. By 1998, sodomy laws were
still on the books in the U.S. while, in Canada, basic anti-discrimination

laws were mandated in *Vriend*. This chapter emphasizes the acceleration of policy divergence over time, a key point of institutionalist analysis (Pierson 2004). However, it also shows how social movements cycle against policy legacies by highlighting the long and expensive campaign by the lesbian and gay movement in the U.S. to reverse *Bowers* and secure basic constitutional protection. In this sense, the chapter continues to highlight the other aspects of the argument—the impact of institutional difference and the role of political parties and partisan electoral competition.

Chapters 5 and 6 trace the emergence of the same-sex marriage issue in the two countries over the most recent period, beginning in 1991 with the filing of the *Baehr v. Lewin* (1993) case in Hawai'i. Chapter 5 shows how the same institutional factors continued to create obstacles for lesbian and gay mobilization as federalism, the separation of powers and the power of legislatures continued to generate backlash against each court decision that recognized lesbian and gay rights in the U.S. The chapter provides a detailed comparative analysis of the ways in which legislatures and governments responded to court decisions showing that the most important differences between the two countries were not in the jurisprudential differences or the attitudes of judges or even the decisions of courts but, rather, in the interaction of courts with other political institutions. The main cases discussed in this chapter are the Hawai'i, Vermont and Alaska same-sex marriage cases in the U.S. and, in Canada, *M. v H.*, *Rosenberg v. Canada* (1998) and other cases that established relationship recognition rights for same-sex couples in Canada over the same time period.

Chapter 6 follows the same-sex marriage issue through *Lawrence* (which, although not on same-sex marriage was an important case for lesbian and gay rights in the U.S.) and *Goodridge v. Dept. of Public Health* (2003) in Massachusetts and, in Canada, through the trio of important same-sex marriage cases of the early 2000s in Ontario, Quebec and British Columbia, the Supreme Court of Canada reference case on same-sex marriage of 2004 and the federal legislation legalizing same-sex marriage in 2005. The chapter shows how, once again, political institutions opened the way for same-sex marriage in Canada, while continuing to place roadblocks in the path of the lesbian and gay movement in the U.S, especially in the form of constitutional amendments and defense of marriage acts (DOMAs) that banned same-sex marriage. In Chapter 7, I summarize the three main aspects of the argument in terms of the empirical material presented and explore the implications of the importance of policy legacies, institutional differences and "politics in time" for theories of law and social movements, judicial behavior and comparative policy analysis.

In making these arguments, I show that a historical institutionalist approach is well suited to understanding cross-national differences in human rights policies just as it has been well suited to explaining cross-national differences in social policy and other areas. By considering lesbian and gay rights policies through the lens of historical institutionalism, rather than as a moral hot-button issue that is somehow divorced from the politics of the welfare state, lesbian and gay rights are linked to other policy areas. The historical timing of the arrival of the lesbian and gay movement and the impact of previous policies—especially policies that evolved from struggles over other sources of difference such as race, language and nation—has had important effects on the evolution of lesbian and gay struggles in the U.S. and Canada and helps to explain the particular obstacles that face the lesbian and gay movement in the U.S. The Canadian lesbian and gay movement was strongly favoured by the historical circumstances of its arrival in the midst of a constitutional crisis that provided legal opportunity for the movement while the U.S. lesbian and gay movement was disadvantaged in arriving in the midst of a backlash against the expansion of the welfare state of the 1960s and against the gains of the civil rights and women's movements. Historical institutionalist analysis also highlights the advantages and disadvantages, the costs and benefits, of particular structures of political institutions in providing opportunities or obstacles for social movement mobilization. Exploration of the lesbian and gay case in comparative perspective provides another demonstration of the importance of political institutions and historical pacing in producing particular kinds of policy and politics. In doing so, the book shows how historical institutionalism can fruitfully be applied to understanding differences in state policies and practices in the area of human rights, a policy area that is of critical importance for the survival and resilience of democratic political institutions in the contemporary era.

2 Starting Points, 1969–1980

Studies of American political development emphasize the importance of evaluating the evolution of the political order over the long term. The historical institutionalist approach specifically emphasizes the ways in which a particular course of action can become locked in over time. Political institutions, established in one period, may have important effects on the subsequent period, in ways that were not intended or anticipated at the time. Whether political institutions are the result of "framers' intent" or whether political institutions can best be seen as the codification of the results of particular power struggles, once in place, the structure of institutions sets limits on policy change and shapes the process of contestation. Policy changes in one historical period constitute policy legacies that foreclose other policy options at later points or that render alternative courses of action expensive or difficult. The political opportunity structure for social movements is also altered by these changes, in particular, creating obstacles and openings for social movements to influence policy and encouraging particular forms of social movement organization and mobilization while discouraging others.

In this chapter, I explore a number of institutional and legal starting points for the lesbian and gay movement that have influenced its subsequent evolution in the U.S. and Canada. The first section discusses the rise of the lesbian and gay movement in the U.S. and Canada in the late 1960s and early 1970s, and the initial policy and political context of the movement. The second section focuses on a critical juncture in the trajectories of the two countries—the 1969 reform of the Criminal Code in Canada to legalize sodomy between consenting adults twenty-one years of age or over—and the lack of a similar policy change in the U.S. in that period. As subsequent chapters will show, the continuing definition of homosexual sexual behavior as criminal in state sodomy statutes in the U.S. has constituted a powerful policy legacy for lesbians and gays and, in many specific ways, has shaped the politics of the movement and the pace and content of legal and policy change. This section explains this critical juncture of policy change in Canada and policy stability in the U.S., highlighting the institutional obstacles to change in the U.S.—in this case, federalism and the separation of powers—and how these obstacles affected the early evolution of anti-discrimination policies. The chapter then presents contrasting legacies of previous policies in the human rights area and describes the main policy developments of the period from 1969 through 1980. Finally, the chapter reviews the context of the emergence of the lesbian and gay movement(s) in terms of the partisan political conflict of the time, demonstrating how the issue of gay and lesbian rights was positioned differently in the U.S. and Canada from the moment the movement burst onto the scene in the late 1960s and early 1970s. As these social movements arose in the two countries, they faced very different partisan political environments, which would affect the way that lesbian and gay rights were defined and framed in public policy in the context of the timing of their emergence. This chapter shows how institutional features of the two political systems, the impact of policy legacies, and the environment of party and electoral competition created obstacles that were more substantial for the U.S. lesbian and gay movement compared to the Canadian movement.

THE EMERGENCE OF THE LESBIAN AND GAY MOVEMENT

While informal networks and subcultures of lesbian and gay life had long existed, especially in American and Canadian cities, World War II was a turning point in the emergence of lesbian and gay politics. During the war, many young men and women were away from home and new networks and subcultures of lesbian and gay life emerged. With the onset of the Cold War, there was increasing state regulation and repression of homosexuality, both through the discharge of gay men and lesbians from the military and through the policing of gay bars and spaces. Entrapment and surveillance were the new techniques of policing gay life and witch hunts against communists and other "subversives" often victimized lesbians and gay men. The security campaigns and surveillance of homosexuals were also linked to the anti-communism of the era as communism and homosexuality were defined as politically and socially deviant, and dangerous identities over this period (D'Emilio [1983] 1998: 23–53). In the U.S., anti-communism was particularly important, given the U.S. role as a superpower; security campaigns against lesbians and gay men reinforced a national image of independence and democracy that was counter-posed to the image of deviant communist subversives. In Canada, anti-communism was part of the federal government's commitment to the NATO alliance and to military cooperation with the U.S. in the Cold War (Kinsman 2000: 143–153).

At the same time, however, World War II had an important impact on the domestic politics of human rights in the U.S and Canada as the revelation of the wartime atrocities raised awareness of human rights and racism. While the U.S. had been criticized in the past for racist practices, this criticism became more intense after World War II and created problems for the credibility of American diplomacy as leader of the West in the Cold War and for its ability to exercise moral and political suasion with other governments or to inspire pro-Western development, especially as the wave of postwar decolonization got underway in parts of Asia and Africa. The first steps in the direction of the recognition of civil rights in this period were taken by President Harry Truman who, among other measures, desegregated the U.S. military (Klinkner and Smith 1999: 208–241). Soon after, legal mobilization resulted in the Supreme Court's decision in *Brown v. Board of Education* in 1954 and a wave of contestation followed the arrest of Rosa Parks in 1955 (Klinker and Smith 1999: 242ff). While in the U.S. World War II had highlighted the position of African Americans in American society, in Canada, wartime experiences and the emergence of international interest in human rights through the newly formed U.N. shone a critical light on the wartime internment of Japanese Canadians and gave strength to domestic campaigns for stronger human rights legislation.

It was in the U.S. that the first organized efforts for lesbian and gay civil rights occurred with the founding of the Mattachine Society by Harry Hay in 1950 and the establishment of the Daughters of Bilitis in 1955. These organizations—usually styled "homophile"—pushed for education about and acceptance of homosexuality, especially in the medical community, hoping that de-pathologization and education would lead to greater social acceptance. The leaders of these organizations had roots in other forms of political activism. Notably, Hay was a member of the Communist Party of the United States. The Daughters of Bilitis organization was founded in 1955 by Phyllis Lyon and Del Martin and was probably the first explicitly lesbian political organization anywhere in the world. Beyond lesbian organizing, Lyon and Martin were also involved in other social justice organizations throughout their activist careers. Through the circulation of newspapers and newsletters (Mattachine's *One* and Daughters' *The Ladder*), these organizations raised consciousness throughout the United States and in other English-speaking countries such as Britain, Australia and Canada, where these materials circulated throughout the 1950s and 1960s prior to the official arrival of the modern lesbian and gay movement (D'Emilio 1983: 298; see also Valocchi 2001: 451–455). Inspired by the example of Mattachine, the Association for Social Knowledge (ASK), founded in Vancouver in 1964, also engaged in early homophile organizing (Kinsman 1996a: 229–233; Smith 1999: 28).

The transformation of the homophile movement into the gay liberation and lesbian feminist movements in the late 1960s and early 1970s occurred in a context of social movement ferment. The youth movements of the 1960s such as the anti-war movement, the student movement and the women's movement encouraged a questioning of the structures of social and political authority. The women's movement was an important precursor of the gay liberation and lesbian feminist movements because of its challenge to patriarchy and entrenched gender roles. The new left generally challenged authority structures and advocated democratic and participatory grass roots politics. The civil rights movement in the U.S. was the model for a rights-claiming movement that would achieve social and political change through litigation, demonstrations and civil disobedience. In this context, the Stonewall riots, which took place in Greenwich Village on June 27–28, 1969, mark the beginning of the modern lesbian and gay movement in the United States. The event is also a significant marker for other lesbian and gay movements throughout the English-speaking world and, certainly, events in the U.S. were watched very closely in Canada, especially among youth from English-speaking Canada who had easy access to U.S. media. Stonewall was the first occasion in which there was a spontaneous, open and direct contestation of the state's regulation of queer sexuality by lesbian, gay and trans people, especially drag queens (Duberman 1993). In both Canada and the U.S., the state had long used direct physical repression to control and regulate the expression of queer sexuality. Through monitoring and arrests of those who frequented gay and lesbian bars, through arresting gays for having sex in public places and through conducting surveillance on queers for state security, the arm of physical repression was ever present in gay and lesbian lives prior to 1969. After the contestation of police authority in the Village in June 1969, symbolically, the emperor had no clothes and the gay liberation movement burst onto the scene in the U.S., closely followed by similar movements in other Western countries, including English-speaking Canada and French-speaking Quebec. Prior to the open contestation of Stonewall, lesbian and gay cultures existed in largely informal networks that were submerged from public view. Stonewall marked the symbolic birth of modern queer movements; ironically, the spontaneous protests at Stonewall were led by trans people whose interests and identities were often marginalized within the subsequent "lesbian and gay" movement (Rudacille 2006: 151–159).

Both lesbian feminism and gay liberation not only asserted the validity and equality of same-sex sexual relationships but also challenged traditional gender roles. Gay liberation, especially in its earliest phases, presaged later groups such as Queer Nation and the genderqueer and trans movements of the 2000s by emphasizing the authoritarianism of the existing sex/gender system and arguing for a broad continuum of sexual rights, which would not force people to choose between gay/lesbian and straight sexual identities. For example, anticipating later debates on "the end of gay" (Archer 2004), the Australian gay liberation theorist Dennis Altman argued in 1971 that the gay world would eventually die, as the full bisexual potential of all people would be realized and that, as traditional gender roles were eroded, people would be free to choose their sexual preference without rewards and stigmas attaching to particular choices. As he put it, "[g]ay liberation . . . is part of a much wider movement that is challenging the basic cultural norms of our advanced industrial, capitalist, and bureaucratic society . . . It is a movement that is political, not in the traditional way that we have used that word, but because it challenges the very definitions and demarcations that society has created" (Altman, [1971] 1993: 244). Similarly, feminist Kate Millet clearly linked sexual and gender identity and captured the spirit of sexual liberation, demanding a "reassessment of the traits categorized into 'masculine' and 'feminine' with a total reassessment as to their human usefulness and desirability in both sexes," "unisex or the end of separatist character structure, temper and behavior so that each individual may develop an entire—rather than a partial, limited, and conformist—personality," "the end of the ancient oppression of the young under the patriarchal proprietary family," an end to "male rule through institutions: patriarchal religion, the proprietary family, marriage, the 'home,' masculine culture, and pervasive doctrine of male superiority," and "the end of enforced perverse heterosexuality, so that the sex act ceases to be arbitrarily polarized into male and female, to the exclusion of sexual expression between members of the same-sex" (Millett 1972: 1).

In both the U.S. and Canada, a lively women-centered culture grew up in the 1970s although lesbians often devoted their activist energies to the women's movement and independent lesbian political action was relatively rare outside of the cultural sphere. Gay liberation groups politicized the issue of sexual orientation and sexual identity more directly and the leadership and organization of the gay liberation groups of both countries was predominantly male, although some women did participate in gay liberation groups in both countries. Following Stonewall, in 1969, a number of gay liberation groups were founded in the U.S. The Gay Liberation Front (GLF) in New York and other gay liberation and radicalized homophile groups across the U.S. made common cause with the anti-war movement and with black nationalists such as the Black Panthers. In part in reaction to debates over alliances with other groups and involvement in other political issues, the GLF splintered and the Gay Activists Alliance (GAA) was established in order to focus solely on the achievement of gay civil rights. These groups mounted important campaigns in the U.S. throughout the 1970s against employment discrimination, police oppression and, importantly, against the medical establishment in order to remove homosexuality from the list of mental disorders in the psychiatric disorders diagnostic manual (Adam 1995: 81–89). In Canada, there were similar developments as a number of new homophile and gay liberation groups were formed or radicalized over this period and, by 1971, Toronto, Montreal, and Vancouver all had gay liberation organizations. In Toronto, the gay liberation newspaper *The Body Politic* was founded in 1971 and the paper would play a lead role in queer politics in the city and internationally until its demise in 1987. Although there was no analogue to Stonewall, the first pan-Canadian lesbian and gay rights demonstration was held on Parliament Hill in 1971 (Waite and De Novo 1971: 4–7). Therefore, by the early 1970s, the first glimmers of the human rights campaigns of the lesbian and gay movement were visible in the initial steps in organizing in major cities in both countries.

1969: CRIMINAL LAW REFORM

Despite the similarities between the two movements, they faced important differences in political environment and political institutions as well as in the legacies of past policies. These differences are exemplified by the different political course taken in 1969 on a key issue of gay rights—the criminal regulation of homosexual sexual conduct. This section outlines the origins and consequences of criminal law reform during the initial period of gay liberation. In subsequent sections, I explore the consequences of these differences for the evolution of the movement and the subsequent development of policy.

In Canada, as in the U.S., the 1960s were still a dangerous time for lesbians and gay men, making political organizing difficult. These dangers were called to public attention by the case of Everett George Klippert, who was convicted of "gross indecency" in the Northwest Territories after admitting that he had engaged in consensual sex with other men. Klippert was labeled a dangerous sex offender, meaning that he could be imprisoned indefinitely, and his sex offender status was upheld on appeal to the Supreme Court of Canada in 1967. As Tom Warner points out, the Court's decision "raised the chilling prospect that any gay man could be imprisoned for life unless he could prove he was unlikely to recommit a same-sex act" (Warner 2002: 46). Partially in response to the public outcry over the Klippert case as well as to advocacy work by ASK and by lawyers' groups such as the Canadian Bar Association, the federal government in 1967 followed the lead of Britain in tabling a bill to decriminalize homosexual acts between consenting adults twenty-one years of age or over. Britain's Wolfenden Report was influential in Canadian legal thinking as, during the 1950s and 1960s, the Canadian bar and Canadian judges still looked to Britain for guidance; in addition, the Canadian Criminal Code was constructed on British models and various sexual offenses such as keeping a "bawdy house" or engaging in "buggery" had been adapted wholesale from English criminal codes. The 1957 Wolfenden Report was not a gay liberation document; on the contrary, it was a set of suggestions for the reform of criminal law in the U.K. The report was strongly influenced by the Kinsey studies emphasizing the plasticity of sexuality and it was based on the frank assertion of the superiority of heterosexuality and the desirability of steering men who had sex with men (especially young men) into heterosexual relationships. Nonetheless, with regard to criminal law, the report suggested that a zone of legal privacy should be created for acts committed between consenting adults in private (McGhee 2000: 120–21). As a number of scholars have argued, the Wolfenden report was aimed at producing the "good" homosexual who would confine sexual activities to the private realm, without disrupting heteronormativity (Kinsman 1996a: 267–270; A. M. Smith 1994: 205–207).

The Canadian Criminal Code amendments, proposed in 1967 and passed in stages between 1967 and 1969, opened up access to abortion, loosened the divorce laws and "legalized" homosexual acts in private between consenting adults twenty-one years of age and older. These provisions on homosexuality, passed in 1969, meant that homosexual sex was "legal" in Canada, although the age of consent was higher for homosexual acts than for heterosexual acts. The 1969 reforms also provided for no-fault divorce and established a procedure by which women could obtain legal abortions. These changes were part of the Liberal Party's modernizing drive of the period and was seen as part of ensuring that law kept pace with the mores and values of a changing society, epitomized by the quotation from then Justice Minister (later Prime Minister) Pierre Trudeau "the state has no place in the bedrooms of the nation" (cited in English 2006: 471). As for Klippert, he was released from prison in 1971.

Just as the Canadian Bar Association and legal elites played a role in the reform of the Criminal Code in Canada over the period 1967–1969, so too in the U.S., there were debates among legal elites about the extent to which private sexual practices between consenting adults (including same-sex sexual practices) should be criminalized. As in the U.K. and Canada, American legal elites distinguished between religious and moral views with respect to the criminalization of such sexual practices between consenting adults in private. In debates of the mid-1950s to the early 1960s, the American Law Institute, an organization of legal scholars and lawyers, voted to decriminalize sodomy and other similar sexual acts as part of its review of criminal law in the U.S. The Institute developed a Model Penal Code, intended to provide a guide for the states and to encourage conformity and consistency in criminal law and procedure among the states (Andersen 2005: 19–20: Bernstein 2003: 360; Cain 2000: 134–142). As Andersen (2005: 22) points out, the Supreme Court's decision in the *Griswold v. Connecticut* case on the right to access birth control indicated an openness to change in this area. In 1967, following *Griswold*, the ACLU also supported the decriminalization of homosexuality arguing that consensual acts between adults were protected by the constitutional right to privacy.

Specific features of the institutional environment impeded policy change in this area in the U.S. while facilitating it in Canada. First, unlike the U.S., the federal division of powers in Canada allocates the criminal law power to the federal government. There was no need for Canadian legal elites to develop a Model Penal Code since they had direct access to the federal government, which had sole responsibility for criminal law in this area. Second, the parliamentary system makes it much easier for a determined executive to pass its legislative agenda unopposed. In contrast, in the U.S., the American Law Institute was conscious of the fact that opposition in state legislatures might torpedo the entire concept of the Model Penal Code, given that the code would have to be adopted by each state (Andersen 2005: 20). In the U.S., the division of powers system provides more points of access for determined opponents and the criminal law regulation of sodomy is a power belonging to the states, not to the federal government. These differences have greatly exacerbated the difficulty of legalizing sodomy in the U.S. In Canada, the question of criminalizing or decriminalization sodomy was framed in a policy package that included changes to ease access to divorce. Hence, the changes were presented as part of a progressive legal change, which would update the country's laws to reflect a changing morality. While some Canadians might have opposed this interpretation, they did not have easy access in influencing the debate beyond making their representation to the party in power. Once the government had decided to pass the reform package, opposition parties could not stop the legislation in Parliament, there was no legal ground for a court challenge against it and the provinces—even those that disagreed with the federal initiatives—had no jurisdiction over the policy area. In this way, institutional factors facilitated policy change. Although the Canadian system is usually seen as more decentralized than the U.S. system, in this particular jurisdictional area, the control of the federal government over criminal law gave the advocates of policy change an important institutional advantage over their counterparts in the U.S.

Canada's 1969 law reforms form a critical juncture in comparison with the failure of U.S. states to decriminalize sodomy, which had important repercussions through policy debates on lesbian and gay rights. The legalization of sodomy was the most important public policy issue in the lesbian and gay rights area in the U.S. until the *Lawrence* decision in 2003, which finally invalidated state sodomy laws. In Canada, sodomy laws were a non-issue. However, the lack of criminal law reform in the U.S. affected a broad range of legal and policy decisions. In a number of areas, the lesbian and gay movement in the U.S. has had to counter the categorization of homosexuals as putative or potential criminals (Cain 2000: 282–283; Rimmerman 2002: 57–64). Legal doctrines such as suspect class status under the equal protection clause, the right to privacy and First Amendment rights were all been shaped, directly or indirectly, by the criminalization of sodomy. Under the equal protection clause, sexual orientation or homosexuality could be treated as defining a category of citizens whose differential treatment requires strict or heightened scrutiny. However, the fact that, until the U.S. Supreme Court's *Lawrence* decision in 2003, homosexual conduct has been defined as criminal has been cited as grounds for denying lesbian and gay citizens the protection of suspect classification on the basis of sexual orientation (Cain 2000: 185–192). Furthermore, criminalization has affected the way in which the First Amendment has been used to create a distinction between conduct and status. While the First Amendment protected the rights of gays and lesbians in the United States to assemble freely and to circulate newsletters and other materials through the mail, it was not legal for homosexuals to engage in certain conduct (i.e., sodomy). In custody battles, judges in U.S. courts have referred to the fact that children of lesbian and gay parents may suffer adverse moral effects from witnessing the criminal behavior of their parents. In discrimination cases, judges have ruled that engaging in criminal (homosexual) behavior cannot form the ground for suspect class protection under equal protection or First Amendment protection for the right of intimate expression (Leslie 2000: 104). Studies of policy dissemination in the U.S. states have shown that states that "criminalize" homosexuality are less likely to recognize lesbian and gay rights in any other policy area including parenting, education, hate crimes or discrimination (Wald, Button and Rienzo 1996).

In contrast, in Canada, the stigma of illegality and criminality of homosexual sexual behavior was not available as a political lever for gay and lesbian rights opponents. This is not to say that Canada was a beacon of tolerance as a result of the 1969 reforms. In fact, Gary Kinsman argues, criminal law was used in other ways to pathologize and stigmatize queers and to attempt to regulate queer sexuality. For example, Canada's archaic "bawdy house" laws were used to close gay bathhouses, to hassle and arrest gays having sex in public places and the term "gross indecency" continued to be applied to homosexual sex and the Criminal Code continued to be used to regulate and police gay sex through such incidents as the infamous Toronto bath raids of 1981 as well as more recent raids in Montreal, Vancouver and in Calgary in 2002 and at the Pussy Palace in Toronto in 2000 (Bain and Nash 2007). For this reason, Kinsman (2003) refers to the legal change of 1969 as a "partial decriminalization" of homosexuality. Kinsman points out that "[t]he 1969 Criminal Code reform is today widely misunderstood as legalizing homosexual sex. It does nothing of the sort. Instead, it is a shifting of sexual regulation and policing. A limited private moral realm for two consenting adults (aged 21 and over) is established in which homosexual sex will be tolerated" (Kinsman 2003).

However, despite the ongoing process of criminalizing certain forms of queer sex, the decriminalization of sex acts between consenting adults in private did mark a key stage in the evolution of Canadian human rights policy and it had a substantial impact on subsequent policy development in others areas. This is because the change in the law signaled the fact that the state did not employ the direct strategy of criminalizing lesbians and gays for engaging in the sexual acts that might be reasonably deemed to define their identity. Courts, policymakers and lesbian and gay rights opponents could not use the argument that lesbian and gay people were *by definition* criminal or *by definition* automatically suspect as potential criminals. Therefore, courts could not deploy this argument either as a justification for their decisions. Hence, the criminal prohibition on sodomy was a factor in the development in American law and policy of the distinction between "conduct" and "status" (see Halley 1999). In contrast, the privatization of sexuality in Canada and the policing of public sexual expression did not entail the same distinction between status and conduct. In Canada, it was legally permissible for homosexuals to engage in conduct, if only in private, and the fact that this conduct occurred in private did not create any *necessary* moral opprobrium.

POLITICAL INSTITUTIONS AND HUMAN RIGHTS PRACTICES

At the time of the emergence of the lesbian and gay movement, the U.S. and Canada had developed different state policies and practices on "human rights" or on what is usually termed in the U.S. as "civil rights." The experiences of other rights-claiming groups in American and Canadian society were directly relevant for the lesbian and gay movement as policy and political battles that were fought over other issues, especially over race in U.S. politics and over Quebec nationalism in Canadian politics, created policy legacies that directly and indirectly shaped the fate of the lesbian and gay movement. For the civil rights movement in the U.S., the courts eventually provided a political opening for change, supported to some extent by leadership from the political executive. The institutional fragmentation of U.S. federalism and the separation of powers system was a major obstacle in the way of the advance of civil rights and, indeed, this was no accident as American federalism reflected the power of the southern states, especially as exercised through Congressional committees in the post-bellum, post-Reconstruction era, to enforce and maintain the Jim Crow system. Therefore, strong federal action combined with clear direction from the high court was necessary to overcome resistance to the dismantling of segregation (Klinkner and Smith 1999). The historical legacy of decentralization of power in the U.S. federal system in areas such as voting and the regulation of private discrimination are legacies of the confederal origins of the U.S., in part designed as the core compromise between northern and southern states at the founding. The political processes of segregation and desegregation shaped the terrain for subsequent rights-claiming by other stakeholders such as the women's movement, the lesbian and gay movement and the contemporary immigration movement. Protecting civil rights in the U.S. was a decentralized and fragmented process, reflecting many possible access points for policy change and social movement influence. At the same time, the many access points in the system also provided many veto points for policy change. As the Canadian comparison makes clear, it is particular noteworthy that policy change at the national level is so difficult in the U.S., while, in other jurisdictions like Canada, action on the federal or national level has become the norm. While this is a well-known feature of American politics, it has not been taken sufficiently into consideration in the area of lesbian and gay rights. The history of claims for very basic political rights by African Americans shows the ways in which entrenched opposition in American politics is amplified by the particular structure of U.S. political institutions.

Federal action through legislation did not seem likely to ensure discrimination protection for lesbians and gays, given the existing structure of federal anti-discrimination policy and enforcement. The Civil Rights Act of 1964 is the most important piece of federal civil rights legislation in the U.S., outlawing discrimination in public accommodation, public education, and employment for the employers covered by the Act and for programs receiving federal funding. The Act established a federal-level commission of enforcement, the Equal Employment Opportunity Commission (EEOC) that, along with state agencies, where they were established, was intended to mediate complaints and assist with civil rights litigation. The Act specifically mandated the Attorney General to investigate and undertake civil litigation where patterns of discrimination occurred. Title VII of the Civil Rights Act 1964 prohibited discrimination in employment and public education based on sex, race, color, religion, and national origin. In turn, state governments developed equal opportunity offices that, in most cases, were responsible for implementing Title VII. As the centerpiece of federal anti-discrimination protection, the Civil Rights Act was a natural target for successor social movements claiming legal protection from discrimination, including the LGBT community. Throughout the 1970s, there were repeated efforts to include sexual orientation within the ambit of the Act. This began with a bill introduced by Bella Abzug in 1974 that would have expanded the scope of protection for women under the Civil Rights Act, as well as including marital status and sexual orientation under the Act. Legislation to extend basic protections to lesbians and gays were repeatedly introduced in Congress throughout the 1970s (Campbell and Davidson 2000: 348–350; Feldblum 2000). The debate over affirmative action in the U.S., obviously linked to debates over racial equality, spilled over into consideration of a "gay civil rights bill" in the period as gay rights opponents consistently argued that extending civil rights protections would require employers to hire a quota of lesbian and gay employees, for example. In this way, debates and policy debate over race informed the consideration of lesbian and gay rights at the national level and, in 1977, when Ed Koch (echoing Trudeau's earlier comment) stated that "the state has no business in the bedrooms of this nation," his gay civil rights bill explicitly prohibited affirmative action or quotas (cited in Feldblum 2000: 156). In contrast, the EEOC, at least during its initial phase, was often criticized as lacking resources and power to enforce civil rights legislation (Pedriana and Strkyer 2004).

The idea of achieving policy change for the lesbian and gay movement through legislative action at the centre of American politics was not likely to succeed however. Unlike the concentration of power in the Canadian federal system that was used to change the criminal law, the dispersed authority of the executive and legislative leadership made concerted action much more challenging in the U.S. Rather than responding to policy changes set by the party leadership, individual legislators had their own priorities, reflecting the electoral calculus for their individual districts and seats. Given that lesbian and gay rights were hardly on the national radar in the 1970s, it was unlikely that the effort to obtain protection in the Civil Rights Act or through stand-alone legislation would succeed. It was in this context that many activists focused on the local level and were successful in obtaining anti-discrimination ordinances and, gradually, over time, in changing sodomy laws state-by-state. One of the most visible successes occurred in 1977 in Dade County, Florida, when a local anti-discrimination by-law was passed. Throughout the 1970s, many local ordinances of this type were passed throughout the U.S.; Werum and Winders's study of lesbian and gay activism from the 1970s to the 1990s shows a substantial increase in lesbian and gay rights measures over the course of the first decade of lesbian and gay activism (Werum and Winders 2001: 396).

Ironically, in Canada, the movement to build stronger human rights institutions during this period was a reflection of the relative weakness of courts. Because of the absence of a constitutional bill of rights, those who felt that their rights had been violated in Canada, had to find other grounds on which to bring rights claims to courts. Just as the U.S. constitution reflected a political negotiation between free and slaveholding states, Canada's constitution reflected a political compromise between francophones and anglophones. The only groups who received recognition of rights or legal standing in the 1867 constitution were the Protestant and Catholic religious minorities in certain provinces, who received constitutional protections in part to protect religious rights but in part also to protect the language and cultural rights of francophones and to secure Quebec's consent to Confederation in the 19th century. However, judicial review was not very well established in Canada initially (Stevenson 1993) and it was only at the turn of the 20th century that courts began to strike down legislation as unconstitutional and to develop a tradition of judicial review in the American sense. Because the Canadian constitution lacked a codified bill of rights (let alone any guarantees like the Fourteenth Amendment), judges in Canada often sought to decide questions of civil liberties under the terms of the federal division of powers and, in general, were decidedly timid on basic rights questions. The relatively tepid nature of judicial review and the lack of any constitutional rights document akin to the U.S. Bill of Rights, meant that the courts were not a very viable avenue of redress for minority groups (see Backhouse 1999).

Nonetheless, in part as a result of these critiques, pressure began to build from the 1930s to the 1950s for increased civil liberties and human rights protections. Following World War II, human rights groups began to develop specifically focused on securing equal treatment for ethnic, racial and religious minorities, especially after the internment of Japanese Canadians (Lambertson 2005; MacLennan 2003; Patrias and Frager 2001). In the movement that developed over this period, civil liberties were distinguished from "human rights," with the latter denoting the terrain of anti-discrimination provisions. Jewish Canadian organizations, especially those based in Ontario, made a key political decision to cast their political demands and mobilization beyond the protection of their own community and to build alliances with other minority groups, especially African Canadians and Japanese Canadians, for the protection of the rights of all religious, ethnic and racial minority groups in the province. In doing so, these groups played an important role in bringing about the first human rights legislation in Canada, which was passed in Ontario in 1961 (Lambertson 2005: 196–239). In addition to the mobilization of minority groups in favor of rights protections, the social democratic government of Saskatchewan set an example for other provinces by passing the first Canadian human rights legislation in 1944, which was quickly followed by other provinces, notably Ontario in 1951. Ontario's act, in particular, followed the example of neighbouring New York State in establishing fair employment and accommodation practices (Howe and Johnson 2000: 6–7). In 1960, the Conservative government of the day, responding in part to this pressure, passed legislation creating a Canadian Bill of Rights. However, this legislation applied only in federal jurisdiction and, unlike later human rights legislation, it had no specific apparatus for enforcement (Lambertson 2005: 318–386; MacLennan 2003: 126–161).

Therefore, it was in part the weaknesses of human rights protection in Canada that led to the creation of human rights commissions. Because the courts were less than proactive in relation to rights questions and because the scope of judicial review of rights questions was more restricted, the provinces adopted the model of the complaints-based human rights commission in order to implement and enforce anti-discrimination measures. Eventually, over the period from 1951 to 1977, human rights commissions were established in every Canadian jurisdiction as bureaucracies charged with implementing provincial and federal human rights policies, adjudicating human rights complaints, especially complaints of private discrimination by employers and landlords, and educating the public about discrimination and human rights. The human rights commission template in Canada left the investigation, mediation and redress of grievance entirely to the commission, which litigated on behalf of the complainant. This strengthened the arm's-length relationship between the commissions and the government of the day, as well as mandating a sizable bureaucracy to implement the complaints and investigations procedures (Howe and Johnson 2000: xiii–xiv).

In this way, by the time of the arrival of the lesbian and gay movement, American and Canadian activists faced very different sets of policy legacies in the area of discrimination law. In addition, the impact of changes in sodomy laws, several provinces, most notably Ontario, Canada's most populous province, already had in place a human rights commission that could serve as a focal point for demands for change and as a potentially important instrument for the rapid dissemination of policy change. If the lesbian and gay movement succeeded in obtaining the inclusion of sexual orientation as a prohibited ground of discrimination in provincial human rights legislation, this would protect lesbians and gay men from many areas of discrimination in provincial jurisdiction at one fell swoop. For example, as cities are the constitutional creation of the provinces, cities within the province would be covered by province-wide legislation. At the same time, employment by the province or by any para-public agency created or governed by the province (e.g., the hospital, university and education sector) would be covered by legislation, as would the behavior of private employers and other private actors such as landlords. The only areas that would not be covered by a provincial level would be the actions of the federal government itself as employer or regulator, which would extend to areas of federal jurisdiction such as transportation and communication. However, the bulk of discrimination with which lesbians and gays were the most concerned such as discrimination on the job and discrimination by landlords would be covered. Actions of the police would also be strongly influenced by this. The human rights commissions constituted a state elite that had an interest in the expansion of human rights protections (Howe and Johnson 2000). Over the years, the staff of the commission and the leaders of the human rights commissions, both provincially and federally, played a key role in advancing public discourse on rights and in undertaking human rights education. Although much of the educational work of the commissions—for example, their anti-racism work—might be dismissed as symbolic efforts of little practical use for marginalized minorities, in the area of lesbian and gay rights, the commissions eventually played an important role in intervening in public debates about lesbian and gay rights and in advocating the inclusion of sexual orientation as a prohibited ground of discrimination (Smith 1999). The establishment of a human rights commission gave state-sanctioned support to the discourse of human rights and, by naming the grounds of discrimination, created the possibility that other groups could be added to expand the list.

In contrast, in the U.S., the legal toolkit for human rights protections was more complicated and not as easily expanded as the experience of the women's movement and the lesbian and gay movement with the Fourteenth Amendment suggests. The historical legacy of the U.S. Bill of Rights and the complex decentralization and fragmentation of U.S. political institutions makes it more difficult to achieve rapid and thorough-going policy change and policy diffusion. Jurisprudence on equal protection under the Fourteenth Amendment has created a hierarchy between strict scrutiny, heightened or intermediate scrutiny and the rational basis test. Race-based classifications receive suspect class status requiring strict scrutiny while sex-based classifications require heightened or intermediate scrutiny. The lesbian and gay movement has not been able to secure a footing in the

Fourteenth Amendment beyond the rational basis test, the lowest level of constitutional rights protection, which is highly deferential to legislative objectives (Gertsmann 1999). Further, although constitutional rights protections existed on paper in the U.S. constitution, enforcement and implementation of the Fourteenth Amendment with regard to African Americans, especially in the South, was effectively absent until the 1960s. The framers of the Fourteenth Amendment were not aiming to protect human rights for a broad range of groups in American society such as women or other stakeholders; rather, in keeping with the historical context of their time, they were seeking to resolve the issue of slavery in the U.S. and to enfranchise blacks as American citizens. Obviously, the timing of the enactment of this cornerstone of U.S. civil rights policies did not reflect the rights-and-equality social movements of the 1960s, as did Canada's human rights legislation but, rather, the limited 19th century idea of civil rights that established former slaves as American citizens with the right to the equal protection and benefit of the laws. The aim of the Fourteenth Amendment reflects a 19th century American view of rights while the Canadian human rights legislation reflects a 20th century rights sensibility in which a broader range of social groups were striving for social, political and economic equality and in which there was a broad international movement toward human rights through the experiences of fascism, genocide, war, and anti-colonial movements. These differences in historical pacing and timing afforded Canada the opportunity to create modern human rights protections. Unlike the Fourteenth Amendment, provincial human rights legislation specifically named grounds of discrimination that were each placed on the same footing in the way that the clause was worded. This provided an opening for other grounds to be added through legislative change.

In the U.S., protection against discrimination could occur through ordinances issued by the executive, through legislation or through litigation. However, these institutional levers could also be used by gay rights opponents to counter the influence of the lesbian and gay movement on public policy. While states or cities could pass gay rights ordinances and laws, these could be undone using the mechanisms of referenda and initiatives and data analysis of the pattern of law-making and un-making from the 1970s through the 1980s shows that this is precisely what happened in many jurisdictions in the U.S. Werum and Winders (2001: 396) demonstrate that, while lesbian and gay rights measures were passed through legislative and executive action (and less often through judicial action), rollbacks sometimes occurred through the institutional mechanisms of direct democracy. The contrasting institutional models of human rights litigation and enforcement in the two countries are a legacy of the differences in the role of courts, judicial review and bills of rights in the two cases, especially with the extensive scope for civil litigation in the U.S., compared to the absence of this opportunity in the Canadian human rights commission model (Suk 2006).

POLICY BATTLES OF THE 1970S

The effect of the differences created by the ongoing criminalization of sodomy in the U.S. and by the institutionalization of different practices on human rights in the two cases can be seen at work over the subsequent historical period. In this section, I provide an overview of developments from the period of the decriminalization of homosexuality in Canada and the Stonewall Riot that ushered in the modern gay liberation movement in the U.S. through to the rise of AIDS in 1980–81.

Chauncey (2004: 30–34) argues that several factors drove the creation of the gay movement in the U.S. in the post-Stonewall period. Most of these factors also affected Canada. Chauncey sees the rebirth of feminism, the building of open gay and lesbian community and the insistence on coming out as essential elements of the post-1960s movement. As for the goals of the gay liberation movement at the outset, these were similar in the two countries as well. Chauncey (2004: 35) characterizes the post-1969 gay liberation movement as pursing the policy goals of ending policy harassment and surveillance of queer spaces; ending the stigmatization of homosexuality by medical science, governments and churches and eradicating discrimination in housing, employment and other areas. Other important social changes occurred in the two countries. In the area of religion, for example, Chauncey describes the movement within American Protestantism to condemn discrimination against lesbians and gays and the establishment of Metropolitan Community Church (MCC), a lesbian and gay friendly congregation, which challenged the traditional religious condemnations of same-sex sexual behavior and relationships (Chauncey 2004: 37).

Over the period between 1969 and 1986, the lesbian and gay movement in the U.S. and Canada began to reflect some of the differences produced by the policy divergence of 1969. In the U.S., the movement focused much of its legal and political energy on overturning the sodomy laws (Kane 2007). While the U.S. movement also sought to enact anti-discrimination measures, its efforts in this area were hampered in part by the ongoing consequences of sodomy laws. The legal opening in Canada provided by decriminalization of homosexual conduct in private provided a framework for demands for further legal change in the area of human rights. Over the 1970s and early 1980s, the movement focused on securing anti-discrimination protections and in pushing back the frontiers of police oppression and legal regulation of public cultural and sexual spaces (Warner 2002).

During the 1960s and early 1970s in the U.S., lesbian and gay organizations did not directly take on the issue of sodomy law reform through legislative change. The measure was defeated at the 1972 Democratic convention and so much stigma was still attached to homosexuality that organizers did not feel that there would be any success in mounting an open challenge; furthermore, lesbian feminists and gay liberationists who wished to transform traditional gender roles and the dominant categories of sexuality were not interested in legal reform. The fact that organizing would have to take place from state to state in order to effect change was also an important factor because the movement did not have the resources in the early period to mount state-by-state campaigns for reform (Bernstein 2003: 361–362). Over the period from 1961 to 1977, eighteen states overturned sodomy laws (Kane 2007; Bernstein 2003: 354). However, many of the changes were undertaken because of quiet legislative action, often through the incorporation of the proposed Model Penal Code without any particular explicit attention to homosexuality. At this time, there was also a proliferation of new lesbian and gay organizations, many of which were institutionalized legacies of the upswing of gay liberation. The radical direction of gay liberation, as exemplified by the Gay Liberation Movement and the Gay Activists Alliance (GAA), was tempered somewhat as the GAA became more focused on state-based lobbying and was reconstituted as the National Gay Task Force in 1973 (now known as the National Gay and Lesbian Task Force or Task Force, for short). The Gay Rights National Lobby was founded in 1978 and renamed itself the Human Rights Campaign Fund in 1980[1] (Rimmerman 2002: 28–34, 55–56). The movement in the U.S. focused on several main goals: enacting anti-discrimination measures to protect lesbians and gays in areas such as housing and employment and overturning the state sodomy laws. A number of organizations sprang up which specifically took on the sodomy laws.

One of the most important of these was Lambda Legal, a litigation fund on behalf of lesbian and gay rights, established in 1973. Together with the ACLU, the organization took on lesbian and gay rights cases over the 1970s and 1980s. The main areas of litigation for Lambda Legal over this period were cases of employment discrimination, dismissal from the military, child custody (i.e., lesbian or gay parents denied custody or access to their children on the grounds of their sexual orientation, usually mothers, denied access to or custody of their children after a divorce), freedom of speech or association (e.g., recognition by a university of a gay and lesbian group on campus), immigration, and sodomy laws. Of Lambda's litigation over its first decade, from 1973–1982, 19% of its docket was comprised of sodomy cases (Andersen 2005: 30–31). Further, according to Andersen's analysis, "[i]n virtually every case Lambda involved itself in, the criminalization of same-sex sexual conduct was invoked by opposing counsel to justify the disparate treatment of the lgb [lesbian, gay, bisexual] litigant" (Andersen 2005: 31). Although there were many more cases of family disputes over custody than there were cases of prosecution under the sodomy laws, Lambda pursued a strategy of prioritizing the fight against the sodomy laws. This was undertaken on the grounds that these laws had an effect on other areas of law and also on the grounds that it was much more difficult to win custody cases in the 1970s than it should have been to win sodomy cases, as lawyers for Lambda were well aware of the fact that there was strong support among legal elites for the decriminalization of sod-omy. For these reasons, Lambda lawyers felt that it would be easier to win the sodomy cases (Andersen 2005: 32–33). Custody cases were most often brought to Lambda when one spouse in a divorce, most often the mother, was denied custody of her children because of her sexual orientation.

Therefore, sodomy cases were pursued as a deliberate political strategy by Lambda and other allies and most of the resources of the organiza-tion went into fighting these cases, especially in New York state. Lambda's position on the importance of countering the sodomy laws was echoed by other organizations in the gay and lesbian movement over this period and there is broad agreement among observers that changing sodomy laws was by far the first priority of the lesbian and gay movement in the U.S. from the 1970s until their final and decisive reversal by *Lawrence* in 2003 (Ber-nstein 2003: 355; D'Emilio 2007: 45; Button, Rienzo and Wald 2000). Lambda, together with the ACLU, hosted a meeting of litigators in 1983 who created the Ad Hoc Task Force to Challenge the Sodomy Statutes. It was this network of litigators who began developing a legal strategy that eventually led to the *Bowers v. Hardwick* case, to be discussed in detail in the next chapter (Bernstein 2003: 365; Cain 1993).

During these same years in Canada, the focus turned to fighting for legal protections against discrimination, much of which took place in the provinces, rather than at the federal level. The 1969 Criminal Code reform had removed the issue of sodomy reform and grass roots gay liberation organizations in Canadian cities were tenuously networked in the national level National (or Canadian) Gay Rights Coalition,[2] which existed between 1971 and 1980 (Warner 2002: 154–161). Although the courts were a weak instrument for making this case, the movement followed the template pop-ularized by the African American civil rights movement in the U.S. in throwing itself at the courts in locally based strategic litigation. Lesbian and gay rights activists of the period understood that attempts to pres-sure provincial governments to include sexual orientation as a prohibited ground of discrimination in human rights codes were likely to fail and that court cases based on discrimination on other grounds, such as the grounds of sex, were also bound to lose in the courts. However, activists believed that these cases could be used to draw attention to the problem of lesbian and gay discrimination and, even more importantly, to build a sense of collective identity, to overturn the stigma associated with homosexual-ity and to bring other lesbians and gays out of the closet (Smith 1999: 41–72). Over the course of the 1970s, the gay liberation movement in Canada deliberately used courts as a means of achieving political change, creating community, and mobilizing the movement. The movement expe-rienced setbacks in a series of challenges including the case of employment discrimination against John Damien, the case of educational discrimi-nation against Doug Wilson, the case of discrimination in the rental of facilities to a gay liberation group and discrimination by the *Vancouver*

Sun newspaper, which refused the publication of an ad (Smith 1998; see also Warner 2002 and Korinek 2003). During the 1970s, many provinces established human rights codes and human rights commissions and this model was also adopted in federal jurisdiction through the passage of the Canadian Human Rights Act[3] and the Canadian Human Rights Commission in 1977. Most notably, pressure from within the caucus of the governing social democratic and nationalist Parti Québécois at the provincial level brought the first victory for the lesbian and gay movement in Canada on discrimination. In 1977, when Quebec passed its own human rights legislation and established the Quebec Human Rights Commission, sexual orientation was included as a prohibited ground of discrimination in the legislation, making Quebec the first province in Canada to prohibit such discrimination.[4]

While the change to the law in Quebec held, a similar law passed in Dade County, Florida, did not. There, a measure to prohibit discrimination against lesbians and gays, passed in 1977, sparked a backlash from the Christian evangelical movement. The most high profile was the mass campaign led by Anita Bryant against lesbian and gay rights recognition. Bryant was successful in her campaign to roll back lesbian and gay discrimination protections in Dade County and, in so doing, demonstrated how concentrated opposition to lesbian and gay rights recognition could be mobilized through the institutional openings provided in the individual states. In particular, the use of direct democracy to roll back the gains made by lesbians and gays in Dade County would be repeated many times in local battles in the U.S. over the 1980s and 1990s. The diffusion of opportunity and obstacles for discrimination protection in the U.S. through the federal, state, city and local levels and the private sector created a complex and multifaceted institutional environment for the small and struggling lesbian and gay movement of the 1970s. The weakness of enforcement measures in discrimination protection, the substantial role afforded to courts and to ligation as options for individual redress against certain types of discriminatory action and the multiplicity of institutional sites at which policies could be changed, created multiple cracks at policy change but, also, as Anita Bryant's campaign illustrated, multiple veto points for policy roll-back (Fetner 2001).

PARTISAN CONFLICT AND HISTORICAL TIMING

The lesbian and gay movement arrived on the scene during a period in which both the U.S. and Canada faced formidable domestic challenges in managing difference and diversity with their own borders. In the U.S., the rise of the civil rights movement, the continued racial inequalities in American society, and the racial unrest of the middle and late 1960s demonstrated that the passage of the Civil Rights Act of 1964 and the Voting

Rights Act of 1965 and other civil rights measures had been insufficient to defuse racial tensions or to bring about economic, social and political equality for African Americans. The United States faced a formidable challenge to its legitimacy and, because of its status as a superpower, this challenge was global. As the U.S. was waging an unpopular war in Viet Nam, supposedly for freedom and democracy, it seemed deeply problematic that the American government could not ensure democracy or even a reasonable measure of social, political, economic and civic equality for African Americans within its own borders (Skrentny 1996: 106ff).

In Canada, during the same period, the rise of Quebec nationalism posed a threat to the survival and legitimacy of the Canadian state. The nationalist movement was successful in calling attention to the political, social and economic inequality of French Canadians within Canada and developed a new national identity as *Québécois* (Quebecers), emphasizing the territorial boundaries of national identity, centered in the province of Quebec. From this definition of territorially based identity, it was a short step to the demand for outright independence of Quebec, put forth by the Parti Québécois, which won a majority government in the Quebec provincial election of 1976 and which held an independence referendum in 1980 (McRoberts 1993).

Therefore, over the 1970s, both the U.S. and Canada faced profound challenges that centered on the way in which difference and diversity would be accommodated within their societies and polities. The lesbian and gay movement arrived on the scene during this period of social and political change. Of course, the rise of the gay liberation and feminist movements as youth movements of this period was connected to the challenges by African Americans (through the civil rights movement and through the Black Panthers) and from Quebec nationalism. All of these movements were part and parcel of the social movement politics, which, in the case of the U.S. civil rights movements, had roots going back to the 1940s, but that clearly exploded on the scene in the mid-1960s. While it has often been noted that the lesbian and gay movement, like many other American social movements that followed in its wake, has to some extent borrowed the template of the African American civil rights movement and, in that sense, can be considered as a "spin-off" movement (McAdam 1995; Minkoff 1997), the impact of the civil rights movement is much more profound for lesbian and gay politics than is captured by the notion of spin-off. Certainly, the civil rights movement and the women's movement were critically important for the lesbian and gay movement for different reasons. The American civil rights movement set the model of strategy, tactics and discursive arguments over citizenship and equality that would be used by successor movements including the women's movement, the lesbian and gay movement and the contemporary American immigration movement. Similarly, the women's movement was also an important precursor movement for the gay liberation movement because it politicized gender and sex in a new way that opened up the discursive space for political claims around sexual orientation and gender identity in various forms. The women's movement also provided the main political home for lesbian feminists, many of whom did not participate systematically in alliances with gay men, especially in the initial period of these movements in the 1960s and 1970s (Faderman 1991).

Nonetheless, beyond its impact as a model of social movement activism, the American civil rights movement was also important because it provoked a massive public policy response from the American state, critically from the Johnson Administration. The lesbian and gay movement emerged on the scene during a period of partisan political change in American politics, when the party system and political discourse were undergoing a seismic shift that signaled the end of the New Deal era. While scholars date this shift in various ways—some date it from the election of Nixon in 1968 while others date it from the election of Reagan in 1980—studies of American development have emphasized the ways in which the public policies of the 1960s helped to create a backlash politics against the welfare state and against public policies that were perceived to benefit African American and other minorities as well as against the women's movement. This analysis rests on the policies designed by the administration of Lyndon B. Johnson to extend the American welfare state through the creation of the Great Society programs of the 1960s. When Johnson undertook the Great Society programs, it was clear that these were seen as an extension of full political and citizenship equality for blacks in the U.S., especially in relation to the central failure of New Deal policies such as Social Security to provide benefits for African Americans. In seeking to enact these programs, the Johnson administration recognized the limits of political equality and the need to deal with grinding poverty in the U.S. It has been argued that the design of these programs focused on the neediest citizens and that, in so doing, the design of the programs caused them to lose support, especially among white working-class Democrats. Because many of the programs benefited African Americans, the Great Society exacerbated the racial divide between African Americans and working-class whites (Skocpol 1988; Weir 1988). In addition, as the Democrats embraced civil rights public policies that benefited blacks, they began to lose their grip on the "solid South." As white male voters moved away from the Democrats and towards the Republicans, the Republicans were successful to some extent in depicting the Democrats as the party of special interests, a party that represented the interests of trade unions, minority groups, feminists, and others who were seeking a special deal from government that would cut against American values of equal treatment, individualism, and fundamental fairness (see Frymer 1999). Lesbian and gay Americans stepped into this cauldron of gender, race, and sexuality and were defined as part of the Democratic constituency at a time when the Democrats were on the political defensive.

Skrentny (1996) has emphasized these factors in his analysis of the evolution of federal affirmative action programs. He argues that, in part because of the Viet Nam War and because of the global audience for U.S. domestic politics, the government faced a serious challenge in the mid-1960s as racial unrest tore apart U.S. cities. The government was very sensitive to this dynamic and international considerations were part of the reason that the Johnson administration undertook the Great Society programs. Skrentny's (1996) analysis of the evolution of affirmative action shows that, originally, civil rights leaders argued for color-blind hiring policies but the legitimacy crisis of the 1960s led to tremendous pressure on federal agencies to get results and that many of these agencies began to slowly shift to hiring preferences. According to Skrentny, Nixon also perceived that he could use the issue of affirmative action to divide the Democrats. The political backlash against the politics of the 1960s in the U.S., in part organized and engineered by the rising Republican ascendance, linked the defense of the traditional nuclear family to the political identity of the working class white voter (the Reagan Republicans) and to a restored and revitalized American national pride after the humiliations of Viet Nam, Watergate, and the 1979 hostage crisis, which culminated in the Reagan election in 1980.

This backlash politics in the U.S. was fuelled in part by the growth of the Christian Right. Wilcox's (2006) work shows that evangelical activism in the U.S. has come and gone in waves over time, beginning with the political activism of the 1920s, symbolized by the Scopes Trial. Anticommunism was also very important in fundamentalist politics over the course of the 1940s and 1950s. However, the anticommunism of the fundamentalist movement of this period was not a major political force in its own right in the sense that anticommunism was widespread in American politics and society during this period. The fervor of the McCarthy period died off and the fundamentalist movement was in decline in the 1960s. According to Wilcox, two important events set off the most recent wave of Christian Right mobilization, which can be dated from the 1970s. These two events were local campaigns by the Christian Right on the issue of gay rights' ordinances and school curriculum symbolized by Anita Bryant's campaign in Dade County and the backlash against the *Roe v. Wade* (1973) decision on abortion and the proposal for the Equal Rights Amendment. Evangelical political mobilization was thus part of the partisan party conflict over the period of the 1970s and 1980s. Like the lesbian and gay movement, the Christian Right must be understood as a dynamic social movement that has evolved over time rather than as a static symptom of the state of public opinion or underlying political cultural values. As Clyde Wilcox defines it: "[t]he Christian Right is a social movement that attempts to mobilize evangelical Protestants and other orthodox Christians into conservative political action" (Wilcox 2006: 5). Recent analyses of the women's movement and social policy by scholars such as Anna Marie Smith (2001) and Sylvia Bashevkin (1996; 2002) have pointed out the ways in which gender equality and sexuality are

linked in social policy in the U.S. The promotion of stable families is linked
to the welfare backlash and to the politics of race as social policy debates
focused on what Bashevkin terms welfare hot buttons (see also Neckerman,
Aponte and Wilson 1988). Therefore, Christian evangelical activism in the
late 1970s and early 1980s can be seen as a backlash or countermovement
to both the women's movement and the lesbian and gay movement and as a
form of gender politics.

In contrast, in Canada, the legitimacy crisis of the 1960s took on a different political form and had a different political outcome, one that strengthened the idea of a human rights policy, increasingly defined as a component
of national identity, in different ways, in both English-speaking Canada
and Quebec. Just as the civil rights movement, the Viet Nam War and the
racial unrest in American cities during the 1960s had nothing directly to do
with the lesbian and gay movement or, directly, with queer sexuality, legitimacy threats to the Canadian state from the Quebec nationalist movement
indirectly shaped the terrain for the lesbian and gay movement. An expansion of lesbian and gay rights was an unintended consequence of a series of
political events, which, like the American crises of the 1960s, constituted a
threat to the legitimacy of democracy and the state from other quarters.

Quebec nationalism posed a powerful challenge to the legitimacy of
the Canadian state and exerted a strong influence on the partisan competition between political parties at the federal level. Quebec nationalists
who argued for an independent Quebec were countered by the centralist
Canadian nationalists of the Liberal Party, led by Pierre Trudeau, which
argued for a pan-Canadian sense of common identity based on a reformed
Canadian constitution with strengthened rights protections. While Quebec
nationalists argued that only a strong or independent government of Quebec could protect the interests of francophones, the Liberal Party put forth
a view of a bilingual Canada in which education and government services
would be available from coast to coast in two official languages. In 1969,
the Trudeau government passed the Official Languages Act[5] putting these
provisions into place and, throughout the 1970s, the Liberals pursued an
agenda of constitutional reform that would revamp Canadian federalism,
establish a formula to permit Canadian amendment of the constitution,[6]
and entrench a new bill of rights in the Canadian constitution. The passage of the new constitution in 1982, complete with the new Charter of
Rights, was in part the Liberal government's response to Quebec nationalism as well as to the centrifugal Western regionalism of the 1970s, which,
in the view of the centralizing Liberals, threatened to balkanize the country
(McRoberts 1997). The opposition Progressive Conservatives during this
period were much more favorable to a decentralized Canadian federalism,
although not as open to the entrenchment of minority language rights. The
expanded welfare state, pioneered from the left by the CCF-NDP in the
provinces and put into place by successive Liberal governments during the
war and, again, in a major period of expansion in the 1960s, was identified

with the Canadian nationalism of the Liberal Party. That is, this form of Canadian nationalism was identified strongly with official language minority rights, the elimination of the race-based immigration system, modernization of criminal law, easier access to divorce and abortion, a moderate welfare state, and a rights-based vision of individual citizenship, which was explicitly designed to counter the political appeal of Quebec nationalism (Russell 2004; Clarkson 2005).

It was into this much more favorable partisan political atmosphere that the lesbian and gay movement arrived in Canada. In contrast, the American movement had to contend with a powerful backlash against "big" government and against the changes wrought by the social movements of the 1960s. Through the partisan electoral contests of the 1970s, the protection of minority rights, eventually through a constitutional bill of rights, was increasingly identified with Canadian nationalism. While this was also linked to the partisan fortunes of the Liberals, it also created a discursive space in which the opposition Conservatives dared not challenge rights cultures as they were increasingly defined as Canadian values. By marrying Canadian nationalism to a new rights culture, the Liberal Party opened up a very favorable environment for lesbian and gay rights claims. In the U.S., the decline of the Democratic party and the rise of the Republicans generated a backlash politics against special interests and minorities, which created a hostile atmosphere for lesbian and gay rights claims.

INSTITUTIONAL FACTORS AT WORK

Historical institutionalist analyses emphasize the importance of "politics in time" (Pierson 2004) and this analysis shows how decisions that were made in one historical period—1969—had a shaping effect on the evolution of public policy in subsequent periods. Because of the structure of American federalism, the lesbian and gay movement in the U.S. was forced to counter the criminalization of sodomy on a state-by-state basis. At the same time, in Canada, this public policy issue was removed from the agenda, permitting the movement to concentrate on other areas, namely, combating discrimination against lesbians and gay men in areas such as employment. In the U.S., civil rights were developed through the Civil Rights Act of 1964, which created the federal Commission on Equal Employment Opportunity, empowered U.S. district courts to hear cases of discrimination in public accommodations and empowered the federal Attorney General to initiate litigation to protect civil rights in public education and public facilities. Efforts to reform this Act to include sexual orientation were unsuccessful. The large scope for litigation in the U.S. created multiple locations for policy change—the private sector, the states, and cities—but also multiple locations for blocking, rolling back or limiting the effect of changing human rights practices that protected lesbians and gay men. In contrast, the Canadian lesbian and gay movement faced an established template of human rights protections governing private and public discrimination, one that provided an obvious target for thoroughgoing and comprehensive policy change that would be implemented and enforced through federal and provincial human rights commissions.

Political institutional factors played an important role in shaping the terms of policy debates over lesbian and gay rights in the early period. This can be seen in the impact of federalism—both with regard to jurisdictional difference and with regard to the presence or absence of state constitutions. It can also be seen in the well-understood impact of the differences between the Westminster parliamentary system and the separation of powers system. As is argued by Tarrow (1998) and other social movement scholars who have focused on political opportunity, external opportunities can be critically important to social movement success. Historical institutionalism can be fruitfully used to build on the concept of political opportunity by offering a more focused and nuanced reading of the specific role of state institutions as a dimension of external political opportunity. In the case of criminalized sodomy, the federal division of powers provided a different structure of political opportunity for lesbian and gay movements in the two countries. The centralization of Canadian federalism with regard to the criminal law power permitted a determined federal government to change the law without regard to the views of provincial governments. The decentralization of the criminal law power in American federalism placed the responsibility of decriminalizing homosexual sodomy squarely with the states, which impeded the reform of criminal law in the U.S. in the 1950s and 1960s. As the discussion shows, there was support in the U.S. for the reform of criminal law on homosexuality at the same time that such reforms were under discussion in Britain, Canada, and other English-speaking countries. However, while the Canadian state provided easy access for expert legal opinion to influence the federal Department of Justice and the centralized political elite in the Westminster parliamentary system, the American state fragmented the jurisdiction and responsibility of criminal law, thus creating barriers to the influence of expert legal opinion.

The institutional mechanisms of the separation of powers system also play a key role in explaining U.S./Canada differences, a conclusion that is well supported in other analyses of U.S./Canada policy differences (Maioni 1998). In the case of the legal reform of criminal law of 1969, the government of the day did not have to contend with opposition in the legislature, because the government enjoyed a majority and, because of its jurisdictional power, it did not have to consult the provinces. In contrast, in the U.S., any initiatives to reform the criminal law would be subjected to the jurisdiction of the legislature, which would provide an opportunity to extensive political mobilization and lobbying by the lesbian and gay movement and by its well-resourced opponents.

In addition to these well-understood differences, which have been discussed in the literature in relation to other policy areas such as redistributive social policies (Weaver and Rockman 1993), this analysis also emphasizes the importance of American federalism in amplifying the fragmentation of power in U.S. political institutions. Specifically, the mechanisms of direct democracy and amendment of state constitutions are available in U.S. states and furnish an important aspect of political opportunity for the political mobilization of social movements. As the lesbian and gay movement in the U.S. started to organize, the countermovement of the Christian Right immediately began to deploy these weapons, beginning with Anita Bryant's infamous crusade of 1977. In Canada, these openings were not available to the evangelical countermovement.

The courts are also an important institutional power in the lesbian and gay rights area. During this early period, courts routinely ruled against lesbian and gay rights; however, in the U.S., the possibilities of challenging the constitutionality of certain laws through the courts (such as the sodomy laws) spurred the organization of litigation funds in lesbian and gay organizing, while litigation in Canada was organized purely in order to mobilize the nascent gay liberation movement of the period. In fact, the relative weaknesses of the courts in Canada on rights issues compared to the U.S. was one of the main reasons that the human rights commission template and deficiencies in constitutional rights protections were later remedied by the adoption of a constitutional bill of rights.

Political parties must be more firmly centered as part of the historical institutionalist analytical universe. Political institutions create specific incentives for particular patterns of party and electoral conflict and partisan politics is a key element in the story of lesbian and gay rights in the U.S. and Canada. From the late 1960s and early 1970s when the gay liberation and lesbian feminist movements arose in the U.S., they were defined as part of the liberal establishment, identified with the Democratic coalition, and caught up in the partisan politics of polarization which saw the Republicans successfully label the Democratic party as the party of special interests, minorities, and big unions. In other words, lesbian and gay politics became defined as part of a universe of political discourse in which race, gender, sexuality, and class were entwined to create a racialized and gendered enemy that was seized upon by the Republican machine and used to marginalize Democrats.

In contrast, in Canada, the reverse political dynamic was set in motion as, from the very moment of the Criminal Code reform of 1969, the movement was identified with the very definition of what it is to be Canadian (at least outside of Quebec), namely, human rights as defined by the Liberal Party, led by Pierre Trudeau. Tellingly, it was Trudeau who had begun work on the Criminal Code revision in 1967 as Justice Minister in the Liberal government of Lester B. Pearson and who brought the Criminal Code revision to fruition. As we will see in the next chapter, this same Prime

Minister, twelve years later, would enact the Canadian Charter of Rights and Freedoms (Charter), systematically entrenching broad ranging human rights protections in Canadian constitutional law.

CONCLUSIONS

The lesbian and gay movements in the U.S. and Canada faced different starting points with regard to policies in areas that directly affected lesbian and gay human rights, namely, the extent to which homosexual sexual behavior would be defined as criminal, as well as differences in pre-existing civil rights or human rights policies. Although sodomy laws were not regularly enforced in U.S. states, these laws were used to regulate gay and lesbian sexuality in ways other than a direct criminal charge of sodomy (e.g., prosecution of solicitation laws, public sex, etc). Furthermore, sodomy laws provided a rationale to deny equal protection to lesbians and gay men in a broad range of areas including child custody and employment discrimination. In contrast, although the 1970s saw very little progress in anti-discrimination measures for the lesbian and gay movement in Canada, the political debate that gave birth to the Charter portended a potential opportunity for the movement. As the Charter's impact on Canadian politics and society unfolded over a twenty-five-year period, the Charter became increasingly popular with Canadians. Lesbian and gay Canadians gained a great deal from the Charter and, hence, lesbian and gay rights were identified with the popular Charter. In the next chapter, I will show how these three main aspects of the analysis—policy legacies as they unfold over historical time, differences in the structure of political institutions (especially, federalism and the separation of powers system) and the nature of partisan electoral conflict between political parties—play out over the critically important period of the early 1980s.

3 *Bowers* and the Charter, 1980–1986

In early 1981, scattered reports began to appear of a new "gay cancer," a "cancer" which would eventually be named AIDS. AIDS quickly became a full-blown health crisis in the gay community and, coming on the heels of the first decade of gay liberation and lesbian feminist organizing, it would have important effects on political mobilization and public policy. However, it did not have these effects unmediated. The crisis intersected with the countermobilization by the Christian Right against gay and lesbian rights, which had been underway throughout the 1970s. This countermobilization included the deployment of ballot initiatives to repeal gay rights measures, epitomized by the Anita Bryant campaign, and the rise of the Moral Majority, symbolized by the election of Ronald Reagan. While the advent of AIDS strengthened the morality framing of lesbian and gay rights in U.S. politics, it also spurred new forms of direct action in the lesbian and gay community, such as AIDS Coalition to Unleash Power (ACT UP). At the same time, gay men with HIV/AIDS suffered discrimination in employment, housing, and medical treatment and their partners and friends were sometimes denied access to, and control over medical decision-making and respect for their wills. In some cases, legally recognized biological families often took control of funeral arrangements and property, barring same-sex partners from funeral services, burials or, in some cases, even access to their own apartments and houses (Shilts 1988). Christian Right mobilization and the stigma attached to "gay rights" in the AIDS era was symbolized by the U.S. Supreme Court's decision in *Bowers*, in which the Court upheld the constitutionality of Georgia's state sodomy statute.

In Canada over the same period, the early 1980s was the era of high constitutional crisis after the referendum on the sovereignty of Quebec in May 1980. Although the federalist side won the referendum, the Trudeau Liberal government entered into a new round of constitutional negotiation with the provinces. This constitutional crisis provided an institutional and political opening for social movement and other actors who wanted to reshape the meta-rules of the political game. Stakeholders in the area of human rights including Aboriginal peoples, the women's movement and ethnocultural minority groups mobilized to obtain and secure an expansive definition of their rights in the recasting of the constitution. The development of human rights commissions provided the backdrop for the proposed Charter of Rights and generated political pressure for an expansive document as well as a proactive interpretation of the document by the courts. As we have seen in the previous chapter, the proposed Charter had nothing directly to do with lesbian and gay rights; rather it was a political response by the federal Liberals to the strength of Quebec nationalism during this period. Nonetheless, the change in the structure of political institutions eventually bore fruit for the lesbian and gay rights movement. Over time, the Charter and the muscular interpretation given to the Charter by Canadian courts created and reinforced a policy discourse of human rights that would send lesbian and gay rights policies in Canada in a much more expansive direction and directly contribute to the widening gulf between Canada and the U.S. in this policy field.

Partisan politics in the U.S. over this period was heading in a very different direction, with the election of Ronald Reagan, the mobilization of the Moral Majority opposition to changes in gender and family politics, especially abortion rights, and the general backlash against big government and affirmative action. As historical institutionalists have emphasized, the abortive expansion of the American welfare state during the Great Society period of the 1960s divided Americans along racial lines, leaving the Democratic coalition vulnerable to the charge that the party stood for big government, special interests and minorities. The *Roe* decision in 1973 mobilized the Christian Right against feminism, the women's movement and the courts (or "judicial activism"), which were held responsible for *Roe* (Wilcox 2006). Lesbian and gay rights in the U.S. were caught up in the countermovement against the women's movement and the racial backlash against the gains that had been made by African Americans in the civil rights movement and the establishment of affirmative action programs. As this chapter shows, the institutional openings provided by state constitutions such as ballot initiatives were successfully exploited to contest advances in lesbian and gay rights protections. This contestation was reflected in the harshness of the *Bowers* decision, the first major decision from the U.S. Supreme Court on lesbian and gay rights.

The chapter begins by exploring the impact of AIDS on lesbian and gay organizing, the rise of the Christian Right countermovement in the U.S. and its use of institutional opportunity. The chapter then compares the background and consequences of *Bowers*—including the scathing attack on gay rights in the U.S. Supreme Court—with the constitutional entrenchment of equality rights in Canada during the same period. Differences in the policy paths taken in 1969 were compounded in the turning point of the mid-1980s, when policy divergence accelerated even further as the U.S. lesbian and gay movement was devastated and radicalized by *Bowers* while the Canadian movement began to explore the potential of the equality rights provisions of the Charter.

AIDS AND THE DEVELOPMENT OF LESBIAN AND GAY ORGANIZING IN THE 1980S

The impact of AIDS in the early 1980s highlighted the link among homosexuality, sexuality and disease and reinforced the stigmatization of gay men. AIDS had important indirect effects on lesbian and gay organizing, by encouraging institutionalized and professionalized organization, contributing to the development of lesbian and gay organization, especially at the federal level in the U.S., and in spurring direct challenges to the stigma of homosexuality through the example of direct action groups such as ACT UP (Epstein 1996; Andriote 1999; Gould 2001; see also Siplon 2002).

In the U.S., AIDS highlighted the state regulation of sexuality through the sodomy laws. Even if these laws were not enforced, they stood as a symbolic statement of the inferiority, stigma, and condemnation of homosexual sexual conduct. The link between homosexual behavior and AIDS only served to reinforce the stigma. Just as in Canada, the change to the legalization or decriminalization of sodomy had occurred with a strong specification of its legality *in private*, efforts to fight the sodomy laws across the remaining states where these laws were still in force during the 1980s emphasized the right to privacy and the link between decriminalization and AIDS education. Activists pointed out that, to the extent that unprotected sex caused transmission of HIV, the criminalization of sodomy impeded education and treatment because it discouraged HIV testing. Activists continued to emphasize the importance of the separation of church and state and, especially in lobbying state legislatures, tended to emphasize that the decriminalization of sodomy did not entail condoning homosexual behavior from a moral or religious perspective (Bernstein 2003: 367–368; see also Altman 1994). The Privacy Project, organized by the National Gay and Lesbian Task Force, did increase the level of organization in the states and these organizations of the 1980s emphasized other issues beyond sodomy law reform such as anti-discrimination and AIDS (Bernstein 2003: 365–369). Nonetheless, the use of the term "privacy" underscored the lines that the movement wanted to draw between private and public and the idea that the movement would have more success by moderating its appeals and emphasizing freedom from state interference with private conduct, especially when lobbying at the state level. The term "privacy" also built on the expansion and solidification of this concept as a legal tool of new social movements of the 1960s that had politicized gender relations. Aside from its use in the *Griswold* case on contraception, the right to privacy concept was also used in *Roe v. Wade* in which women's right to choose, at least during the first trimester, was situated in the context of the right to privacy.

AIDS had complex effects on lesbian and gay organizing in both the U.S. and Canada. Over the course of the 1970s, lesbian and gay organizing in both countries was primarily local and grass roots. AIDS resulted in a professionalization of organizing in both countries as the first institutionalized links were formed in the 1980s among governments, funding agencies and non-profits in the AIDS area, organizations that were predominantly organized by lesbians and gay men such as the Aids Committee of Toronto (ACT) (Kinsman 1996b; Rayside and Lindquist 1992). Reflecting the state-by-state battle over sodomy law reform, litigation strategies were viewed as the most effective means to counter the criminalization of sodomy in the U.S. and, as we have seen in the last chapter, national level litigation organizations such as Lambda emerged to undertake that campaign. In the U.S., the federal role in health funding and the federal government's lack of action on AIDS, spurred national organizing. Analyses of the AIDS crisis have also shown the important urban effects of organizing, especially for self-help. For example, Andriote (1999: 83) contrasts the ways in which AIDS organizations were built up in New York in order to serve the needs of the community through self-help because of the failure of city, state, and federal governments. In contrast, in San Francisco the city government played an active role in providing AIDS-related services. Furthermore, the rise of the Christian Right also spurred the centralization and nationalization of lesbian and gay organizing (Fetner forthcoming). During the AIDS crisis, problems of discrimination against individuals in employment, housing, and health care as well as problems related to discrimination against couples in areas such as health decision-making, wills, and even the right to visit in hospitals highlighted the lack of equality in the most distressing and tragic of circumstances. Between 1983 and 1992, Lambda Legal's docket of cases grew to include AIDS cases and, over this decade, 30% of its case load concerned AIDS discrimination (Andersen 2005: 38). At the same time, even where anti-discrimination measures existed in the U.S., there were often not enforced. As Andersen describes, much of Lambda Legal's docket during the 1980s was taken up with enforcement and implementation of anti-discrimination measures where these existed, especially at the state and local levels (Andersen 2005: 40).

The lesbian and gay movement used multiple avenues of political opportunity in seeking legal and policy change in the U.S. While, during the 1970s, a few anti-discrimination measures had been passed, these measures tended to spark an anti-gay backlash from evangelicals who used state constitutions to initiate referenda and initiatives to strike down gay rights. Over this period in the U.S., the lesbian and gay movement and its allies were most successful in passing antidiscrimination measures at the level of cities (especially college towns). Often, ordinances were used because of the support of executive leadership at the city or state level. State courts were also an important avenue for gay rights advocates. In contrast, the Christian Right and other opponents of gay rights were most successful using ballot initiatives and referenda, whether at the local, city, or state level. Therefore, the opponents of gay rights tended to draw on institutional levers that would mobilize popular support while gay rights advocates tended to draw on institutional levers that required concentrated political leadership (Adam 1995: 109; see also Fetner 2001; Werum and Winders 2001: 398).

The lesbian and gay rights movement in the U.S. over the 1970s and 1980s did not have many clear-cut successes until the *Romer* decision from the U.S. Supreme Court in 1996. Success tended to come at the state, city, and local level and, once these successes were achieved, they became the target of rollback through ballot initiatives and referenda. Werum and Winders (2001) find that from the 1970s to 1994, gay rights advocates focused increasingly on the local initiatives while opponents focused increasingly on ballot initiatives. Button, Rienzo and Wald (1997) argue that hostility at the federal level focused lesbian and gay action to the subnational level. State courts, state legislatures, cities and localities have been the main battlegrounds for gay rights battles in the U.S. from 1974 to 1994 (Donovan and Bowler 1998). According to Haider-Markel and Meir who extensively examined these lesbian and gay rights campaigns, between 1972 and 2001, ballot initiatives or referenda were held in at least 122 cities, counties and states and, of these, 71% resulted in losses for lesbian and gay rights (Haider-Markel and Meier 2003: 676; see also Haider-Markel 2003). These campaigns illustrate the vulnerability of lesbian and gay anti-discrimination measures when the issue moves to a broader audience, as in the case of an election campaign. Haider-Market and Meier demonstrate that supportive elites, entrepreneurial politicians, and a strong civil rights record facilitated local or state-wide anti-discrimination protection while the assault on such measures through initiative or referenda permitted anti-gay forces to mobilize politically and to frame the issue in black and white "morality politics" terms (2003). In general, a number of scholars have established the fact that minority rights are vulnerable when exposed to the processes of initiative and referenda (see also Gamble 1997 and Donovan and Bowler 1998).

Canadian and American political institutions offered different routes to political mobilization and opposition for Christian Right mobilization and the legacy of previous policies that stigmatized lesbians and gay men made it much easier for the Christian Right to mobilize in the U.S. In the U.S., the Christian Right could exploit the association between criminality and gay male sex and then draw on the crisis of AIDS to cement the connections among criminality, illness, sex, and stigma. Further, the criminalization of sexual acts reinforced the distinction between "hating the sin, loving the sinner" that formed a key part of Christian evangelical proselytizing on the AIDS issue. In the U.S., every step in the direction of protecting lesbians and gay men from forms of discrimination in areas such as housing and employment, was met with a discourse of fear-mongering that associated homosexuality with pedophilia and claimed that any measure to protect gays and lesbians from discrimination would create special rights for homosexuals to engage in criminal behavior and to convert children to the homosexual "lifestyle," possibly through means of child sexual abuse (Herman 1997).

These fears existed in Canada as well as in the U.S. Evangelical opposition and mainstream discomfort with homosexuality were part of Canadian society in the 1980s, as they were in the U.S. Evangelical subcultures were relatively strong in Canada over this period and church attendance remained steady among these churches, even as church attendance dropped off for other denominations (Bibby 2002: 20; Reimer 2003). Studies of Canadian religious attitudes over the period from the 1970s to the 2000s show that a majority of Canadians adhered to religious or spiritual beliefs and values, even though church attendance had declined (Bibby 2002; see also Bibby 1987, 1993). However, as Reimer's (2003) study shows, while American and Canadian evangelicals held similar political views, they differed in terms of political participation; Reimer concedes that differences in political opportunity for evangelical mobilization may play a role in explaining these differences in what he conceptualizes as a common evangelical subculture that spans the border. In Canada, among other factors, the policy legacy of the criminal deregulation of homosexuality made it more challenging for evangelicals and gay rights opponents to mobilize. Attempts to criminalize gay male sexual behavior through raids on gay baths and through the prosecution of Toronto's *Body Politic* newspaper for having published an article on gay men having sex with underage boys backfired on the police. Raids on the baths and the locking of the *Body Politic* offices outraged the gay community and led to one of the largest public demonstrations in Toronto's history (Jackson and Persky 1982). The political mobilization of the lesbian and gay community at the local level to counter police behavior created new networks of legal organizing that would be exploited in the Charter era. Police raids had no lasting effect in countering the growing human rights discourse in Ontario and elsewhere in Canada and, if anything, spurred elite political opinion (especially legal opinion) in the direction of supporting and calling for much stronger human rights protections from the courts. In the evolution of these developments, evangelicals, and other gay rights' opponents in Canada were hampered by the lack of political legitimacy in the police attack on gay men. The dominant Liberal party's new brand of Canadian nationalism had built in a commitment to personal privacy in sexual matters as part of Canada's modernization from the deferential colonial mindset to the assertive and modern nation depicted by Liberal politicians under Trudeau's leadership in the 1970s and 1980s. The commitment to withdraw the stigma of criminality from gay men was a policy legacy that had become bound up with the political and constitutional visions of the political parties.

In addition, the Canadian countermovement lacked access to political institutional resources. The most that the movement could hope for would be to dominate a provincial government in a particular province such as Alberta. While the movement might have been able to exert influence within a political party such as Social Credit in a province such as Alberta which tended to support one party, the evangelical movement was not able to stop local action on lesbian and gay human rights at the city level in places such as Toronto or at the provincial level in Quebec. Most importantly, the countermovement was not able to use the institutional weapons of initiative and referenda to attempt to roll back antidiscrimination measures when they were passed. The concentrated political authority of the Westminster parliamentary system also blocked policy change as well as facilitating it. Where the political will existed for policy change, Westminster institutions facilitated rapid and thoroughgoing change that was difficult to reverse, as was the case with the Criminal Code reform of 1969 (see Weaver and Rockman 1993). At the same time, these institutions also facilitated blockage when the government in power did not want to touch a political issue or did not want to undertake policy change. While the independent commission model of human rights protections facilitated an ongoing public debate about human rights, demands for the inclusion of sexual orientation as a prohibited ground of discrimination were largely unsuccessful in Canada (except Quebec) until they were forced on governments by the courts in the wake of the entrenchment of the Charter.

BOWERS V. HARDWICK (1986)

The coordinated attempt to overturn the criminality of sodomy statutes through quiet legislation in the U.S. had secured changes in many states and the *Bowers* case was the result of a multi-year multi-pronged strategy by Lambda Legal and the ACLU to decriminalize sodomy laws through litigation. While sodomy reform remained a major objective of Lambda's litigation, AIDS issues, and family and relationship recognition were also becoming important issues in gay and lesbian rights litigation by the mid-1980s (Andersen 2005: 39; Cain 2000: 169–172). It is in this context that the *Bowers* case was heard by the U.S. Supreme Court.

The main question in *Bowers* was the constitutionality of the Georgia statute that prohibited oral and anal sex. Michael Hardwick had been arrested by a police officer for having consensual, anal sex in his own home, after the police had been let into the house by a guest, unbeknownst to Hardwick. Although the local prosecutor decided not to seek an indictment, Hardwick challenged his arrest under the Georgia law in district court with Michael Bowers, Attorney General of Georgia (and others) as defendants. Because the Georgia law also prohibited heterosexuals from engaging in such acts, a heterosexual married couple joined Hardwick's case. After a defeat in district court, the U.S. Court of Appeals for the Eleventh Circuit ruled in favor of the plaintiffs and the case was then heard by the U.S. Supreme Court on appeal. In 1986, in *Bowers,* the Court ruled against Hardwick and the other plaintiffs, arguing that the there was no constitutional grounds to strike down the Georgia law (Cain 2000: 172–179; Brewer, Kaib and O'Connor 2000: 390).

The process of legal mobilization in *Bowers* conformed to the model that was best symbolized in U.S. cause litigation by the National Association for the Advancement of Colored People (NAACP) and deployed by the women's movement and other groups seeking protection from discrimination in U.S. public policy. In the case, Michael Hardwick was represented by Laurence Tribe, a Harvard law professor who was supported by the ACLU. There were a large number of *amici curiae* supporting the challenge, including the National Gay Rights Advocates and the Lesbian and Gay Rights Project as well as the American Psychological Association, the American Jewish Congress, the Presbyterian Church, the Association of the Bar of the City of New York and the Attorney Generals of New York and California. On the other side, briefs were filed by, among others, the Catholic League for Religious and Civil Rights and the Rutherford Institute, a conservative litigation fund (*Bowers*: 190). Very clearly, for the lesbian and gay movement, the *Bowers* case was a concerted legal action, which aimed to obtain a ruling from the U.S. Supreme Court striking down criminal laws in the states that prohibited sodomy.

The main disputes in *Bowers* concerned the application of due process, equal protection, and the right to privacy. In U.S. constitutional jurisprudence, two of the central doctrines that govern civil rights policy are the idea of substantive due process and the idea of equal protection. An important line of jurisprudence in U.S. courts since the 1960s had established the right to privacy as an aspect of substantive due process under the Fourteenth Amendment. The idea of incorporating substantive due process into the Fourteenth Amendment is in itself controversial. Critics of judicial activism have argued that the Fourteenth Amendment refers to procedural rights and not substantive rights and that its purpose was to ensure the incorporation of African Americans into citizenship by ensuring that they could not be deprived of liberty without a process in which their legal rights were respected and implemented. In the 1920s, U.S. courts begin to incorporate the doctrine of substantive due process. This doctrine was used to recognize the substantive right not to be interfered with by the state, even when the process of interfering with life, freedom, or property had been undertaken according to the rule of law. In other words, rather than focusing solely on process, substantive due process, as its name implies, entails a consideration of the actual substance of the state's action in relation to the liberty of the individual. There are a number of ways that this can be done. One of these doctrines is the "fundamental rights" theory, namely that the state may not abridge rights that fall under the general meaning of the term "liberty" in the Fourteenth Amendment, even if these rights are not specifically enumerated elsewhere in the Constitution. Such rights may be "deeply rooted" (although not explicitly mentioned) and, hence, deemed worthy of constitutional protection (see Eskridge and Hunter 2006: 7–10, 113–124).

One of the rights that has been protected under this rubric is the right to privacy. This right had been defined in cases such as *Griswold* (1965) in which the Supreme Court stated that the right to privacy within marriage includes the right to use contraceptives. In *Loving v. Virginia* (1967) on interracial marriage, the U.S. Supreme Court also ruled that the right to interracial marriage was permissible not only on equal protection grounds, but also on the grounds of substantive due process given that freedom to marry constitutes a fundamental liberty interest (Abreu 2002). The right to privacy was also developed by the Court very famously in *Roe* (1973) on women's reproductive rights. In *Roe*, the right to privacy was defined as the right to terminate a pregnancy during the first trimester of pregnancy and freedom from state interference with a woman's right to choose. In *Griswold* and other cases, the right to privacy was deemed to be incorporated into the substantive due process clause of the Fourteenth Amendment (DeCew 1997).

In *Bowers*, the question arose as to whether or not the state could prohibit private sexual conduct in the home, including oral and anal sex, when this conduct was carried out by homosexuals or by married heterosexuals. By including married heterosexuals in the case, the case played down the issue of sexual orientation discrimination. That is, both heterosexuals and homosexuals were affected by the Georgia statute, even though, in practice, it was homosexuals who had been directly affected by it in terms of arrests and prosecution and indirectly affected by it in terms of its use as a justification for discrimination and the denial of recognition of same-sex relationships and parenting rights. This was a deliberate strategy because the plaintiffs wanted to litigate the case under the right to privacy with which, given the results of the line of right to privacy cases since *Griswold* and *Roe*, advocates felt that they would be on much stronger ground. However, the heterosexual couple was denied standing in the case in the Supreme Court and did not challenge their exclusion from the case. The fact that a heterosexual couple had been added to the case even though they had not been arrested or charged demonstrated the caution with which the plaintiffs and the legal organizations were proceeding. That is, rather than focusing very squarely on the question of equal protection under the Fourteenth Amendment on the grounds of sexual orientation or, in other words, on the idea that the state discriminated against Michael Hardwick because he was gay, the case focused mainly on the ground of privacy, given that the legal precedents in that area seemed promising and that the conduct occurred in his own home. Therefore, there was a reasonable hope that the case would be successful on privacy grounds. As Nan Hunter, director of the Lesbian and Gay Rights Project at the ACLU at this time commented, "[w]hat brought us within striking distance on this case was the essential conservatism of the claim—a privacy argument based on the intersection of core values of individual identity and a-man's-home-is-his castle locational sanctity" (cited in Deitcher 1995: 146).

Nonetheless, the Court found that homosexual sodomy was not a fundamental liberty interest, nor was it deeply rooted in the nation's history or derived from a liberty interest in marriage, family and procreation (*Bowers*: 190–192; see also Abreu 2002). They rejected the idea that previous privacy cases such as *Roe* or *Griswold* sanctioned a right to privacy in sexual behavior between consenting adults and pointed out that the expansive and substantive interpretation of the due process clause of the Fourteenth Amendment required that such rights be recognized in this way had to be "implicit in the concept of ordered liberty." In this case, the Court rejected the view that homosexual sodomy had anything to do with family, stating that "[n]o connection between family, marriage, or procreation on the one hand and homosexual activity on the other has been demonstrated" (*Bowers*: 191). Furthermore, the argument that the right to engage in sodomy is "deeply rooted the history and tradition of this nation" was "facetious," in the words of Justice White, writing for the majority (*Bowers*: 192; see also Lewis 1997). In making these statements, the Court made it clear that it was concerned about its own legitimacy if it took an expansive view of due process:

> Nor are we inclined to take a more expansive view of our authority to discover new fundamental rights imbedded in the Due Process Clause. The Court is most vulnerable and comes nearest to illegitimacy when it deals with judge-made constitutional law having little or no cognizable roots in the language or design of the Constitution. That this is so was painfully demonstrated by the face-off between the Executive and the Court in the 1930's, which resulted in the repudiation of much of the substantive gloss that the Court had placed on the Due Process Clauses of the Fifth and Fourteenth Amendments. There should be, therefore, great resistance to expand the substantive reach of those Clauses, particularly if it requires redefining the category of rights deemed to be fundamental. Otherwise, the Judiciary necessarily takes to itself further authority to govern the country without express constitutional authority. The claimed right pressed on us today falls far short of overcoming this resistance (*Bowers* 1986: 194–195).

The Court also rejected the claim that there was no rational basis for the law because it was based on a particular view of morality, arguing that all law is based on morality, although in his separate concurrence, Justice Powell pointed out that the plaintiff might have a case under the Eighth Amendment's prohibition against cruel and unusual punishment if imprisoned for a full twenty years as provided for under the Georgia law (*Bowers* 1986: 197–198).

However, the dissent in *Bowers* highlighted the right to privacy as protecting a right to intimate association and as protecting the sanctity of the home (*Bowers:* 199ff). Furthermore, the dissent took strong issue with the majority's comments about the deeply rooted test, arguing that the case concerned the fundamental right to be left alone in one's own home and that the infringement of the right to privacy and intimate association in the home could not be justified by reference to traditional morals or religious values. The dissent argued that the law could not hew to the morality of the past and pointed out that, according to the American Medical Association, homosexuality was no longer considered to be an illness or a disease (*Bowers:* 203). The dissent also contested the majority's refusal to treat the question as one of equal protection under the Fourteenth Amendment making it clear that the state of Georgia had repeatedly raised the issue of homosexuality in its presentation of the case, indicating that the state had a particular interest in prosecuting homosexual activity, despite the fact that a heterosexual couple had joined the case (*Bowers:* 203). According to equal protection doctrine, citizens could not be segregated based on characteristics that are "irrational" (*Brown*). If a classification discriminated against a particular class, it had to be established which level of scrutiny applied to the particular class in question. For example, racial classification was subject to the highest level of scrutiny—strict scrutiny—and race was deemed a suspect class under equal protection. Gender discrimination was subject to heightened scrutiny as sex was defined as quasi-suspect class. In other cases, such as sexual orientation, classifications or distinctions among groups of citizens could not be arbitrary. In other words, classifications must pass the "rational basis" test (Hubins 2001). As the dissent argued, the majority failed to consider the *Bowers* case from the perspective of equal protection doctrine. Rather, the case was decided on the grounds of due process and the right to privacy. Therefore, the *Bowers* decision only applied to sexual behavior and not to sexual orientation, thereby maintaining the conduct/status distinction (Hubins 2001). The *Bowers* decision did not discuss same-sex marriage but the decision does state that there is no connection between marriage, family and procreation and this was one of the grounds on which the decision was made in favor of the constitutionality of the sodomy laws (see J. P. Kelly 1997).

The application of equal protection to lesbian and gay citizens in the U.S. has been the subject of much debate. In the U.S., the immutability of the individual characteristic that distinguishes the (potentially) suspect class under the Fourteenth Amendment is a key part of the concept of equal protection under the law, i.e., it is unfair for people to face discrimination because of a characteristic they are not able to change or a characteristic that is not their fault (Levay and Nonas 1995: 274–275; see also Epstein 1987). In *Bowers*, it was clear that the Court did not accept the view that

homosexuality was immutable and this was a major obstacle to the recognition of lesbian and gay rights in the decision. Because of this strong
statement in *Bowers*, it was understood that the jurisprudential regime in
the U.S. did not define lesbians and gays as belonging to even the quasi-
suspect class. The Court clearly stated that, even with respect to the idea
of a "rational basis," the most minimal level of protection, the state could
use public morality as a sufficiently "rational basis" to criminalize sodomy
(Cain 2000: 179).

IMPACT OF *BOWERS*

The *Bowers* decision had important effects on the political mobilization
of the lesbian and gay community, the jurisprudential regimes governing
the litigation of lesbian and gay rights claims in the U.S., and the policy
discourse surrounding lesbian and gay rights. The decision reinforced
a policy trajectory that was very different in the U.S. from in Canada.
As *Bowers* was litigated, Canada took the first steps toward the creation
of the new Charter-based human rights regime that would increasingly
define lesbian and gay rights as a human rights issue. The *Bowers* decision
reinforced the existing policy on lesbian and gay sodomy, perpetuating a
morality framework in which homosexual acts were defined as not only
a moral wrong but as potential violations of criminal law. The ruling
implied in the starkest possible terms that legal mobilization at the level
of the U.S. Supreme Court was not a viable or effective political strategy
for lesbians and gay men.

The impact of the strong denial of lesbian and gay dignity by the
nation's highest court and the vigorous condemnation of homosexuality by certain members of the Court in writing their decision galvanized
the anger of the lesbian and gay community. The ruling in *Bowers* was
roundly condemned in the legal community (Leslie 2000); within hours
of its release, there were spontaneous demonstrations in New York and
other cities. In Washington, there was a demonstration on the steps of
the Supreme Court that drew a stark connection between AIDS and the
court's decision in *Bowers* by staging a "die-in" on the steps of the court.
In March, 1987, 500,000 marched in the March on Washington for gay
rights and 600 people were arrested for civil disobedience after a protest
on the steps of the U.S. Supreme Court (Andersen 2005: 45). Lambda
Legal was able to use the setback in *Bowers* to mobilize further and
to fundraise successfully and the ACLU and Lambda organized public
appearances for Michael Hardwick in order to publicize the human face
of *Bowers* and spur public discussion and political mobilization (Cain
2000: 179–180). Following *Bowers*, there was a threefold increase in
individual contributions to Lambda (Andersen 2005: 45–46). As Deborah Gould (2001) emphasizes, the decision in *Bowers* and the ongoing

inaction on AIDS galvanized a new period of radical organizing through direct action protest movements such as ACT UP.

From a jurisprudential perspective, the *Bowers* decision was a significant obstacle to the legal recognition of lesbian and gay rights in the U.S. Like the *Plessy v. Ferguson* decision of 1896 on segregation, the *Bowers* decision seemed to say that recognition of the rights of the marginalized groups was virtually impossible under existing constitutional law. Both advocates and opponents of lesbian and gay rights exploited *Bowers* for their own legal ends. Discussion of the case centered on the fact that it had not dealt directly with the question of equal protection. Because the Supreme Court in *Bowers* had not been invited to directly include or exclude gays and lesbians from the suspect or quasi-suspect status class of the Fourteenth Amendment, gay and lesbian rights advocates argued that *Bowers* did not affect other areas of law such as discrimination on the basis of employment, housing or child custody. Nonetheless, gay and lesbian rights opponents, as well as many judges and courts throughout the U.S., took *Bowers* as implicitly excluding lesbians and gays from equal protection. After all, if it was constitutional to criminalize homosexual conduct, even between consenting adults in the privacy of one's own home, it was difficult to see how gays and lesbians—whose difference from heterosexuals was defined by their sexuality—were entitled to the protection of the Fourteenth Amendment with respect to other forms of discrimination.

Despite the fact that sodomy laws were infrequently enforced, *Bowers* was taken as a license to discriminate with regard to employment, housing and family law (Lewis 1997; Larsen 2004; Robson 2004: 397). Diane Hassel describes how sodomy laws have been used in three areas of civil law—family law, public employment law, and immigration law—to deny rights to individual gays and lesbians and to queer couples and families (Hassel 2001; see also Leslie 2000). Hassel points out that, in civil law, no proof of sodomy is required—homosexuality and sodomy are treated as one. Therefore, the distinction between conduct and status is blurred and the idea that gays and lesbians are violating sodomy laws is the basis for denying custody. For example, a judge in a custody case stated:

> [A] lesbian mother has harmed these children forever. . . . Until such time that she can establish, after years of therapy and demonstrated conduct, that she is no longer a lesbian living a life of abomination . . . she should be totally stopped from contaminating these children. . . . Some courts have taken a position, under 'sodomy statutes' that a homosexual partner (parent) is a criminal and therefore not a fit parent. . . . It appears that homosexuals . . . are committing felonies, by their acts against nature and God (11). (*Chicoine*, 479 N.W.2d at 896, cited in Hassel 2001: 833).

Again, in a 1996 Georgia case, the judge stated:

Sodomy is against the criminal law of Georgia. . . . Here, it is undisputed that the father engaged in pre-divorce sodomy, and currently is in a homosexual relationship. . . . Thus, the father has a demonstrable past and present history of engaging in conduct, which is against the criminal laws of this state. In determining the father's visitation rights, this criminal conduct . . . cannot simply be ignored by the courts. (In *re* R.E.W., 472 S.E.2d 295, 296 Ga. 1996, cited in Hassel 2001: n109).

Sodomy laws were used to discriminate against lesbians and gay men in cases such as *Padula v. Webster* (1987) and *Shahar* (1995) on employment discrimination, especially in law enforcement, as it was argued that the fact that lesbians and gay men would engage in criminal conduct would make them open to blackmail. In these cases, there was no proof of sodomy and no action was taken against heterosexuals (Hassel 2001: 11–13). This reasoning was used to deny naturalization and to invoke deportation (see Hassel 2001: 15). People did not have to be criminally convicted of violating a sodomy law in order for the law to come into play in civil cases. In the cases cited above, none of the individuals involved had been convicted of the crime of sodomy as it then existed in Georgia or other states. In addition, sodomy laws were not used in the same way against same-sex and opposite sex partners or former partners or against straight individuals in deciding employment, immigration, and custody cases. Criminal law was being used "as an expression of hostility toward homosexuality" as Hassel puts it, rather than cited in relation to any concern about criminal conduct (Hassel 2001). Hassel argues that this deployment of sodomy as a means of undermining lesbian and gay rights in other areas was a violation of equal protection. In sum, in *Bowers*, the Court "established a justification for a host of prejudicial injustices ranging from discrimination in employment and accommodations to loss of custody over one's child and expulsion from employment in the U.S. military" (Hassel 2001: 148).

THE ADVENT OF THE CHARTER

While important policy change had been achieved in Canada through executive leadership with regard to removing sodomy from the criminal law in 1969, thoroughgoing human rights protection proved to be difficult to achieve for the Canadian lesbian and gay movement. Because of the lack of constitutional human rights protections, there were few venues for policy change through litigation. By the 1980s, there was a transition in the movement from gay liberation to other forms of organizing. This was symbolized by the collapse of the Canadian Lesbian and Gay Rights Coalition in 1980. This organization had been a federation of gay liberation groups from major cities across Canada and, importantly, a collaborative link between gay liberation groups in English-speaking Canada and gay liberation groups in Quebec. However, the fount of organizing had always been at the level of the cities and urban communities and in the urban level community institutions that were constructed and solidified over the course of the 1970s. The gay liberation political agenda had been exhausted and, at the end of the decade, the movement had not succeeded in altering much policy at the federal level.

Yet, at the same time, during this period, the partisan political battle yielded results that would have important long-term consequences for lesbian and gay rights in Canada. The lesbian and gay movement was only very tangentially involved in these battles and took little notice of the momentous changes in constitutional politics that were afoot in the early 1980s (Smith 1999). Yet, these political institutional changes turned out to be critically important for the evolution of the movement and for its policy successes of the 1990s and 2000s. Just as the Fourteenth Amendment in the U.S. reflected the codification of battles over how to end slavery and how to accord full rights of citizenship to African Americans, so too the shaping of the Charter reflected a constitutional codification of the dominant approach to defusing the challenge posed by Quebec nationalism and by internal linguistic and national diversities.

As we have seen, the Liberal government led by Prime Minister Pierre Trudeau aimed to blunt the rising forces of Quebec nationalism and Western regionalism through constitutional discussions, which took place throughout the late 1960s and 1970s. Western provinces felt that they were underrepresented in the federal government which, they argued, was dominated by Ontario and whose politics reflected Quebec's demands and concerns. When the Parti Québécois (PQ) government of Quebec held a referendum on a proposal for the negotiation of sovereignty-association with the rest of Canada in 1980, Prime Minister Trudeau promised that, if Quebecers voted against sovereignty, the constitution would be amended in order to recognize and enhance the representation of Quebec in federal political institutions. Following the referendum loss for the sovereignist option, the federal government entered into constitutional negotiations with the provincial premiers and finally reached an agreement on constitutional reform with all of the provinces, except Quebec. It was this agreement that formed the basis of the 1982 constitutional revision and this version of the constitutional reform was passed and enacted in 1982, despite the fact that the provincial government of Quebec did not agree to it. The absence of Quebec's agreement would leave an open issue that the federal government would attempt to resolve through further founds of constitutional agreement in the later 1980s and the early 1990s with no success (Russell 2004; see Clarkson and McCall 1990).

In addition to the goal of strengthening the protection of human rights through the creation of a justiciable constitutional bill of rights, the Trudeau Liberals also had more explicitly political goals for the Charter of Rights. Trudeau wanted to counter the political appeal of both Quebec nationalism and Western regionalism by entrenching a bill of rights that would secure political loyalty between citizens and the federal state (McRoberts 1997; Russell 1983). Specifically, by improving the constitutional protections for francophones outside Quebec, by entrenching the Official Languages Act in the constitution and by protecting the educational rights of both anglophone in Quebec and francophones outside of Quebec in provinces where they were the minority, Trudeau hoped to blunt the appeal of Quebec nationalism by claiming that the rights of francophones were protected throughout Canada. Furthermore, by recognizing equality rights, Trudeau built alliances with a number of allies in the ethnocultural communities, Aboriginal communities and the women's movement that supported the stronger constitutional protections against discrimination and provisions for equal treatment and equal benefit of law (Russell 1994: 107–126: 107–115; Kome 1983; James 2006: 67–90). The Quebec government objected to the Charter, not because of any opposition to the constitutional recognition of human rights, which were already recognized in Quebec's provincial human rights legislation, but because of the rights for linguistic minorities, which were included in the new Charter. The Quebec government recognized the Canadian nationalist agenda of the Liberal government and, particularly, its expression through the clauses that would set provincial language policies in areas such as education. The Quebec government, especially under the sovereignist government of the PQ, but also under the auspices of the opposition Liberal Party of Quebec, asserted that language policies should be set in provincial jurisdiction and that the federal government should not intervene in the matter of the protection of the French language in Quebec. The Quebec government viewed its role as the protector of the francophone minority in Canada and put forth a vision of a territorially defined Quebec nationalism that clashed with the pan-Canadian nationalism of the federal Liberal Party under Trudeau (Rocher and Smith 2003; Gagnon and Iacovino 2007). In this way, the Charter expressed the triumph of a pan-Canadian nationalism, a nationalism that would take root in the years to follow in the rest of Canada.

Similarly, although from a regionalist perspective, the assertive and restless Western provincial premiers worried that the Charter would detract from provincial jurisdiction and provincial powers. In general, a number of critics were concerned that the proposed Charter of Rights was not a good fit with Canada's Westminster political institutions (see Hiebert 2007). Because of this opposition and in order to outflank Quebec, the Trudeau government included a constitutional override on certain sections of the Charter, including legal rights and equality rights (but not language rights); in this way, provincial or federal legislatures could pass legislation notwithstanding these sections of the Charter for a period of five years. Thus, a provincial or federal government that wanted to circumvent a court ruling in these areas could do so for a limited period (Russell 2004: 92–126). In addition, all of the rights enumerated in the Charter were subjected to a general limitation clause—section 1 of the Charter—that allows the courts to balance Charter rights against the government's legitimate objectives.

The importance of these developments for the lesbian and gay movement was momentous even though few could have foreseen this at the time. At the moment of the Charter's entrenchment, the national or pan-Canadian level Canadian Lesbian and Gay Rights Coalition had collapsed and the only voice of the Canadian gay and lesbian movement in federal politics was a very fragile organization that was not able to mount a major national push for the inclusion of sexual orientation in the Charter. In the absence of effective national organizing to represent gays and lesbians during this period, the longstanding local group Gays of Ottawa (GO) and NDP MP Svend Robinson (who would later become Canada's first openly gay Member of Parliment) proposed an amendment to add sexual orientation to the equality rights section of the Charter. Furthermore, Robinson asked Jean Chrétien, Justice Minister (later Prime Minister), if, given that section 15 contained an open-ended list of grounds of discrimination, "you (the government) are allowing for the possibility that the courts might interpret this to include additional grounds of discrimination" (Canada 1981: 36–17). Chrétien's answer was "yes." Ultimately, the committee voted 23–2 against Robinson's amendment to include sexual orientation in section 15 (Canada 1981: 40–12). Nonetheless, the exchange between Robinson and Chretien made it clear that the government (as the key "framer" of the Charter) was well aware that the open-ended list of grounds of discrimination in the proposed Charter would permit the courts to add other grounds at a later date (see also Ryder 1990; Jefferson 1985; Young 1983).

In 1984, the Progressive Conservatives (known as Tories), led by Brian Mulroney, were elected with a majority government. Throughout its two terms in office (1984–1993), the Mulroney government was internally challenged by a Family Caucus of MPs, which opposed abortion and gay rights and supported traditional "family values." Many of these MPs had religious or evangelical roots in Western Canada or in rural and small-town Ontario. However, in stark contrast to the role of the right wing and evangelical movements in the Republican Party, this Family Caucus was unable to successfully challenge the moderate party leadership of the Conservative Party. While political culture explanations of Canadian/American difference would cite this as an example of the "Tory" touch of social progressivism in the Progressive Conservative Party of Canada (Horowitz 1968), a structural institutionalist approach would emphasize the institutional limitations on political parties in the first-past-the-post Westminster system as playing a central role in these developments. The fusion of executive and legislative authority centralizes the parties and allocates substantial resources into the hands of the party leader, who can use these carrots and sticks to keep individual MPs in line.

The centrist approach to the Charter was exemplified by the parliamentary committee hearings on the Charter, which took place in 1985, and by the federal Tories' commitment to including lesbians and gays within the ambit of the new Charter. Section 15 on equality rights of the Charter came into effect in 1985, three years after the entrenchment of the Charter itself. The three-year delay had been provided to give governments time to bring statutes and legislation into line with the new provisions. The government appointed a sub-committee on equality rights of the House of Commons Standing Committee on Justice and Legal Issues to undertake a consultation on the questions outlined in the discussion paper (Hiebert 1985) and these hearings drew a large number of submissions from lesbian and gay groups (Canada 1985: 161–176; Smith 1999: 80). The hearings also galvanized a group of lawyers and trade union activists to form an Ottawa-based coalition that, in 1986, established itself a new lesbian and gay rights organization at the federal level named Egale (Smith 2005a).[1] Following the committee report and recommendations, the government stated that it would interpret section 15 of the Charter as including sexual orientation and stated that the Tory government would take "whatever means are necessary" to ensure that sexual orientation was a prohibited ground of discrimination in federal jurisdiction (Canada 1986). For the Tories, it was clear that the new Charter had been popularized by the opposition Liberals and had been seized upon by the federal Department of Justice as a new set of legal limits on policy development (J. Kelly 2005). Therefore, rather than fighting against the new Charter or dragging their feet on human rights policy, the Conservatives chose to undertake the policies and consultations that were necessary to effectively implement the popular new rights document. Thus, in the U.S., while there was a backlash against "special rights" over this period, in Canada, in the mid-1980s, even the Progressive Conservative Party embraced the new Charter, followed a moderate approach on the abortion issue and, four short years after the writing of the Charter, gave a firm and clear commitment to respect the addition of a new ground of discrimination—sexual orientation—in federal jurisdiction.

CONCLUSIONS

In the U.S., evangelical and right-wing movements were on the rise over the course of the late 1970s and the 1980s as a backlash against the rights secured for women in *Roe* and against the other social changes ushered in by the rise of movements such as feminism and gay liberation. The rise of Reagan Democrats, the demise of the solid South, the backlash against bussing, affirmative action and social programs, and the highly gendered and sexualized links between gender, race, and class generated a backlash movement. The disdain and stigma expressed in the *Bowers* decision demonstrated the repugnance of the evangelical right for the morals and values of the sexual revolution as a whole and against lesbians and gays in particular as symbols of social change. At the same time, these changes occurred during a period in which rights for lesbians and gays had even greater material stakes as larger queer urban communities had emerged and newly formed community institutions were managing the AIDS crisis. In light of the fact that the Reagan administration had ignored AIDS, the *Bowers* decision seemed yet a further statement of the stigma attached to lesbians and gays by the mainstream of American society and American political institutions.

The impact of the *Bowers* decision intersected with the partisan and political party divide in U.S. politics of this period reinforcing the negative impact of AIDS on the framing of policy discourse on lesbian and gay rights. The evangelical opposition was given a strong weapon for its fight against homosexuality as a deep and profound moral wrong. Further, the focus in *Bowers* on the conduct of homosexuals meant that the distinction between conduct and status was strengthened, a distinction that fit neatly with the evangelical insistence on hating the sin (conduct) and loving the sinner (status). In all these ways, *Bowers* reinforced the earlier legacy of the failure to decriminalize sodomy and continued the U.S. down a path that would result in dramatically different policy outcomes in this area of human rights policy. During this same period, the mid-1980s, Canadians were taking the first constitutional steps towards a new regime for human rights policy, a regime in which lesbians and gay men would become stakeholders and beneficiaries.

4 Discrimination, From *Romer* to *Vriend*, 1986–2000

By the mid-1980s, the U.S. and Canada were firmly set on divergent trajectories in lesbian and gay rights policy. The failure of the U.S. to enact policy changes to modernize the criminal law on homosexuality stood in contrast to the decisions made in other similar democracies over the same period, notably Britain and Canada. As the historical institutionalist approach emphasizes, the legacies of past policies shape the choices available to policymakers and political actors in contemporary debates. In the U.S., the obstacles for the lesbian and gay movement were that much greater than they were in Canada because of lack of protection for lesbians and gay men from state laws criminalizing homosexual acts. The institutional openings provided by the U.S. political system permitted evangelical organizations and gay rights opponents to organize against the passage of ordinances at the local level that provided protection from discrimination. In contrast to the Canadian model in which politically and institutionally muscular human rights commissions acted as advocates for expanded human rights protections, civil rights policies in the U.S. were more decentralized and fragmented, given the multiple obstacles to the passage of legislation in the separation of powers system.

In this chapter, I survey the period following the *Bowers* decision in the U.S. and the coming into force of section 15 of the Charter in Canada in 1985. The chapter traces the story of lesbian and gay rights policies in the two countries through the 1990s, a period in which lesbian and gay politics emerges for the first time in U.S. presidential politics with the debate over "gays in the military." It highlights the process of mobilization and countermobilization between the lesbian and gay movement in the U.S. and the Christian Right through the use of referenda, voter initiatives, and amendments to state constitutions, focusing specifically on Colorado's Amendment 2. This amendment constitutionally prohibited anti-discrimination measures against gays and lesbians and was struck down by the U.S. Supreme Court in the *Romer* case in 1996. The next chapter takes up the story of the same-sex marriage issue, beginning in the early 1990s with the first Hawai'i same-sex marriage case. Thus, while the two chapters overlap in time, both considering events of the 1990s, this chapter focuses on discrimination—especially in employment—while the next chapter traces the specific development of the same-sex marriage issue.

There were a number of common factors that influenced the direction of lesbian and gay politics in both countries over this period, including the role of AIDS in spurring different forms of organization in the gay and lesbian community (Andersen 2005; Andriote 1999) and the impact of the growth of lesbian and gay families on generating demand for legal change to recognize same-sex relationships and parenting rights (Chauncey 2004). In the U.S., the defeat in *Bowers* and the pressure brought to bear by the growing power of the Christian Right, helped spur lesbian and gay organization (Gould 2001; Fetner forthcoming). Through the analysis of the key cases on lesbian and gay rights in both countries over this period, the chapter emphasizes the ways in which legal and policy discourses on lesbian and gay rights in Canada and the U.S. were formulated in different ways relative to the broader policy discourses of which they are a part. The chapter ends by comparing two U.S. cases on public accommodation and employment discrimination (*Dale* and *Shahar*, respectively) with a key Canadian case on employment discrimination (*Vriend*). The comparison shows the acceleration of legal and policy divergence between the two cases. In Canada, the *Vriend* decision signaled a public discourse on human rights linked to English-speaking Canada's national identity and associated with the governing Liberal party while, in the U.S., the *Dale* and *Shahar* decisions demonstrated the legal and policy obstacles to the implementation of basic anti-discrimination measures in U.S. public policy, the discursive construction of lesbians and gays as associated with "special interests" and the particular obstacles created by the claims of immutability and their intersection with U.S. legal arguments.

MOVEMENTS AND COUNTERMOVEMENTS

In the late 1980s and 1990s, there were a number of important changes in the social and political context for lesbian and gay organizing. The defeat in *Bowers*, combined with the impact of AIDS, drove the U.S. gay and lesbian movement in a more radical direction in the late 1980s. Groups such as ACT UP and, in the early 1990s, Queer Nation, engaged in direct action such as demonstrations, "die-ins" and media events designed to capture the public's attention on the AIDS crisis. In addition to radicalizing the movement, however, Lambda Legal was heavily involved in litigating on AIDS discrimination issues throughout this period as its caseload of AIDS cases increased exponentially in the 1980s and 1990s (Andersen 2005). Organizations such as the National Lesbian and Gay Task Force, founded in 1973, experienced substantial growth in this period, adding staff and resourcing while competitor organizations such as the Human Rights Campaign were founded with the specific goal of countering the rise of the Moral Majority (Human

Rights Campaign 2004). In Canada, there was a growth in lesbian and gay professionals working in social services and the health sector as well as links between government (especially local health agencies) and organizations representing people with AIDS in urban communities (Kinsman 1996b).

The 1980s and 1990s was a period in which gay and lesbian community organizations flourished at the urban level. While much of the urban growth of queer space was associated with burgeoning consumer and commercial zones, nonprofit, and community organizations spanning many spheres of cultural life were also established in this period (R. Bailey 1999; Nash 2005; Smith 2005b). From a time in the early 1970s in which there might have been one gay group in an entire city, by the 1980s most major cities in the U.S. and Canada had begun to develop a recognizable infrastructure of lesbian and gay community organizations ranging from recreational, social, and sports organizations to AIDS service organizations, parents and friends' groups, queer-friendly churches, whether within liberal Protestant denominations or through the growth of the lesbian- and gay-friendly Metropolitan Community Church. From the annual Pride celebrations to gay and lesbian media and gay and lesbian businesses, the LGBT community grew, expanded and diversified over this period in the major urban centers and the base of this developing community was an ever-larger group of lesbians and gay men who identified as part of the LGBT community and who were out, at least in some ways, in some parts of their lives, some part of the time. Along with these sociological changes, the late 1980s and early 1990s saw the growth in numbers and visibility of lesbian and gay families as a social fact, a new phenomenon that had been hidden from view in the previous generation. Many queer families were composed of lesbians and gay men who had children from previous heterosexual relationships; however, increasingly, over the course of the late 1980s and 1990s, gay men and, especially, lesbians, undertook deliberately to have families of their own through the use of medical technology or adoption (Arnup 1995). The growth in the understanding, access and use of new reproductive technologies over this period made this possible and lesbian mothers, in particular, would form a key group pushing for relationship recognition and parenting rights for same-sex couples over the coming decades.

Political mobilization to forestall or roll back lesbian and gay discrimination protections continued unabated in the U.S. over this period. The Christian Right was concerned about efforts to ban anti-gay discrimination in the states, which had occurred first in Wisconsin in 1982 and in Massachusetts in 1989. The balance sheet on these ordinances was largely affirmative, with gay rights ordinances increasing from eughty in 1990 to more than two hundred in 2000 (Chauncey 2004: 52). Another count of local laws prohibiting discrimination based on sexual orientation highlights their growth; in 1993, twelve cities and counties had banned such discrimination but, by 1996, there were over one hundred communities that had implemented such measures (Button, Rienzo, and Wald 2000: 273–274). At the same time, anti-gay ordinance campaigns succeeded most of the time. In other words, when anti-gay mobilization was undertaken in a state, it was more than likely to be successful in repealing such ordinances. The mobilization of right wing groups affected lesbian and gay mobilization as well as many more local level groups at the state, city and local levels were established. Throughout this period, the social conservative movement continued to use direct democracy and initiatives were often supported by national level organizations that assisted individuals or local groups. In Oregon, Maine, and Colorado, local groups attempted to forestall attempts to pass anti-discrimination ordinances by banning them throughout the state (Wilcox 2006: 70–86), although, as we will see, the Colorado ban was found to be unconstitutional by the U.S. Supreme Court in the *Romer* case. Political institutions in Canada did not provide the same mechanisms for the mobilization of social conservatives.

Moreover, through the period from 1986 through 1996, the Christian Right pursued a strategy of bringing pressure to bear in American party politics through the Republican Party. In the U.S., the structure of the parties permits group mobilization and the Christian Right and other conservatives were especially successful in permeating Republican Party organization in states that used such methods such as caucuses to select nominees. Even in states with primary systems, the Christian Right and its allies were able to mobilize financial and organizational resources to threaten moderate Republican candidates. Although the Christian Right was a minority in the Republican Party, it was able to gain control of some state level parties that set the rules for the nomination process. The movement also influenced the presidential nomination process through its control of state parties in many states, through the publication of voter guides that are distributed through churches, and through its financial resources. School board elections were another major arena although where the Christian Right candidates are out in the open, they are often defeated (Kaplan 2004: 68–90; Wilcox 2006: 70–85).

Through the campaigns of Ronald Reagan and George H.W. Bush, there were constant links between the themes of special interests and special privileges and the tie between "special treatment" for certain groups and its association with political liberalism. This highly race-coded political discourse around issues such as affirmative action, quotas, welfare, and crime suggested that African Americans received special treatment while hardworking white Americans were ripped off by "big government." This rhetoric was critically important to the Reagan victories and to the emergence of the Reagan Democrats in the north—working class and unionized constituencies that had once voted Democratic—and the gradual shift of the South to the Republican camp over this period (Teixeira and Rogers 2001). Public opinion evidence shows that Americans increasingly defined welfare and poverty as racial terms and the electoral problems of the Democratic party were increasingly viewed in terms of the party's positions on what were seen as racially coded welfare programs (see Soss and Schram 2007: 111–113). Chauncey points out the important links between lesbian and gay discrimination and other issues. Campaigns by the Christian Right against laws that protected lesbians and gays from discrimination argued that such measures would give lesbians and gay men advantages over heterosexuals and even over other minority groups such as African Americans and Hispanics. As Chauncey argues, "the charge that gays were demanding 'special rights' also allowed Christian conservatives to play on the growing white hostility toward affirmative action" (Chauncey 2004: 46). A number of other scholars of the lesbian and gay movement in the U.S. have pointed out the links between the discourse of special rights and anti-gay political mobilization (Goldberg-Hiller 2002; Herman 1997; A. M. Smith 2001).

In this context, Bill Clinton's commitment to a centrist strategy for Democratic presidential victory reinforced the political strength of conservative Christian political mobilization in the U.S. In particular, Clinton played into the racial backlash through a number of highly visible actions that were designed to cement the loyalty of anti-black white voters, critically, the Reagan Democrats. As Frymer (1999) has shown in his analysis of the position of African Americans in U.S. electoral politics, black Americans were a captured group; because they were unlikely to support the Republican Party, the Democrats took black votes for granted. However, Frymer also shows that the political support of African Americans in U.S. elections tended to drive away white voters. To the extent that blacks were deemed to be a "special interest" group that received "special privileges" such as preferential hiring, welfare, and lax criminal enforcement, some white voters did not want to support political parties that were openly associated with black voters. Rather than exercising political leadership in seeking to shape policy discourses surrounding race, gender, and sexuality in the U.S., Clinton's centrist political strategy and his policies and discourse on crime and welfare reinforced it. Similarly, Clinton's stance on gay and lesbian equality emphasized the similarities between gay and lesbian voters and black voters. Like black voters, gay and lesbian voters were largely captured by the Democratic Party, despite the efforts of the gay group, Log Cabin Republicans, to win support from lesbian and gay economic conservatives.

In contrast, social conservatives faced barriers to political mobilization in Canadian politics despite the election of a Progressive Conservative government in 1984. Although the 1984 election signaled a shift to the political right on social and economic policy, social conservatives were a minority within the Progressive Conservative caucus and had few policy successes. The government's attempts to build a pan-Canadian brokerage coalition drove its strategies to the political center in the search for votes (Bercuson et al. 1986; Petry 1999). Despite the criticisms of the Family Caucus, the party leadership directed a strategy through which the government supported the new Charter and engaged in discussion of the meaning of the new equality rights guarantees. As we have seen, the Tory government committed itself to a fair interpretation of section 15 equality rights as the clause came into effect in 1985, issuing policies and discussion papers that clearly committed the government to supporting an expansive definition of equality.

The fate of the Family Caucus within the Progressive Conservative Party at this time forms a stark contrast with the success of the Moral Majority in the U.S. The role of political institutions in relation to political parties is critically important in this respect. In the U.S., political parties were more open to the influence of outside groups and they were not controlled as strongly by legislative leadership. After the demise of the seniority system in Congress during the 1960s and 1970s and with the growing role of the media and of money in Congressional campaigns, candidates became more independent from the party machinery while, in Canada over the same period, MPs were even more beholden to party leaders to set the direction of the parliamentary party and even less able to challenge the party leadership (Savoie 1999; Bakvis and Wolinetz 2005). The concentration of power in the hands of the prime minister and direct control by the central party and the party leader over the process of securing the party's nomination made it very difficult for outside groups to penetrate the process of candidate nomination. Although anti-abortion groups tried to organize to overturn party nominations in favor of pro-life candidates, they were largely unsuccessful in this because of the institutional control of the party center. Similarly, there were no other avenues for social conservatives because of the fact that constitutional amendment, referenda, and initiatives were all closed to them. Attempts to use the courts to strike down abortion were not successful as the Canadian Supreme Court continued to rule in favor of legal abortion and denied access to the courts by an individual pro-life crusader who sought to have a fetus declared a person under the new Charter (Brodie, Jenson and Gavigan 1992). Again, in response to a Supreme Court of Canada decision on abortion, which struck down the existing provisions of the Criminal Code as Charter violations, the government was torn between the Family Caucus's demands for an abortion bill that would restrict access and its desire to put forth a moderate image that would reap the most votes in the center of the political spectrum. When the Family Caucus succeeded in galvanizing the government behind proposing a new abortion bill that would have re-criminalized abortion and reduced access to it, the government was strongly attacked by the women's movement and by the Liberal opposition for undermining women's equality and the government retreated, devising a compromise bill that was eventually defeated (Brodie, Jenson and Gavigan 1992).

The government's defeat on its own bill only occurred because it allowed its own members a "free vote" in the House of Commons and Senate. Under the free vote, MPs are freed from the party discipline and the control of party leaders and many Conservative Senators and MPs wanted to restrict access to abortion. In the end, the compromise bill did not satisfy either side in the abortion debate and, in an unprecedented turn of events, it was defeated in the Senate. These events showed that there was support for taking a more socially conservative direction in the Progressive Conservative party during this period; however, the control of party leaders and the impact of party discipline gave the individual MPs very little independence from the wishes of a party leadership that was most interested in winning a majority government through centrist politics. The requirement for moderation on social issues was well understood in this period by the leadership of the Progressive Conservative Party and this moderation was one of the contributing factors in the fracturing of the electoral coalition and the founding of the Reform Party, a populist Western party in which evangelicals played a leading role (see Harrison 1995).

Finally, race played a completely different role in relation to partisan party competition in Canada than in the U.S. While racism and racialized inequality were important political problems in Canada, the dominant "race" issue in party politics has historically been the conflict between Quebec and the rest of Canada, a conflict that was particularly important over this period, which saw a virtually 50/50 vote on Quebec independence in 1995 as well as numerous rounds of constitutional talks aimed at the constitutional conciliation and recognition of Quebec. Like African Americans (or "minorities") in U.S. politics, Quebec was often seen as a province that unfairly received "special treatment" and advantages not extended to other provinces. However, this "special treatment" discourse did not extend to other political issues such as crime or social policy but was cast in terms of federalism and constitutional recognition (Russell 2004; Cairns 1992; 1995). Therefore, in Canada, over this period, there was not a major link between political issues such as crime and social spending on one hand and issues of race and sexuality in partisan political conflict.[1]

INSTITUTIONAL STRUCTURES AND THE *ROMER* CASE

The case of Amendment 2 in Colorado demonstrates the process of mobilization and countermobilization by the lesbian and gay rights movement and its opponents in the U.S. through the use of initiatives for state constitutional amendment. The story of Amendment 2 is well known and the *Romer* case is one of the most important gay rights cases to reach the U.S. Supreme Court. Rather than considering the case solely as an expression of the strength of the religious right in the U.S., a comparative analysis sheds light on the role of state constitutions, direct democracy and federalism in shaping policy outcomes in the legal arena.

In the 1970s and 1980s, a number of jurisdictions in the U.S. had moved to recognize sexual orientation discrimination. However, such moves were most likely to occur through executive action or as an effect of court decisions, rather than through legislative action. When "gay rights" was thrown out into the process of majoritarian politics in the legislature, the lesbian and gay movement faced powerful opponents who were able to pressure legislators to stymie anti-discrimination laws (Werum and Winders 2001; Green 2000: 130–136; Donovan, Wenzel and Bowler 2000: 161–190). In constructing human rights legislation and commissions in Canadian jurisdictions (federal and provincial), the executive did not face legislative obstacles to building human rights protections through legislation and through the building of new institutions (the human rights commissions) for implementation. In the U.S., by 1993, a number of states and cities had banned sexual orientation discrimination, many by executive order. In Colorado itself, these included the cities of Aspen (1977), Boulder (1987) and Denver (1991). In 1990, Colorado governor Roy Romer banned sexual orientation discrimination in state government in Colorado by executive order (Cain 2000: 259; Bodi 1999: 667–668). At this time, public opinion in the U.S. was moving in the direction of supporting lesbian and gay rights and, in particular, supporting the specific right of lesbians and gay men to be free of discrimination based on sexual orientation (Yang 1997; Lewis and Rogers 1999; Brewer 2003a). Yet, lesbian and gay opponents mobilized to pass Amendment 2, which prohibited anti-discrimination protection on the basis of sexual orientation. The passage of Amendment 2 in the 1992 Colorado election sparked a boycott of Colorado tourism and a court challenge by the lesbian and gay movement, which eventually led to the *Romer* case, decided by the Supreme Court in 1996. In this case, the second major lesbian and gay rights case to be heard in the U.S. Supreme Court and the first case since *Bowers*, the Supreme Court struck down Amendment 2 as unconstitutional (*Romer v. Evans* 1996; see also Cain 2000: 202–222).

The role of policy legacies and political institutions in the context of the partisan political party competition of the period sheds light on the role of institutional structures and past policies in shaping the field of political conflict in the area of lesbian and gay politics. First, the lesbian and gay rights movement and the Christian Right countermovement were able to mobilize using political institutional weapons. In Colorado, as in other states, the state constitution could be amended using ballot initiatives, thus setting new constitutional limits on the actions of the executive and the legislature and forestalling or rolling back the recognition of lesbian and gay rights. The Christian Right was successful in mobilizing the money and numbers of voters needed to mount an initiative campaign. As Cain points out in her comparative discussion of the development of women's rights and civil rights in the U.S., progress for blacks and for women in securing protection from discrimination often bubbled up from the local level through city ordinances against discrimination and through fair practices legislation at the state level, legislation that had been passed in twenty states since the Civil Rights Act of 1964 (Cain 2000: 203; see also Gamble 1997). In the case of racial discrimination, in the late 1960s, the U.S. Supreme

Court ruled that states could not amend their constitutions to prohibit such protective measures for minorities and, similarly, city charters could not prohibit them either (Cain 2000: 205). In the absence of federal intervention, these policy options and political strategies were open to the anti-gay movement in the U.S. and, as had been the case for other minority groups and for women, opponents were able to use direct democracy to roll back gay rights. Between 1978 and 1996, there were eleven anti-gay initiatives and two state-wide referenda on gay rights, many of them aimed at rolling back employment and housing protections for lesbians and gays. Over the same period, there were five initiatives to secure gay rights (Donavan, Wenzel and Bowler 2000: 162–163). In the case of Colorado, as in many of the other cases of "rollback," the evangelical movement was able to mobilize to pass Amendment 2 as a state constitutional amendment. In this way, the constitutional design of American political institutions provides openings for the mobilization of backlash movements, including backlash movements against the rights of minorities.

On the other side of the coin, the constitutional status of judicially enforced rights protections through the Bill of Rights also provides a strong weapon for minority groups, a weapon that did not exist in such a strong form in Canada until the entrenchment of the Charter in 1982. As the case of Colorado illustrates, political institutional openings created possibilities for political mobilization by the lesbian and gay rights movement. The lesbian and gay movement used elite pressure on the executive at the level of the governor, combined with local measures, to implement rudimentary human rights protections in Colorado even though these protections were then rolled back by popular initiative. This rollback of minority rights then became the subject of litigation. This seesawing movement in civil rights policy development in the U.S. is produced in part by the nature of the political opportunities that are provided through the structure of American federalism, the separation of powers system, and the presence of mechanisms of direct democracy in many U.S. states, such as Colorado.

At the same time, the *Romer* developments also demonstrate a second feature of this comparative analysis: the impact of the legacy of previous policies in shaping human rights' debates. Previous policies shaped the debate in Colorado, particularly, through the impact of the ongoing constitutional sanction for the criminalization of lesbian and gay sexual behavior and through the impact of the legacy of the African American civil rights movement. With regard to the legacy of the criminalization of sodomy, this was used by the conservative movement in the Colorado debate to stigmatize gays and lesbians by arguing that, because the sexual conduct of gays and lesbians was criminal in many parts of the U.S., there was no need for lesbians and gays to claim "civil rights," a term reserved for African Americans, and, to a lesser extent, for the claims of the women's movement on certain issues (such as non-discrimination in the labour market and in education). Instead of "civil rights," according to conservatives, lesbians and gays were asking for "special rights," including—by implication—the right to engage in criminal behavior. Therefore, according to conservatives, lesbians and gays were demanding rights that were not accorded to other citizens. The Christian Right could point to the fact that the slippery slope of "gay rights" might lead to people having to rent rooms in their houses to gays and lesbians, it might allow gays and lesbians to have contact with children in areas such as teaching or scouting, and it might even lead to same-sex marriage. The Amendment's authors were successful in framing the debate in terms of private rather than public contexts of discrimination, i.e., the idea that individuals would be forced to accept homosexuality in the private sphere (Goldberg-Hiller 2002: 50–56; Alexander 2002: 277–279).

During the debate on Amendment 2, Colorado for Family Values (CFV) and other conservative groups asserted that gays already had the same rights as others but that Amendment 2 would prevent them from having more rights than others. At the same time, however, CFV was able to draw on the template of civil rights by arguing that other groups such as African Americans had suffered real disadvantage and needed the protection of the law while homosexuals were a well-heeled minority that did not need the law's protection. This had an effect on public opinion as gay rights were equated with special rights or special treatment in Colorado public opinion. In addition, by calling attention to the discourse of "special interests," evangelicals highlighted the stereotype of gay men as rich and politically powerful; therefore, any measures to protect them from discrimination would be adding to the "special rights" they already possessed by virtue of their alleged wealth and political power (Rimmerman 2002: 143; Herman 1997). Therefore, as Gerstmann (1999: 91–93) points out, the debate over Amendment 2 raised the specter that lesbians and gays—already stereotyped as a privileged and white group—would be able to receive special treatment such as access to affirmative action programs and preferential hiring. Even though race was depicted by the CFV as "real" grounds for anti-discrimination protection, many racial minority organizations in Colorado opposed Amendment 2 as a potential threat to all civil rights protections in the state. The rhetoric of "special rights" was also coded to appeal to the politics of racial backlash, which viewed programs such as affirmative action as a form of "special rights" in which one group was given "more rights" than other groups. In this way, policy discourses that had been defined in relation to previous debates in American politics were linked to gender, race and sexuality by emphasizing the racialized contrast between the law-abiding, tax-paying, and hard-working citizen and those who were not. The implicit status of this hard-working, tax-paying citizen as a breadwinning, white, working, heterosexual male was all too clear in the appeals of the CFV to the "traditional" family.

Therefore, the debate over special rights for gays and lesbians in Amendment 2 was widely credited with having assured its success because, even as 52% of voters in Colorado supported Amendment 2, polls taken during the same period show that 70% of Coloradans supported measures to protect gays and lesbians from discrimination. Clearly, some percentage of voters did not believe that Amendment 2 would affect discrimination protections for gays and lesbians even though the Amendment constitutionally prohibited precisely such protective measures (Alexander 2002: 279–280).

THE *ROMER* CASE

In reaction to the passage of Amendment 2, the Colorado Legal Initiatives Project filed suit, arguing that Amendment 2 was a violation of the first amendment and equal protection provisions of the U.S. Bill of Rights. Because the Supreme Court had ruled in *Bowers* that sodomy laws were constitutional, federal courts of appeal had ruled that homosexuals could not constitute a suspect or quasi-suspect class under the equal protection clause of the Bill of Rights (Joslin 1997: 227). For example, in *Padula v. Webster*, a federal appeals court found that it was legitimate for the FBI to deny a position to a lesbian. The Court found that homosexuals did not qualify as a suspect class because their behavior may be criminalized by the state. Under the rational basis test, the Court had to decide if the measures taken by the state were rationally related to legitimate goals or ends. Given that homosexual conduct could be criminalized, it was much easier under the *Bowers* ruling for courts to conclude that the state should attempt to prevent or forestall the commission of criminal acts (Joslin 1997: 228).

In the first hearing of *Romer* in the Colorado Supreme Court, lesbian and gay rights advocates argued that Amendment 2 prevented gays and lesbians from participating in the democratic process. Lesbians and gays could not vote for representatives who would seek to pass legislation that would protect them from discrimination, because such legislation would be unconstitutional according to the state constitution. The Court agreed that Amendment 2 impaired the fundamental rights of lesbians, gays, and bisexuals. The case was remanded to a trial court where the state had the burden of showing the reasons for such an impairment and, at this stage, the trial court ruled that Amendment 2 violated federal equal protection because the bar for the achievement of anti-discrimination legislation would be set higher for gays, lesbians, and bisexuals than for other groups (i.e., any anti-discrimination measures would require the amendment of the Colorado constitution). Such a burden was not warranted or justified by any compelling reason as required in constitutional law (*Evans v. Romer* 1994; see also Chrisman 1995: 521; Cain 2000: 206–207). The Supreme Court of Colorado agreed with this decision and, at this point, the state of Colorado asked the U.S. Supreme Court to review the case.

The U.S. Supreme Court decision in *Romer* rejected the state's argument that Amendment 2 was a denial of special rights for homosexuals. The Court determined that Amendment 2 did single out homosexuals, that it treated them differently than other citizens, and that this was a violation of the equal protection clause. First, the Court argued that Amendment 2 was a literal violation of equal protection since it denied lesbians and gays protection that was afforded to other citizens. Second, the Court argued that Amendment 2 failed the rational basis test, a test that is usually considered to be highly deferential to the legislature and that, historically, has given wide scope to the state to argue in defense of its own interests. However, in this case, the Court dismissed the arguments made by the state, namely that the Amendment protected the right of free association and that Amendment 2 freed up resources that could be used in protecting other groups from discrimination. The latter was a clear attempt to pit the interests of marginalized groups against each other, i.e., by suggesting to Hispanics or African Americans that the state would not have the resources to protect them from discrimination because it would be forced to protect well-heeled "special interests." The majority's view of the rational basis test was attacked in a dissent by Scalia who suggested that, if the conduct was criminal, it was rational to deny any protection to those who engage in it (*Romer v. Evans* 1996; see Joslin 1997: 234–235; Alexander 2002: 292–297).

Therefore, the positive decisions in the Colorado courts and the decision in the U.S. Supreme Court were reached on somewhat different grounds. While the Colorado Supreme Court had focused on the right of gays and lesbians to participate in the political process, agreeing with the plaintiffs that this right was impeded by the state prohibition on anti-discrimination protections, the U.S. Supreme Court took the simpler tack of stating that Amendment 2 was a straightforward violation of equal protection (Alexander 2002: 288; Kimpel 1999: 995). In this sense, the *Romer* decision of 1996 was a step away from the legacy of *Bowers*. The U.S. Supreme Court clearly indicated that animosity toward a particular group could not provide a rational basis for a violation of equal protection. Most commentators on this have agreed that the Supreme Court's decision in *Romer* was important in part because of the fact that if the rational basis test was used successfully by lesbians and gays, it would make it more difficult for anti-gay forces to use "compelling state interests" to justify discriminatory measures. Sharon Alexander, staff lawyer for the Human Rights Campaign, makes a distinction between public and private discrimination, arguing that, in the U.S., courts have been more willing to recognize the right of lesbians and gays to be free from discrimination in the public sphere than in the private sphere. This was demonstrated in *Romer* as the anti-gay proponents of Amendment 2 could not convince the courts that the Amendment principally concerned private discrimination or that there was any compelling state interest in guarding against homosexual "special rights" (Alexander 2002: 297). Yet, at the same time, as other scholars have pointed out, *Romer* only protected the right of lesbians and gays to seek to change the law so that the law would protect them from discrimination. As Karlan comments, "it was a procedural, rather than a substantive, right" (Karlan 1997: 295). Karlan argues that it was because lesbians and gays had been successful in obtaining protections in Colorado that their opponents wanted to deny these protections by striking at the right of lesbians and gays to participate in the political process (Karlan 1997: 296).

Therefore, the debate in *Romer* concerned the issue of the constitutionalization of lesbian and gay rights. At the same time as this debate was underway in the U.S., Canada was similarly debating the inclusion of sexual orientation as in section 15 and whether or not it could be overridden by the Section 1 "reasonable limits" clause. The difference was that, in Canada, the question was moved quickly to the issue of the constitutional requirement to protect lesbians and gays from discrimination, rather than an argument about the procedural foreclosure of this option. The discussion of the right to participate has no analogue in Canadian legal struggles over lesbian and gay rights. Because of the legal and quasi-legal bars to participation for African Americans in the U.S. and the opening up of the legal route to policy change through the courts in the modern civil rights movement from the 1940s on, there is a huge amount of case law in the U.S. on the right to participate in the political process from debates on poll taxes and literacy requirements for voting through to contemporary litigation on race and redistricting (Epstein and O'Halloran 1999). This course of litigation and its jurisprudential legacy does not exist in the same extensive form in Canada, given Canada's different history of racially coded legal discrimination (see Walker 1997; Backhouse 1999). For example, in Canada, exclusion of blacks from the right to vote in some parts of the country was carried out through segregationist local practices rather than formal law. Formal legal bars to voting, participating, and mobility affected Asian Canadians and Aboriginal peoples and conflicts over these issues played out in different ways from the massive civil right struggle in the U.S. The right to participate and the right to receive substantive protection from discrimination in the public or private spheres are very different issues. In the *Romer* case, the Supreme Court did not want to offer lesbians and gays substantial protection from discrimination or rule that this was a constitutional requirement. In contrast, for African Americans, these protections were constitutionally required, as U.S. judicial decision-making has evolved in the post-*Brown* era (Karlan 1997: 296).

At the conclusion of the legal and political debate over *Romer*, it was not clear which direction had been signaled by the U.S. Supreme Court on lesbian and gay rights. On one hand, the *Romer* case seemed to constitute an inconsistency with *Bowers* in the general sense that *Romer* was seen as a positive recognition for lesbian and gay rights. However, the two cases dealt with different legal issues in that the *Bowers* case focused more on due process while *Romer* focused on equal protection. If equal protection could be afforded to lesbians and gays or if the categories of sexual orientation and gender identity were defined as suspect classifications for the purposes of equal protection analysis, this would afford lesbians and gays much stronger constitutional protection than a due process approach. Equal protection explicitly recognized rights while due process tended to focus on liberties traditionally rooted in the U.S. constitution. Due process opened up debates over constitutional intentions and living trees, a discourse that cast deviations from framers' intentions as a potentially illegitimate exercise of so-called "judicial activism" (Robb 1997). Between 1986, when the Court ruled in *Bowers,* and 1996, when the Court ruled in *Romer,* there had been shift in U.S. public opinion toward gays and lesbians and the *Romer* decision reflected that change (Yang 1997). While attitudes about homosexuality were changing among the liberal moderates on the Supreme Court, the Court was clearly cautious about extending lesbian and gay rights recognition and had generally taken a more conservative direction in the 1980s after the appointment of William Rehnquist as Chief Justice in 1986 (Feldblum 2002). However, while *Bowers* focused on sexual behavior, *Romer* concerned the status of lesbians and gays and their right to equal protection. In this sense, one might argue that the two cases had nothing to do with each other, as they dealt with distinct issues and, indeed, the Supreme Court majority in *Romer* did not even cite the *Bowers* decision (Hassel 2001; Michaelson 2000).

As the *Romer* case developed, a similar case arose in Cincinnati (*Equality Foundation v. City of Cincinnati, 1997*). In a familiar pattern, the Cincinnati City Council passed ordinances that banned discrimination based on sexual orientation in city employment in 1991 and discrimination in private employment, housing and public accommodation. Gay rights opponents proposed an amendment by ballot initiative to the Cincinnati Charter, following the pattern in which such opponents attempted to cement opposition to gay rights through amending the state and federal constitutions or, in this case, city charters or constitutions. The proposed amendment stated that sexual orientation did not entitle an individual to any protection or to a claim of minority or protected status. This local initiative provoked a bitter campaign and debate over special rights. When the initiative was successful, lesbian and gay rights supporters went to court to stop Issue 3 (as the initiative was called) under the banner of the Equality Foundation of Greater Cincinnati. An injunction to stop the implementation of Issue 3 was granted by a district court. Lesbian and gay rights claimants made their case under the First and Fourteenth Amendments, asserting their rights to free association (First Amendment) and equal protection (Fourteenth Amendment). As in the debate over Amendment 2, the rhetoric of the political debate over Issue 3 emphasized that gays and lesbians were asking for special rights for the protection of their choice of lifestyle, a lifestyle that was associated with pedophilia (Kimpel 1999: 995–996).

In reply, a large number of experts contested claims of "special rights" before the court by deploying what Steven Epstein (1987) has called the "ethnic model" of gay rights in the U.S., namely, the claim that sexual orientation, like race, is an immutable characteristic and that, as such, it should be grounds for protection from discrimination. According to Kimpel's account of the testimony, the experts established that "sexual orientation is a characteristic which exists separately and independently from sexual conduct or behavior," "sexual orientation is set in at a very early age—three to five years—and is not only involuntary, but is not amenable to change" and "sexual orientation bears no relation to an individual's ability to perform, contribute to, or participate in, society" (Kimpel 1999: 995). In reply, the court found that sexual orientation was a quasi-suspect class and that Issue 3 violated the right of lesbians and gays to participate in the political process (Kimpel 1999: 998–999). This decision was appealed to the U.S. Court of Appeals and the decision was reversed. This court did not agree with the findings of fact regarding the nature of homosexuality and the history of disadvantage and, by disagreeing with this, the court reversed the ruling. Once the positive decision of the lesbian and gay claimants had been heard in Cincinnati, this decision was in turn appealed to the U.S. Supreme Court. As the Court was in the process of deciding *Romer*, it turned the case back to the Sixth Circuit to reconsider in light of *Romer*. After a further Sixth Circuit ruling in favor of Issue 3, the case was again appealed to the Supreme Court, which declined to hear the appeal. This was a disappointing result and indicated that the Court was taking a cautious and moderate stand in extending lesbian and gay rights, despite the *Romer* decision (Cain 2000: 214; Feldblum 2002: 135–138). Further, as Cain points out, "unlike the Supreme Court opinions in the late 1960s that struck down racially discriminatory ballot measures and put a stop to that practice, *Romer*, by its vagueness and its refusal to apply anything other than rational basis review, left huge holes for antigay forces to use to their advantage" (Cain 2000: 213).

These events show how legal reasoning heightens and reinforces litigation strategies that rely on the distinction between conduct and status and on asserting the immutability of homosexuality as well as the historic disadvantage of gays and lesbians. In Canada, in contrast, the arguments have been straightforwardly based on historical disadvantage and dignity, with little reference to the origins or mutability of homosexuality, especially in comparison to the legal importance of immutability in these critically important American legal decisions. These differences in jurisprudential regimes provided an easier path for Canadian lesbian and gay claimants. Moreover, lesbian and gay rights opponents in Canada were not able to mobilize through ballot initiatives and direct democracy at the local level as in these cases in Colorado and Cincinnati. Through the entrenchment of the Charter and the rulings of the courts under the Charter on sexual orientation, human rights protections for lesbians and gays were federalized or, to put it another way, dealt with at the national level. In contrast, in the U.S., the courts declined to intervene to establish a national standard or floor for lesbian and gay rights protections, other than the very weak standard created by *Romer.*

In seeking to understand these jurisprudential differences and their discursive function in policy debates over gay rights, it is possible to simply ascribe them to differences in political culture. For example, Jason Pierceson (2005) argues that differences in the attitudes of courts in the U.S. and Canada on lesbian and gay rights issues stem from differences in political culture. Judges operate within the parameters of a political culture that deems certain policy pathways more or less acceptable and Canadian political culture encapsulates a form of liberalism that is more open to the recognition of difference within a democratic polity. However, this inert concept of political culture overlooks the role of collective actors and, in particular, social movement organizations, in putting forth particular views of rights and interests in the policy process, operating within specific institutional structures. In both Canada and the U.S, Christian Right (and other religious organizations) intervened as third parties or participated as amicus curiae in such lesbian and gay rights cases. In the U.S., however, the role of the Christian Right has been much more extensive than it has been in Canada, in particular, through the deployment of measures such as Colorado's Amendment 2 in a deliberate and systematic strategy to block the recognition of gay rights across the states. While the Christian Right in Canada sought to influence the executive leadership in the federal government by organizing an emasculated Family Caucus within the governing Progressive Conservative Party, the Christian Right in the U.S. was organizing on a state-by-state level to gather signatures on ballot initiatives and engaging in city and state campaigns for the passage of measures such as Amendment 2 or the Equality Initiative in Cincinnati. The political culture differences between Canada and the U.S. must be placed in an institutional context, recognizing that there are many more opportunities for Christian Right mobilization in American political institutions while the Christian Right movement in Canada is institutionally blocked through the centralization of the parliamentary and party systems and the lack of direct democracy mechanisms that have been used with such effect in the U.S.

"DON'T ASK, DON'T TELL": THE SEPARATION OF POWERS AND FEDERAL PROTECTION

The policy challenge of providing for anti-discrimination protections in the U.S. has been compounded not only by federalism and direct democracy but also by the separation of powers system. This is epitomized in the consistent failures of efforts at the federal level to pass non-discrimination measures to protect lesbians and gay men, from their first proposal by Bella

Abzug in 1974 to the contemporary debate over ENDA. Most proposals to protect gays and lesbians from discrimination in the U.S. must surmount the multiple hurdles of the separation of powers system. The separation of powers system and the undisciplined political parties in the U.S. system open up the process to pressure and political mobilization from conservatives and other opponents to mobilize to influence legislators. As with other marginalized groups in American politics, it is difficult for the lesbian and gay movement to muster the resources to pressure politicians on this scale. The complex legislative process of the U.S. Congress in which legislation emerges through log rolling, coalition-building, and compromises is a stark contrast to the parliamentary system in which neat and ordered legislation is vetted by bureaucrats and presented to the legislature by the government for certain passage under most political circumstances. The idea of initiating a major change in governmental policy by attaching riders to legislation is anathema in the Canadian parliamentary process and commonplace in the U.S. Congress.

Before and after his election, Clinton proposed to put into place an executive order that would end the military ban against lesbians and gay men. However, at the outset of the debate, Republican legislators seized control of the political agenda for purposes of their own and placed the issue of "gays in the military" before the newly elected President Clinton in early 1993. While the lesbian and gay community had hoped that President Clinton would sign an executive order to permit gays and lesbians to serve openly in the armed forces within the first hundred days of his presidency, Senator Bob Dole deployed his power of initiative to place the issue on the policy agenda by proposing a rider upholding the ban to an unrelated piece of legislation (Rayside 1998: 222). In the parliamentary system, this type of legislative initiative cannot be undertaken by one member. One member can propose a private member's bill and, if they are fortunate, they will be allocated a few minutes of parliamentary time in one of the few free periods that are not reserved for government legislation (Docherty 2004). Clinton had already used his executive authority to alter federal policy on other issues during the initial period of his administration, notably on measures affecting women's equality, and conservatives were watchful of the president's use of the executive order (McFeeley 2000: 240–244). At the same time, conservative Democrats in Congress, led by the chair of the Senate Armed Services Committee, Sam Nunn, opposed the lifting of the ban, although Clinton secured an agreement from conservative Democrats to hold hearings on the issue. The hearings were swamped by opponents of lifting the ban. In the end, Congress enacted the policy "don't ask, don't tell," which was condoned by President Clinton (Mezey 2007: 158–164; Feldblum 2000; Rayside 1998: 219–234). In contrast, in a parliamentary system, Clinton would have controlled his own party and would have been able to change these policies either through an order-in-council (similar to an executive order) or through the government's power to control the legislature without the necessity of compromise with opposition parties. Further, in the Canadian system, it is very likely that the party leader, as prime minister, would have the tools to ensure that the caucus stayed in line behind the leader while, in the U.S. system, Clinton was attacked by members of his own party.

The policy effects of the separation of powers system are also highlighted by the fate of ENDA, the federal legislation that would have banned discrimination based on sexual orientation and, in some versions of the bill, gender identity. As will be discussed in detail in the next chapter, after the first *Baehr* decision on same-sex marriage in Hawai'i in 1993, Republicans and other conservatives in Congress had pushed for and passed the federal Defense of Marriage Act (DOMA) in 1996. This act prohibited the recognition of same-sex marriage in federal law and purported to ensure that states would not be forced to recognize same-sex marriages from other states. As a condition for the passage of DOMA, Senator Ted Kennedy unsuccessfully proposed the passage of ENDA (which would ban sexual orientation discrimination) and throughout the following decade, ENDA continued to be introduced again and again, only to go down to defeat in the face of conservative opposition in Congress (Mezey 2007: 215–221). Given the lack of party discipline in the U.S. and the separation of powers, the Democratic Party had no concerted leadership to present a united front on the issue, even when the party had the support of the executive. Clinton supported ENDA, although after the gays in the military debacle, he was not willing to place his own political capital behind the passage of the bill. At the same time, however, he used his executive authority to ban discrimination on the basis of sexual orientation in the federal government as well as prohibiting discrimination on this ground in access to classified government information (Mezey 2007: 220–221). Considering that the Canadian federal government reluctantly agreed to amend federal human rights legislation in 1996 only after it was enjoined to do so by the decisions of courts and the imprecations of its own federal human right commission (see Smith 1998), the support for the passage of ENDA in Congress and at the executive level during the same historical period in the U.S. demonstrates once again that differences in public opinion or political support for lesbian and gay rights recognition cannot explain public policy outcomes in any straightforward fashion.

Clearly, during this time period, Clinton and some liberal Democrats in Congress were willing to enact federal discrimination protection based on sexual orientation. If Clinton had enjoyed the power of a prime minister and, critically, the ability to control his own party in the legislature, it seems very likely that ENDA would have passed at this time. Aside from the direct policy effect of this critically important policy change, this would also have indirectly affected litigation and court rulings as it would have indicated a federal commitment to equal treatment and equal opportunity for lesbians and gays under Title VII of the Civil Rights Act of 1964 or under stand-alone legislation. Thus, the failures of the Clinton years were important to setting the future pathways for lesbian and gay rights in the U.S. In a parliamentary system, a determined executive would not face a situation in which his or her actions or potential actions could be sandbagged by the opposition nor would the executive face quasi-independent legislators among whom support would have to be built for executive action. As public attention was drawn to the gays in the military debate, the separation of powers system left Congress open to lobbying and, in the lobbying game, gay rights opponents were able to muster substantial resources. By taking the legislative initiative, they were able to set the agenda of public debate. In this way, institutional structures set limits on the ways in which supporters and opponents of lesbian and gay rights have mobilized and the separation of powers system has militated against policy success for the lesbian and gay movement.

Although Clinton's proposal to ban discrimination against gay men and lesbians in the military was not passed, the debate over discrimination against lesbians and gays in uniform also demonstrated the extent to which the idea of banning discrimination was becoming politically thinkable in the U.S. The massive 1993 March on Washington for lesbian and gay rights highlighted the issue of discrimination, especially in the military, and, in a portent of the future politics of lesbian and gay rights in the U.S., the demonstration featured a mass wedding reception for same-sex couples as well as thirteen same-sex marriages, which were performed on the steps of the Internal Revenue Service in order to highlight the taxation discrimination suffered by same-sex couples (Deitcher 1995: 155).

CHARTER-BASED LEGAL MOBILIZATION IN CANADA, 1986–1996

Despite the dominance of the right-of-center Progressive Conservatives, who were in power from 1984 to 1993, there were several important lesbian and gay rights cases over this period, which began to generate legal pressure for relationship recognition and for the inclusion of sexual orientation in section 15 of the Charter and in federal human rights legislation. Once again, it is important to underline the impact of policy legacies on the evolution of the lesbian and gay rights debate. While the cases of *Bowers* and *Romer* concerned the criminalization of sodomy and the right of gays and lesbians to participate in the political process, Canadian cases tackled discrimination and relationship recognition. These cases were not planned or financially supported by Canada's new lesbian and gay rights group, Egale, which, in any case, did not have the resources to fund litigation, although it acted as a third party intervener in several of them. To say the least, Egale was no Lambda Legal, let alone an organization with the scale or resources of the Human Rights Campaign or the National Gay and Lesbian Task Force. The organization did not have a single full-time employee until 1995 and, even then, most of its funding came from a very small volunteer base, supplemented with some federal government funding to pay for legal research and legal services (Smith 1999; 2005a).

Two of the key cases in the late 1980s and early 1990s were *Veysey v. Correctional Services (Canada)* (1990) and *Haig and Birch v. Canada* (1992). In these cases, courts ruled that the exclusion of sexual orientation from federal human rights legislation violated the rights guarantees of the Charter. As would occur under the Liberal government on the same-sex marriage issue in the early 2000s, the federal government, under the leadership of the Progressive Conservatives, quietly declined to appeal the decisions. Because of these decisions, it was widely understood in the legal community that sexual orientation had been "read into" the Charter of Rights and into the federal human rights legislation through court decisions, despite the lack of a formal federal legislative amendment and despite the lack of a ruling from the Supreme Court of Canada. The Canadian Human Rights Commission, the enforcer of the federal human rights code, was itself a strong supporter of the inclusion of sexual orientation within its ambit and immediately recognized the implications of the *Veysey* and *Haig and Birch* decisions by accepting over two hundred complaints based on sexual orientation after 1992 (Iyer 1993; Sanders 1994). This change enabled lesbian and gay rights claimants to challenge discriminatory laws in federal jurisdiction.

The Progressive Conservative government had staved off some of the direct lesbian and gay rights challenges by settling issues out of court and by incrementally adjusting policies on the armed forces and immigration, although these policy changes fell short of the clear and enforceable policy directions favored by Egale and other lesbian and gay rights activists. The direction from the courts was critically important to the government's reactions as the Department of Justice quickly came to take a central place in policymaking in the Charter era. Department of Justice lawyers played an increasingly important role in advising the government on Charter cases and the direction of key court decisions such as *Haig and Birch* was taken as an indication of the likely direction of Charter litigation on lesbian and gay rights (see Hiebert 2002; J. Kelly 2005). The Progressive Conservative government was hemmed in by the advice of the lower courts and the advice of its lawyers; even if the government of the day had wanted to challenge these lower court rulings, there was every indication that these challenges would be defeated and that the government might be depicted as a party of extremism or social conservatism, a label that might have prevented the party from reaping the rewards of the moderate political center.

The *Egan* case was a turning point in lesbian and gay litigation (*Egan v. Canada* 1995). In this case, the Court ruled that sexual orientation was included within the ambit of the equality rights clause of the Charter, although the Court ruled against Egan on other grounds. At the time of this landmark case in 1995, there had been fourteen cases concerning sexual orientation under the Charter (McIntosh 1999: 157–163). Cases concerning the inclusion of sexual orientation as a prohibited ground of discrimination in the federal human rights legislation—*Veysey* and *Haig and Birch*—had been successful, while cases concerning relationship recognition had not. In addition, cases that concerned discrimination in the Armed Forces (*Douglas v. Canada* 1992) and immigration (*Morrissey and Coll v. the Queen*)—the right of lesbians and gay men to sponsor their partners for immigration to Canada—had been settled favorably out of court by the federal government. In *Egan*, the Supreme Court of Canada ruled that sexual orientation was analogous to other grounds of discrimination enumerated in section 15 of the Charter and that, hence, it was included (*de facto*) or "read in" to the Charter, thus confirming the implications of the earlier judgments in *Haig and Birch* and *Veysey*. In response to this, the Liberal government (elected in 1993), came under increasing pressure to amend federal human rights legislation to include sexual orientation, a change that had already been informally included because of the *Haig and Birch* judgment. Led by Egale and by the Canadian Human Rights Commission itself, the Liberals acted to amend the law in 1996 (see Smith 1998).

Therefore, the early litigation on Charter issues with regard to lesbian and gay rights was influenced by the impact of political institutional factors and policy legacies. Through the historical timing of the advent of the Charter—timing that had nothing directly to do with lesbian and gay politics—the lesbian and gay movement enjoyed a clear opening to secure legal recognition, an opportunity that was not available to the U.S. lesbian and gay movement. While the U.S. movement faced an equal protection clause that had already been profoundly shaped by a century of conflict over racial inequality, the Canadian movement faced a Charter that had been written in part to respond to the demands of the modern women's movement, one that left the door open to additional rights-seekers, one that explicitly protected equity measures, and one that explicitly placed race, ethnicity, religion, sex, and any unnamed grounds (i.e., sexual orientation) on an equal footing. The U.S. experience was profoundly influenced by the policy legacies of race in the interpretation of equal protection, while Canadian lesbian and gay litigants and their advocates faced a much shorter history of litigation under section 15. In addition, the Charter was a centralizing document, thus reinforcing one of the key differences between the U. S. and Canada, namely, the role and impact of federalism. In securing rights recognition under the Charter, the lesbian and gay movement was able to change policies throughout Canada. In the U.S., most positive court decisions in recognizing lesbian and gay rights have been located at the level of state courts, in part because of judicial federalism and in part because of state jurisdiction over key policy areas such as criminal law and marriage. Hence, in the U.S. the process of policy change proceeded on a piecemeal basis as battles were fought from state to state.

Another key factor that we see at work in the early treatment of lesbian and gay claimants by the Progressive Conservative government in Canada during the period from 1984 to 1993 is that Christian evangelical opponents did mobilize to exercise political influence. While this group did not have the extensive resources of the U.S. Christian Right or "Moral Majority" as developed through the 1970s and into the Reagan presidency, this group also lacked the political opportunities provided by American political institutions. Christian evangelicals could not pressure the Progressive Conservative party from the inside because there was no primary process for party nominations. Because of parliamentary political institutions, the impact of the Family Caucus within the Progressive Conservative Party was moderated by party leaders and this was one of the factors that led to the breakup of the party. The establishment of the evangelical-influenced Reform Party in 1987 did not alter this landscape as the new party was unable to break through to majority status (Laycock 2001). While this drive to the center might be seen as a reflection of Canadian political culture, the passive measurement of religiosity or public opinion does not capture the dynamic of party competition. When the Liberals were elected in 1993, they had increasingly defined the values of the Charter as the values of Canada. This was not an equation that was given in public opinion but an equation that was made over this period in the dynamic process of party competition and in which party leaders chose to mobilize "Charter values" as "Canadian values" in relation to the political struggle over Quebec sovereignty and national unity. The centralized party leadership of the parliamentary system, therefore, curtailed the influence of the Christian Right in Canada, and the partisan conflict over national unity and Quebec secession boosted the commitment of the main political parties to the new terrain of the Charter as a nationalist symbol for English-speaking Canada in its battle for unity. Lesbian and gay litigants were able to take advantage of these circumstances.

THE ACCELERATION OF POLICY DIVERGENCE: A COMPARISON OF *DALE, SHAHAR,* AND *VRIEND*

During the late 1990s, a number of legal cases arose that dealt with issues of discrimination against lesbians and gays and with expressive rights regarding the stigmatization of homosexuality in the public square. These cases exemplify the divergent paths taken by the U.S. and Canada on lesbian and gay rights issues and the impact of policy legacies, institutional differences, and partisan political conflict playing out over time. As Canadian jurisdictions moved to include sexual orientation in human rights codes, legal struggles continued over the constitutionality of discrimination against gays and lesbians in the U.S. These arguments centrally concerned the stigma associated with homosexuality and the extent to which the relatively conservative U.S. Supreme Court and the political leadership would defend the view that heterosexuality was better than homosexuality and that heterosexuality should be promoted over homosexuality. Although the level of religiosity is often cited as a factor that differentiates the U.S. from Canada, religion played an important role in several important cases touching on discrimination and education in Canada during this period. A comparison of the two important lesbian and gay rights cases in the U.S. at this time—*Shahar* and *Dale*—with one of the key Canadian cases of the same time period—*Vriend*—highlights the ways in which arguments over lesbian and gay rights were shaped by policy legacies, the institutional context (specifically the role of judicial review) and the overall shape of the partisan political battle between the main political parties.

The 1998 Supreme Court of Canada decision in the *Vriend* case forms a stark contrast with the 1997 decision of a Georgia federal court in the case of *Shahar* and the U.S. Supreme Court decision in *Dale* (2000). The Canadian case concerned the constitutionality of human rights legislation in Alberta and its exclusion of sexual orientation as a ground for human rights complaint in the Western province. As Canada's most socially conservative province with a longstanding Conservative government, Alberta had declined to include sexual orientation as a prohibited ground of discrimination in its provincial human rights legislation. The issue in *Vriend* was the constitutionality of the exclusion of sexual orientation from provincial protection as a ground of complaint under the Charter. Delwin Vriend, an openly gay teacher in a Christian college in conservative Alberta, had been fired from his job, allegedly because he was gay. He argued that his human rights had been violated and he attempted to lodge a complaint under Alberta's human rights legislation. Because the legislation did not explicitly include sexual orientation as a prohibited ground of discrimination, he was denied the opportunity to lodge a complaint. He then took the government of Alberta to court, arguing that Alberta's human rights legislation violated section 15 (equality rights) of the Charter which, by 1998, had been deemed by the courts to include sexual orientation (*Vriend v. Alberta* 1998; see also Gotell 2002).

The *Vriend* case illustrates the limits of the political culture approach to explain policy divergence between Canada and the U.S. on lesbian and gay rights. Although Alberta is considered to be Canada's most socially conservative and politically right-wing province, in part due to the legacy of American immigration to the province, its degree of conservatism is somewhat similar to that of Massachusetts, according to Adams's (2003) analysis of public opinion in Canada and the U.S. According to Adams, Canada is so much more socially liberal than the U.S. that even the most conservative part of Canada—Alberta—is only as "conservative" as Massachusetts. Adams uses this comparison to demonstrate differences in public opinion and political culture between Canada and the U.S. While Adams's analysis of political culture may be accurate, differences in political values and beliefs do not translate neatly into policy outcomes. In Massachusetts, political values and beliefs have translated into a pioneering role for the state with regard to same-sex marriage. In Alberta, the same degree of "conservatism" or "liberalism," as defined in Adams's data, translated into government opposition to the inclusion of sexual orientation as a prohibited ground of discrimination in the province's human rights legislation. Therefore, the same political culture, as measured by Adams, led to very different policy results in these two locations.

By using the Charter, Vriend was able to argue that the Alberta human rights legislation was unconstitutional because it did not protect lesbians and gays from discrimination and the Supreme Court of Canada agreed, ruling that the exclusion of sexual orientation from Alberta's human rights legislation infringed the Charter. Despite Alberta's opposition to including sexual orientation within its human rights legislation, its right-of-center government chose not to go as far as to invoke the notwithstanding clause of the constitution to set aside the result of the court decision. The government's decision was influenced by the fact that litigation on other Charter equality issues was pushing governments across Canada to recognize spousal and parenting rights for same-sex couples; moreover almost three-quarters of Albertans supported such human rights protections for lesbian and gay Albertans (Alberta 1999). In light of the extensive policy changes underway across Canada, Alberta would have risked looking like a human rights backwater if it had invoked the highly visible notwithstanding clause to prevent gays and lesbians from lodging complaints regarding private discrimination in areas such as employment or housing.

In contrast to the fate of Delwin Vriend, the case of Robin Shahar demonstrates the acceleration of policy divergence between Canada and the U.S. in this period. While there are many cases of employment discrimination against gays and lesbians in the U.S. over the same period, Shahar's case is noteworthy because of the fact that it was denied a hearing by the Supreme Court on appeal and because it engages questions of both religion and same-sex marriage. Most importantly, it provides a striking case of the open and explicit deployment of the criminal law as the means of providing a rationale for firing a woman on the grounds of sexual orientation. In 1991, Robin Shahar, a staff attorney for the Georgia Attorney-General's office was fired by Michael Bowers (of *Bowers v. Hardwick* fame) after it became known that she and her female partner had celebrated a Jewish wedding ceremony. In his role as Attorney-General, Michael Bowers was the legal counsel and senior legal advisor for the state of Georgia and, therefore, the firing of Robin Shahar sent a strong message that firing lesbians and gays was viewed as justifiable by the state's most senior legal advisor. Shahar contested her firing with the assistance of the ACLU Lesbian and Gay Rights Project and Lambda Legal, which initially filed the case.

On June 1, 1997, a Georgia federal court ruled against Shahar, finding that there had been no employment discrimination.

Shahar's claims in the case rested on her right to intimate association, her freedom of religion, and her right to equal protection. In reply to Shahar's claim, the full panel of the court decided that her Jewish marriage to her female partner would disrupt the workplace. The Court disagreed on whether or not her right to marry formed part of the right of intimate association and, if it did, what implications this would have for her right not to be fired from her job (*Shahar v. Bowers* 1995: 1; see also Wildenthal 1998). Further, this case, as so many others in American jurisprudence on lesbian and gay rights, was directly affected by the illegality and criminality of homosexual conduct under the law. This seems to have been the clear intention of Michael Bowers who, at the time of *Bowers,* had argued that state sodomy laws were not a form of discrimination against homosexuals, since the specific sodomy laws at issue in *Bowers* applied equally to heterosexuals and homosexuals. Despite his disavowals at the time that he litigated the *Bowers* case on Georgia's sodomy laws, in *Shahar,* Bowers used *Bowers* for the express purpose of justifying employment discrimination. According to *Bowers,* there was no due process right to homosexual conduct and, as there was no due process right to such conduct, such conduct could not form any basis of a religiously performed or sanctioned marriage that would furnish a right to intimate association or a right to expressive association. Bowers explicitly stated the connection between the discrimination against Shahar when he explained that "[r]egardless of whether [p]laintiff has actually committed sodomy, [p]laintff's Amended Complaint admits that she has purportedly 'married' her female companion, and that she made such 'marriage' public knowledge. On these facts alone, the Attorney General is justified in withdrawing the offer of employment in order to ensure public perception (and reality) that his [d]epartment is enforcing and will continue to enforce the laws of the State" (cited in Cain 2000: 218). The Court also found that equal protection did not provide any legal footing for Shahar's claim. She was fired because she got married and not because she was a lesbian, according to the majority opinion *(Shahar* 1995: I). Lambda Legal's Beatrice Dohrn commented of this decision, "Most Americans oppose job discrimination. It is ironic that a government employer would want to discriminate by exempting from constitutional rules those whose very job it is to uphold the Constitution (Lambda Legal 1997)." Yet, despite this, Robin Shahar lost her case and the Supreme Court declined to hear her appeal in 1998.

At the same time that the Supreme Court seemed to recognize that the motivation to discriminate against homosexuals was illegitimate in *Romer,* the Court also moved in the other direction in the case of *Boy Scouts v. Dale.* Once again, this case revived the discourse of the morality of homosexuality (S. Kelly 2002); in this case, the Court ruled on the conflict between freedom of association and anti-discrimination provision in the case of a gay scoutmaster who was expelled from the Scouts because of his sexual orientation. This case went to the heart of the traditional association between homosexuality and pedophilia, often used by the religious right to justify discrimination against gays and lesbians. In this case, the Court drew on First Amendment case law in which private organizations were held to have interests in expressing certain values, opinions, and goals (McGowan 2001: 126–128; Lim 2003, 2006). In a previous case on the right of an Irish-American gay and lesbian group to march in the St. Patrick's Day parade in Boston in 1993, the Court had found that the parade organizers had the right to free expression and could exclude from the parade those who did not fit in with the message they wanted to express (*Hurley v. Irish-American Gay, Lesbian & Bisexual Group,* 1995;[2] see also Yalda 1999). Hence, the gay and lesbian group was barred from participating in the parade.

In the *Dale* case, the Supreme Court ruled 5–4 that the young scoutmaster (aged 18 when expelled from the Scouts) had no right to be protected against discrimination by the Scouts. James Dale had a distinguished career as a Scout but was expelled when he came out as a gay man and joined a local gay rights group. Despite the fact that New Jersey law required no discrimination in public facilities on the grounds of sexual orientation, Dale was denied recourse on the grounds that the purpose of the Scouts was to instill certain values in its young charges and that Dale's actions in openly acknowledging his homosexuality and in actively working in favor of gay rights came into conflict with the goals and values of the Scouts. The Court distinguished between Dale's gay activism and the actions of heterosexual Scout leaders who supported him (*Dale*: 660; see Lim 2003: 2618). The Court thus ruled that the freedom of expressive interest was not outweighed by a compelling state interest and accepted the Scouts' assertion that its function was to teach moral values to young people and that homosexuality was contrary to its values. The majority of the Court stated that, if the Scouts accepted Dale's open homosexuality, this would be similar to permitting a gay and lesbian group to march in the St. Patrick's Day parade in the *Hurley* case. The Court ruled that the First Amendment outweighed the state interest in the issue of discrimination (*Dale*: 655ff; McGowan 2001: 122; S. Kelly 2002: 248–250). Supporters of the *Dale* decision emphasized the rights of intimate association and the right of parents to raise their children as they saw fit in protecting the right of parents to send their children into organizations that upheld the values and teachings they favored (Lim 2003: 2622).

The decision was very close in this case, as the Court split 5–4. However, even the dissent, written by Justice Stevens, emphasized the undesirability of homosexuality in the context of the Scouts. Stevens argued that the *Dale* decision was wrong because it created a "constitutional shield" for discrimination based on sexual orientation. He emphasized that the Scouts did not have a clear-cut policy on homosexuality, that the Scouts were a non-sectarian organization and hence could not have policies that would be deemed offensive to various religious organizations that might have different beliefs on the issue. Further, Stevens argued that Dale was expelled because of the fact he was homosexual, not because he had engaged in homosexual conduct. A key part of Stevens's dissent concerned Dale's expression of his homosexuality in the Scouts. Stevens argued that there was no reason to think that Dale would express his homosexuality, encourage others to homosexuality or even discuss sexual matters (the policy of the Scouts is to forbid discussion of sexual matters; *Dale*: 663ff; see also S. Kelly 2002: 250–255). However, this begged the question of whether Dale's open expression of his sexual orientation would tend to encourage others to come out or that it would validate the experiences and feelings of other gay scouts, even when there was no discussion of sexual matters.

The Court's decision in *Dale* indicated the depth of moral approbation toward homosexuality on the U.S. Supreme Court as the Court accepted the characterization that homosexuality was not "morally straight" and "clean" and that the Scouts did not want to "promote homosexuality as a legitimate form of behavior" (*Dale* 2000: 667). Even Stevens, who dissented from the decision and who was concerned about the creation of an exception in constitutional jurisprudence that would permit discrimination against lesbians and gays, upheld the stigmatizing of homosexuality and, specifically, homosexual conduct by arguing that, if Dale had expressed his homosexuality openly or if he had a boyfriend who had been seen by other scouts, he would have had no right to any protection from discrimination whatsoever. In Stevens's view, if Dale had any ground at all, it came from the fact that he had not expressed his homosexuality during his actual scouting activities. This is a very restrictive sort of freedom for anyone and, even that much freedom was denied to James Dale.

Therefore, the policy legacies continued to shape the legal and policy discussion of homosexuality in the U.S.; the stigma surrounding homosexual conduct remained very strong, evidenced by the Court's ready acceptance of open and evident discrimination against Robin Shahar and the open and evident discrimination against James Dale. This same type of open discrimination against Canadians was becoming less acceptable to the Supreme Court of Canada, as evidenced in the *Vriend* decision. As the U.S. continued to battle with basic questions about the legitimacy of discriminating against gays and lesbians, litigation under the Charter in Canada had moved public policy toward recognition of the rights of same-sex couples in relationships and parenting. While Alberta was an outlier province with regard to the basic issue of private discrimination, it was brought into line with other provinces through the *Vriend* decision. In the meantime, private discrimination against lesbians and gays in the U.S. continued to be defined as politically legitimate in public policy, even though some private employers began offering same-sex partner benefits and recognizing workplace diversity (Human Rights Campaign 2007d).

These differences in the legitimacy of private and public discrimination in public policy and law reflected the twenty-year period in which homosexual behavior had been stigmatized as criminal in U.S. states and in which this stigmatization had been constitutionally sanctioned by the U.S. Supreme Court in *Bowers*. Thus, over time, despite the changing social attitudes toward homosexuals in the U.S. that are evidenced in public opinion polling, public policy was stuck in the past and reflected the legacy of criminalization, a legacy that clearly defined homosexuality as inferior to heterosexuality and that legitimated public and private discrimination against individual lesbians and gay men as well as against same-sex relationships.

PARTISAN CONFLICT

Over the ten-year period from the *Bowers* decision in 1986 to the passage of the federal Defense of Marriage Act in 1996, there was an acceleration of policy divergence between Canada and the U.S. In 1969, the difference between the adoption of the Wolfenden recommendations by Canada and the failure of similar legal reform measures in the U.S. may have seemed like a relatively minor policy difference, coming as it did before the rise of the modern lesbian and gay rights movement, signaled by Stonewall and the birth of gay liberation in 1969. Yet, over the decades following 1969, cross-national policy divergences accelerated. As of 1996, the stance of the two countries on the issue of same-sex marriage was quite similar, as Canada was far from adopting such a policy in 1996 and, in fact, the House of Commons passed several resolutions reaffirming the heterosexual nature of legal marriage over this period and would continue to do so into the early 2000s (Smith 2002). However, cross-national differences are demonstrated through a comparison of progress on the issue of basic anti-discrimination protections for lesbians and gay men, especially for people fired from their jobs because of their sexual orientation or people denied public accommodation because of their sexual orientation. In this sense, the contrast between cases such as *Dale* and *Shahar* on one hand and the case of *Vriend* on the other hand, shows the difference between the two countries as of the late 1990s, prior to the take-off of the public debate over same-sex marriage. In addition, in Canada, there was increasingly legal recognition of parenting rights and of rights for co-habiting same-sex couples over this period, even if there was still a consistent public commitment to the maintenance of traditional marriage.

Throughout this ten-year period, partisan party politics on the lesbian and gay issue can be read as a stalemate between supporters and opponents. The election of the Liberals in 1993 signaled some openness to lesbian and gay rights claims. As the party that had brought Canada the Charter, the Liberals prided themselves on their commitment to human rights, which provided a lever for lesbian and gay activists to hold the government accountable for its actions. The 1993 election also signaled the transition from a three-party Parliament to a five-party Parliament with the fracturing of the Progressive Conservative Party and the rise of the Western right-populist Reform Party (later Canadian Alliance) and the Quebec-based nationalist Bloc Québécois (Carty, Cross and Young 2000). The Reform Party, in particular, was a consistent opponent of lesbian and gay rights claims and was backed by evangelical Christian supporters from western Canada. The Bloc Québécois was largely supportive, although the issue was peripheral for the party. Within the Liberal caucus, there was some opposition to lesbian and gay rights from a small group of pro-family MPs. Liberal governments were highly sensitive to the opposition to lesbian and gay rights from within their own party and from the right-wing Reform/ Canadian Alliance party.

In this sense, the Liberal government would have stalemated on the issue and ignored it had it not been for the impact of judicial empowerment. Court rulings provided the lesbian and gay movement with the policy resources to force policy change on reluctant legislators. The establishment of legal networks and the formation and strengthening of Egale increasingly assisted litigants in bringing forward successful Charter challenges. Judicial empowerment served the interests of legislators who were sensitive to the relatively strong opposition to lesbian and gay rights which had a strong voice in Parliament in the Reform Party[3] and, to a lesser extent, within the Liberal caucus. The government preferred to deflect pressure from lesbian and gay rights opponents by shifting responsibility for the issue to the courts. At the same time, the government continued the Trudeau-era policies of supporting litigation for disadvantaged groups in the equality rights and language rights areas. Lawyers working in favor of lesbian and gay rights, as well as Egale itself as an organization, undertook legal research funded by these programs (Egale 1998: 1–2). Thus, while the government was reluctant to legislate in favor of lesbian and gay rights unless forced into it by the courts, its policies continued to provide part of the support structure for lesbian and gay rights litigation (Epp 1998: 178–220).

In contrast, in the U.S. over this period, the partisan divide continued to reflect the shift of the South to the Republican Party, the role of the Christian Right in Republican Party politics and efforts by the Democrats to dissociate themselves from the perceived liberalism of the 1960s through the adoption of more centrist positions. Despite the fact that there were few occasions on which lesbian and gay rights were explicitly debated in national party politics, the discursive construction of policies such as anti-discrimination or affirmative action as policies reflecting "special interests" or "special rights" reinforced the backlash against the civil rights gains of the 1960s and the advent of expanded welfare state programs, with welfare increasingly encoded in racial terms (Goldberg-Hiller 2002; Soss et al. 2003b). Over this period, there were important public debates over abortion and over the enduring legitimacy and constitutionality of the *Roe* decision, and the extent to which the federal courts should enforce a common vision of civil rights and equality in the U.S. continued to be a hotly debated question. Minority groups such as gays and lesbians were clearly associated with the liberalism of the Democratic Party and were a liability to a centrist political leadership that felt itself to be vulnerable to the Christian Right attack on "family values." The association in American politics between gender, race, and sexuality placed the stability of traditional heterosexual families squarely at the heart of concerns over social stability and racial peace, as evidenced by the extensive social policy debate of the 1980s over the stability of the black family, the anxiety over single mothers (especially black single mothers), and the rate of illegitimate births in the U.S. The foundation of American social policy in the heterosexual nuclear family was clearly established through these debates and centrist Democrats in the Democratic Leadership Council (such as the Clintons) embraced the policy discourse linking the stability of families to social policy (especially welfare policy).

The entwining of these issues as the historical legacy of the effects of the New Deal and the Great Society led some scholars to call for the revamping of U.S. social policy in ways that would make these policies less racially divisive and that would appeal to working class whites. However, most of these recommendations contained an undercurrent of stable heterosexuality that continued to marginalize lesbian and gay citizens and to define same-sex relationships as outside of family. The emphasis on stable families in U.S. social policy reinforces the normativity of heterosexuality, especially because of the anxieties that were focused on children, especially black inner-city children. There was no discussion of two mothers or two fathers as providing stable homes for such children (Cahill et al. 2002; Cahill and Tobias 2007). The increase in the number of same-sex couples and children living together in the U.S. over this period was completely elided in social policy debates that presumed, assumed, and explicitly discussed the fact that it was the lack of fathers or the lack of the two-parent heterosexual unit that was the cause of urban instability and poverty.

In this context, the main debates on lesbian and gay rights in national politics in this period highlighted the fundamental issue of the inferiority of homosexuality and homosexual relationships. The debate on "gays in the military" was a moment that highlighted and reinforced the political and social stigma toward lesbian and gay citizens in the U.S. Pat Buchanan's homophobic attack on gay men during the 1992 Republican Convention clearly condemned homosexuality as a sin and suggested that AIDS was a fitting punishment. While this episode may be seen as another example of a political cultural difference between the U.S. and Canada as no Canadian politician (even an evangelical such as Preston Manning) has ever made such an open statement, again, it is important to note the institutional underpinnings of the Buchanan episode, which formed part of an ongoing campaign by Buchanan as a presidential candidate and by the Christian Right to permeate the Republican Party. In turn, this campaign was facilitated by changes to the process of nominating candidates in both the Republican and Democratic Parties during the 1960s, which had opened up the candidate nomination process to primaries. In turn, this provided opportunities for social movements to exercise influence within parties and, in the case of the Christian Right, this effort paid off as many energized and ideologically committed evangelicals entered Republican Party politics over this period (Kaplan 2004; Wilcox 2006). These episodes show the ways in which same-sex relationships are subordinated compared to the normativity of heterosexuals and opposite-sex relationships.

CONCLUSIONS

In the mid-1980s, lesbian and gay rights policies in the U.S. and Canada underwent a process of accelerating divergence, a process that had been underway since the Canadian Criminal Code revision of 1969. The evolution of policies on discrimination shows the striking differences in the evolution of policy. Over this period, a majority of Americans and Canadians believed that discriminating against lesbians and gay men in areas such as employment was wrong. Yet, American public policy did not reflect the positions that were actually supported by public opinion or by political culture as measured in beliefs and values. U.S. political institutions opened up every opportunity for the emergence of a backlash against gender equality and against any sign that lesbian and gay rights would receive legal recognition in the U.S. The idea that the U.S. Supreme Court ruled based on law and law alone in the *Bowers* decision cannot explain how the same court broke with its own precedent in the *Lawrence* decision seventeen years later. The vitriol expressed in the Supreme Court decision seems an excellent example of the power of judicial attitudes in play (Pinello 2003). Despite the power of the attitudinal model in providing explanations for specific judicial decisions in particular time periods, the ruling of the Court in *Bowers* and *Dale* and the Court's refusal to hear *Shahar* (and, hence, to overturn it) does not provide the main explanation for the policy outcome in which the U.S. lagged far behind Canada in provision of legal protection against discrimination. Judicial attitudes do not develop in a societal vacuum. Over this period, the Christian Right undertook a sustained assault against lesbian and gay rights, sparked by the initial victories in securing basic anti-discrimination measures in localities and states across the U.S. Threatened by the spread of these local measures, measures which were often undertaken by executive action or as a result of decisions of state courts, the Christian Right mobilized to stop these measures. The U.S. system offers political opportunity for the mobilization of the Christian Right, opportunities that do not exist in Canada.

As we have seen in this chapter, the Christian Right was active in using the mechanisms of direct democracy in constitutions such as that of Colorado, to repeal gay rights measures. In doing so, the Christian Right put a chill on these types of legal protection and greatly increased the costs for the lesbian and gay movement in fighting battles such as this on a state-by-state basis across the U.S. An extraordinary coordinated litigation effort was required by the lesbian and gay movement to challenge Amendment 2 and, while these battles contributed to the development of professionalized and well-resourced lesbian and gay organizations in the U.S. compared to Canada, these battles also resulted in an uneven pattern of policy development in which the lesbian and gay movement was constantly on the defensive. This uneven pattern, combined with the continuing criminalization of sodomy and the constitutional recognition of this inequality in the *Bowers* decision, reinforced the stigma attaching to homosexuality and opened the door for the justices of the Supreme Court to indulge traditional prejudices, whether dealing with the "homosexual right to sodomy" in *Bowers*, the "straight" and "clean" Boy Scouts in *Dale*, the implicit criminality of Robin Shahar's marriage, according to the state of Georgia (given Georgia's criminalization of homosexual sodomy),[4] or the "special interests" of Amendment 2 and Cincinnati Equality, who were supposedly imposing their way of life on everyone else.

The openings provided by state constitutions and by the separation of powers, as well as the jurisdictional decentralization and fragmentation of responsibility for human rights in the U.S. system among states, localities and the federal government contrast with the relatively closed and centralized Canadian parliamentary system. There are simply fewer points of access for gay rights opponents in Canada, which means that opponents are not offered multiple opportunities to strike down lesbian and gay rights and to put forth homophobic views. The development of U.S. party politics over this period and the backlash politics against gender, racial and sexual equality that was epitomized by the permeation of the Republican Party by the religious right and the swing of the southern states into the Republican camp also reinforced the association of lesbian and gay rights with the Democratic party of minorities and special interests. In contrast, the development of Canadian party politics over this period created the opposite dynamic as conservatives were imprisoned in the chains of social liberalism, which had become associated with English Canadian nationalism in part through the mechanism of the new Charter. In this context, it was only a matter of time before lesbians and gays in Canada would walk through the door opened by the Charter.

5 The Emergence of Same-Sex Marriage, 1991–1999

By the late 1990s, same-sex marriage had emerged as the dominant "gay rights" issue in national politics in the U.S. and Canada. State courts in the U.S. set the policy agenda by finding in favor of same-sex couples in a series of decisions beginning in Hawai'i in 1993. By 2005 when Canada legalized same-sex civil marriage, American policy outcomes were much more diverse, with marriage available in Massachusetts, civil union available in Vermont (and pending in other states), and domestic partnerships recognized in Hawai'i and other states. Same-sex marriage had been rendered unconstitutional in some state constitutions, banned by statute in other states, and its recognition in federal law had been prohibited through the passage of the federal Defense of Marriage Act (1996), which had also explicitly recognized the right of the states to refuse to recognize same-sex marriages from other states. While Canada legalized same-sex marriage, the U.S. Congress tabled a constitutional amendment to ban it, an amendment supported by President George W. Bush. These divergences show the long-term impact of policy legacies on the definition of this public policy issue in the two contexts, the ongoing impact of institutional differences in shaping policy discourse, political struggles and policy outcomes, and the contrasting dynamics of partisan conflict.

While lesbian and gay rights struggles from the late 1960s to the 1990s focused on the rights of the individual, the late 1990s saw a shift of the legal and political terrain from the rights of the individual to the rights of couples and families (Chauncey 2004: 94). Yet, the way in which the issue of discrimination against individuals had been resolved (or not) set the parameters for the recognition of the legal rights of same-sex couples. From the modest policy variance of 1969, when homosexuality was decriminalized in Canada, the policy variance between the two cases had been compounded as the U.S. was unable to decriminalize sodomy on a nation-wide basis or offer basic anti-discrimination protection let alone relationship recognition and same-sex marriage. At the same time, these policy challenges had forced the U.S lesbian and gay movement to develop its political skills and resources to an extent unparalleled in Canada (see Fetner forthcoming). Federalism also compounded the complexity of policy change in the U.S. Just as criminal law is allocated to the states in the U.S. and to federal jurisdiction in Canada, so too civil marriage is allocated to federal control in Canada and to state jurisdiction in the U.S. Just as the decriminalization of sodomy proceeded on a state-by-state basis in the U.S., so too policy shifts on same-sex marriage took place in state-by-state battles rather than, as in Canada, by way of a policy change in federal jurisdiction. State constitutions provided openings for opponents of same-sex marriage in the late 1990s and the first decade of the 2000s, just as these constitutional arrangements had provided opportunities for gay rights opponents in Dade County for Anita Bryant in 1977, in Colorado for the proponents of Amendment 2 in 1992, and across many other states where discrimination protections were rolled back. The federal Defense of Marriage Act (DOMA) was signed into law by Bill Clinton in 1996 in response to the first spate of same-sex marriage cases in Hawai'i; DOMAs and state constitutional bans on same-sex marriage were widely diffused through the states between 1996 and 2004.[1]

This chapter and the next chapter outline these factors at work by examining the evolution of same-sex marriage from the *Baehr* case in Hawai'i in the early 1990s to the legalization of civil marriage in Canada in 2005. This chapter discusses the general context for the same-sex marriage debate in the two countries, including the sociological factors that underpinned the contemporary marriage movement as well as the role of marriage in relation to social policy debates. By surveying the three key cases on same-sex marriage in the U.S. in this period—cases that occurred in Hawai'i, Alaska and Vermont—as well as the Canadian cases on same-sex relationship recognition over this period (especially the *M v. H* case), I emphasize the ways in which the institutional context for these court decisions led to very different policy outcomes in the U.S. and Canada. In the next chapter, I survey the subsequent developments, including the pivotal *Goodridge* case in Massachusetts, which resulted in the legalization of same-sex marriage in that state. Through a close comparison of each step in the litigation and the response to it, the chapter shows that an understanding of institutional context is critically important to understand how differences in human rights policy develop over time.

MARRIAGE AND POLICY LEGACIES
IN THE U.S. AND CANADA

By the early 1990s, there was a new generation of lesbians and gay men living openly, some in relationships, some with children, either from previous relationships or from adoption or new reproductive technologies.[2] The fact of these new forms of family in the U.S. and Canada ineluctably led to demands for the legal recognition of these family relationships. Sociological changes—namely, the expansion of "out" lesbian and gay communities and families—helped to drive the debate on lesbian and gay rights beyond the previously debated public policy issues of criminalization of sexual conduct or the need for protective measures for individual lesbians and gay men against discrimination and toward the demand for the recognition of same-sex couples and parental relationships. While sociological change and societal demand for the legal recognition of parenting, family and relationship rights evolved in both the U.S. and Canada over the course of the 1990s, these demands produced different results in the two cases.

There were several important factors driving the same-sex marriage debate: the impact of the AIDS crisis, the growing number of same-sex couples (especially women) who were deliberately choosing to have children, the growing egalitarianism of gender roles in heterosexual marriage, the decline of religious authority, and the growing importance of marriage to obtaining public and private benefits (Chauncey 2004: 59–86). Some of these changes occurred in similar ways in the U.S. and Canada. For example, AIDS had a similar impact in both countries and the lesbian baby boom occurred in Canada, as well as the U.S. (Arnup 1995). Changing mores with regard to marriage have also developed in both countries including the right to choose one's partner, the decline of religious authority, and changing gender roles within marriage. There is some evidence that gender roles are more egalitarian in Canada than in the U.S. Michael Adams (2003) finds that far fewer Canadians agree with the patriarchal exercise of male authority in the household than Americans. Similarly, with respect to religion, Americans are somewhat more religious than Canadians, although the political implications of this are complex (Bibby 2002). Even if Americans are more religious than Canadians, the U.S. has undergone shifts in gender roles, increased female labor force participation, an increase in the divorce rate, an increase in the number of people living alone (U.S. Census Bureau 2006), and a general decline in the role of traditional religious, family and community authority over the choice of marriage partner (Frank and Mceneaney 1999). Given the magnitude of the sweeping changes that have characterized both societies over the 20th century and given that same-sex households and same-sex couples with children are an identifiable population in both societies where they were not thirty years ago, the sociological setting of the two societies is similar, especially by international standards.

However, despite sociological similarities prior to the rise of the same-sex marriage debate, there were important differences in law and policy between the two countries with respect to marriage, especially with regard to the legal legacy of slavery, the relationship between marriage and the welfare state, and the extent of legal recognition of common law conjugal relationships. First, with regard to slavery, after the demise of Reconstruction, many states passed laws barring interracial marriage or even interracial sex. These bans were common not only in the states of the former Confederacy but across the

U.S. Even states such as Vermont and Massachusetts, which did not ban interracial marriage, did pass laws barring recognition of interracial marriages for couples from states that outlawed the practice. After World War II, two important civil rights cases—*Perez v. Sharp* (1948) and *Loving v. Virginia* (1967)—established that interracial marriage bans were unconstitutional under federal equal protection doctrine and that the right to marry and to form intimate relationships was constitutionally protected (Chauncey 2004: 62; see also Eskridge 2001: 424–433). In the U.S., the demands of the contemporary marriage movement recall debates on interracial marriage and raise some of the same legal and constitutional issues with respect to the recognition of the marriage laws of other states and the potential impact of federal intervention under equal protection through a federal court decision (as in the Supreme Court's 1969 *Loving* decision on interracial marriage).

The explicit analogy between interracial marriage and same-sex marriage has been made repeatedly in the legal and constitutional debate over same-sex marriage in the U.S. (Koppelman 2006). In 1999, Alabama was still debating the removal of its law on interracial marriage from the books, even though the law had not been enforced since *Loving*, and some of its legislators expressed the fear that repealing the interracial marriage law would open the floodgates to same-sex marriage (Cabell 1999). While some commentators, including African American political leaders, have criticized the use of the civil rights analogy in the same-sex marriage movement in the U.S. (Duchschere 2004), it is important to note that the marriage movement includes people of color as well as interracial couples, who are all too keenly aware of how their relationships are doubly stigmatized (for example, see Nicol and Smith 2007). Most importantly, the origins of the analogy are carved into U.S. constitutional law because of the legal legacy of slavery encoded in the crafting of the Fourteenth Amendment, and the emergence of a right to marry and a right to intimate and family life as important freedoms claimed by African Americans after Emancipation. While the analogy between the process of social movement mobilization by African Americans and by lesbians and gays may be false in the sense that the experiences of the two groups are very different (to the extent that these groups can be separated from the perspective of LGBT racialized minorities), the jurisprudence resulting from the presence and the eradication of slavery in the U.S. has important effects for the contemporary marriage struggle.

In Canada, it does not make sense to speak of a legal "right to marry" in part because, prior to the Charter, constitutional rights for the individual were not as clearly enunciated as in the U.S. Bill of Rights. Further, although many laws in Canada were "color-coded" in the words of Canadian legal historian Constance Backhouse (1999), there was no analogue to the interracial marriage bans in the U.S., the legal campaign to overcome them, or the establishment of a legal and political claim to a "right to marry" or a right to form intimate relationships.[3] Although slavery was practiced on a small scale in the territory of what would become Canada, both the slave trade and slavery had been outlawed in the British Empire by 1833 and, in any case, slavery had never been widely practiced in what would become Canadian territory in either New France or British North America. Bans on interracial marriage were suggested and debated at various times in Canadian history, in particular during the 1920s when the Klan made significant incursions into Canada; however, such legislation was not passed (Backhouse 1999: 186). Even the right to privacy does not exist in the same legal form in Canada as in U.S. jurisprudence. It has been established most clearly in the Charter era (post-1982) as a right against search and seizure under the Criminal Code rather than, as in the U.S., in relation to questions such as the right of married couples to access contraception (*Griswold*), women's reproductive rights (*Roe*) or the right to engage is same-sex sexual conduct (*Bowers*). In this context, it is important to recall that Canada shares with the U.S. a common law heritage that implies certain rights against state intrusion but that Canada differs from the U.S. in having lacked a codified constitutional bill of rights prior to 1982. The right to privacy in Canada can best be described as a nascent right in Canadian jurisprudence (Chaffey 1993; Davies 2006). Therefore, it has not played a role in the same-sex marriage debate in Canada. Moreover, the problem of the recognition of the marriage laws of other states does not arise in Canadian provinces because the determination of the capacity to marry falls under federal jurisdiction (Hogg 2006).

Second, marital status plays a more important role in the American welfare state than in the Canadian welfare state. Gay and lesbian political mobilization intersects with the legacies of previous policies that were put into place for very different reasons and as a result of the struggles of other social movements. In the U.S. and Canada, as in other countries, social provision was based on certain assumptions about the relationships between states and markets, but also on assumptions about gender and family relationships. The male breadwinner model of welfare state provision was based on a highly gendered division of labor in the household and that women are providing household labor while men work in the paid labor force. In the welfare state literature, the U.S. and Canada are regarded as similar systems, that is, as liberal and residualist welfare states compared to the more generous social welfare systems of Europe (Esping-Andersen 1990). Yet, there are important differences between the welfare state in Canada and the U.S. In particular, the U.S. allocates many benefits in accordance with marital status rather than as citizenship rights. Perhaps the most important of such benefits is health care. Despite cuts to Canadian Medicare, basic health care is provided to all Canadians as an individual citizenship right. In the U.S., with the exceptions of Medicare and Medicaid, health care is often a private benefit that is provided through the employer and social security is firmly linked to labor market participation. This means that same-sex benefits are very important and valuable in the

U.S., raising the stakes for spousal recognition and marriage for same-sex couples (Cahill and Tobias 2007; see also Harder 2007).

Anna Marie Smith has analyzed the intersection between the sexual regulation of social assistance recipients in Bill Clinton's 1996 welfare reform with the movement against same-sex marriage, epitomized by the passage of the federal Defense of Marriage Act in 1996 in response to the Hawai'i marriage decision. Smith argues that these policies mark a linkage between neoliberalism with its emphasis on individual market-drive solutions and the discourse of the Christian Right, which favors patriarchal and heterosexist sexual regulation (A.M. Smith 2001; see also A.M. Smith 2007). The state interest in and promotion of heterosexual reproduction in these policy areas reflects the influence of Christian Right organizing through religious and social organizations and through Republican party politics in reinforcing the heterosexual male-dominated nuclear family as the privileged social unit. As Jacobs (1996), Eskridge (2000) and other legal scholars have pointed out, the lesbian and gay rights frame engages and provokes the Christian Right because the rights frame inevitably "promotes" homosexuality, that is, it questions the political superiority of heterosexuality. These analyses link race, gender, and sexuality, and highlight the ways in which the lesbian and gay rights frame intersects with the framing of other political issues in the U.S. (see also Goldberg-Hiller 1999). These policies have been further reinforced in the Bush era, in which the federal government has implemented faith-based marriage promotion campaigns and other faith-based initiatives. Because federal funding to the states is conditional on such policies, many observers worry that these measures will reinforce gendered inequality in heterosexual relationships; privatize social provision; stigmatize singles, the divorced, and gays and lesbians; and undermine legal claims for custody of queer parents (Payne 2003; see also Hamilton 2004).

A third important difference between the two countries is that, in Canada, there has been much more political and legal willingness to extend the benefits and obligations of marriage to heterosexual couples who are living together while, in contrast, in the U.S., such relationships have not been accorded the same legal status as marriage or as many of the benefits of marriage as have such relationships in the Canadian case (Barlow and Probert 2004). While this might be seen as a function of religious differences between the two countries, like the issue of the "right to marry," it is also strongly related to social policy trajectories that are shaped by the race and sex debates of the 1960s. The question of common law relationships and, especially, having children out of wedlock, is a lightening rod in the U.S., in part because it is linked to the politics of race. Barlow and Probert (2004) show that there is a distinctive stratification of heterosexuals in the U.S. and that co-habiting couples have lower incomes than married couples. These relationships are linked to anxieties about the black family and the American welfare state that have constituted a major theme in debates over welfare reform (see Soss et al. 2003a). Debates over marriage are not just a question of religious attitudes in the U.S; they are also a question of racial attitudes and the gender politics of regulating the sexuality of single women (Sparks 2003). These differences in the political debate and public discourse over social policy are linked in turn to the nature of electoral competition between Democrats and Republicans since the 1960s and the backlash against racial and gender equality that has been mobilized by the right through the Republican party over the period from 1968 through to the early 2000s.

THE ORIGINS OF SAME-SEX MARRIAGE LITIGATION

While same-sex marriage had been litigated in both the U.S. and Canada in the early 1970s, the issue reemerged anew in the early 1990s. In 1991, Ninia Baehr and Genora Dancel, and other same-sex couples filed their historic marriage case in Hawai'i (*Baehr v. Lewin* 1993). Shortly after, in January 1992, Todd Layland and Pierre Beaulne filed a similar case in Ontario, in an attempt to secure immigration status in Canada for Layland, an American citizen (*Layland v. Ontario* 1993). In both the U.S. and Canada, there was hesitancy among lawyers in the lesbian and gay movement in moving forward with a legal case claiming the right to legal civil marriage for same-sex couples. There was concern that the cases would be unsuccessful and that the cause of lesbian and gay rights in other areas of law would suffer a setback (Fisher 2001; Wolfson 2006). In the U.S., in the early 1990s, many states still had laws criminalizing sodomy, the Christian Right was on the rise, and many jurisdictions did not have enforceable anti-discrimination protections for lesbians and gay men. In Canada, in the early 1990s, the Supreme Court had not ruled on whether sexual orientation was an analogous ground of discrimination under section 15 of the Charter and, therefore, it was not clear that lesbians and gays were covered by the equality rights clause. In both countries, lawyers were concerned that proceeding too quickly with a court case would create a negative precedent for lesbian and gay rights (Elliott 2002; Fisher 2001; Wolfson 2006). In the U.S., the filing of the *Baehr* case was an audacious legal and political move, coming as it did only five years after the infamous *Bowers* decision. If same-sex relationships entailed sexual behavior that was criminal in some states and, if the U.S. Supreme Court had stated that criminalization of such sexual behavior was constitutional, how could same-sex relationships receive the legal, political, and symbolic recognition of legal marriage with all of the material benefits bestowed by such status in U.S. policy and law? The case was based on the hope that state courts would act where politicians feared to tread and that the state courts of Hawai'i would be more favorable to lesbian and gay rights claims than courts in other state jurisdictions or the U.S.

Supreme Court. As evidenced by the impact of *Baehr*, the process of legal mobilization in which individual plaintiffs have been mobilized through a coordinated process of litigation, supported by groups such as Lambda Legal and non-governmental organizations, set the agenda of lesbian and gay rights in the U.S. during this period (Solokar 2001).

Baehr was quickly followed by other states, notably, the *Brause v. Bureau of Vital Statistics* case in Alaska (1998) and the *Baker v. Vermont* (1999). These cases laid the foundation for the pivotal *Goodridge* ruling in Massachusetts in 2003, which resulted in the legalization of same-sex marriage in that state. The litigation of these cases resulted in a substantial recognition of lesbian and gay rights and demonstrated that some state courts in the U.S. were prepared to recognize legal equality for same-sex conjugal relationships. While the U.S. Supreme Court could not bring itself to protect the rights of James Dale or hear an appeal in a straightforward case of employment discrimination in the case of Robin Shahar, judges in state courts were prepared to rule that the state had to provide a compelling reason to bar same-sex couples from the benefits of marriage.

In Canada, in contrast, the transition to same-sex marriage occurred by way of the recognition of co-habiting same-sex couples in a series of cases, beginning with *Egan* in 1995, continuing through *Rosenberg* and, in 1999, culminating in the most important relationship recognition case in Canada, *M v. H*, which established that co-habiting same-sex couples should be accorded the same legal status as co-habiting opposite-sex couples. These cases overlapped in time with the cases on individual discrimination, discussed in the last chapter (e.g., *Vriend*, *Dale*, and *Shahar*). Despite the filing of the *Layland* case in Ontario in the early 1990s, the case was not pursued after the initial dismissal of the claim in the Ontario Court of Justice in 1993 because of fear of a loss at higher levels. Legal networks, led and coordinated by Egale, were successful in managing the course of litigation for much of the 1990s after *Layland*. This permitted a legal breathing space in which other lesbian and gay equality issues were litigated (Fisher 2001; Elliott 2002). The positive results from other cases such as *Vriend* (1998), discussed in the last chapter, as well as from other cases that recognized same-sex relationships to varying degrees (e.g., *Egan*, *Rosenberg*) set the stage for successful litigation of same-sex relationship recognition and, eventually, same-sex marriage in the early 2000s. Nonetheless, in the first cases on same-sex marriage of the 1990s in the two countries, it was a U.S. state court that first ruled in favor of the applicant couples and it was an Ontario court that rejected the claim out of hand.

U.S. SAME-SEX MARRIAGE CASES, 1993–1999

The *Baehr* case began when two lesbian couples and one gay couple filed a case against the state's decision to deny them a marriage license.[4]

They lost in the first hearing and appealed to the Supreme Court of Hawai'i, arguing that the denial of the marriage license was a violation of the right to privacy as well as the right of equal protection and the right to due process of law. It is noteworthy that the plaintiffs made these claims not under the U.S. Bill of Rights, but under the constitution of the state of Hawai'i (*Baehr* 1993: 4). Like eighteen other states in the U.S., Hawai'i had enshrined the Equal Rights Amendment (ERA) in its constitution, even though the federal ERA had failed to pass. The plaintiffs also stressed that that Hawai'i had amended its constitution to explicitly recognize the right to privacy and that, in so doing, it had taken note of decisions such as *Griswold* and *Roe*, which had located a right to privacy in the U.S. Bill of Rights.

On behalf of the state of Hawai'i, Lewin made arguments that were to become the standard in government responses to same-sex marriage challenges. First, he claimed that marriage is heterosexual by definition (*Baehr* 1993: 5). This definitional restatement of the longstanding legal definition of marriage as heterosexual was once considered the first and only rebuttal needed to a same-sex marriage legal challenge and, undoubtedly, in looking back at the same-sex marriage cases of the 1970s (see Earl 2003), it had only seemed reasonable to begin with an argument that had convinced courts so completely and utterly only twenty years earlier. However, in the same-sex marriage cases of the 1990s and 2000s, this argument would have much less traction with courts in the U.S. and Canada. Of the same-sex marriage cases of this later period in the U.S. and Canada that are discussed in this time period, very few courts have given credence to this definitional answer (the initial hearing of *Baker* in Vermont and two lower court cases in Canada, *Layland* in 1993 and *Egale v. Canada* in 2001).[5] Second, Lewin claimed that the state's marriage laws did not burden same-sex couples, that they did not interfere with the couples' right to carry on their relationship or with their right to privacy, and that the state had no positive obligation to recognize such relationships. Third, Lewin argued that heterosexual marriage was intended for the protection and nurturing of children as well as the protection of the family as a social unit (*Baehr* 1993: 5) and that marriage laws "constitute a statement of the moral values of the community in a manner that is not burdensome to [the] plaintiffs" (cited in *Baehr* 1993: 5). Finally, Lewin argued that, after all, lesbians and gays did not form a suspect or quasi-suspect class under federal equal protection doctrine and therefore, the state was not obligated to extend any specific legal protection. Thus, the fact that lesbians and gays (and the category of sexual orientation) are excluded from equal protection was an important factor for the state.

The Hawai'i Supreme Court rejected the right-to-privacy ground of the plaintiffs' case in *Baehr* with respect to the "deeply rooted test." For the court, it was clear that the plaintiffs were requesting the recognition of a new right and not one that was deeply rooted in U.S. history. Nonetheless, the court recognized that the couples had suffered discrimination based on sex, which was prohibited under the Hawai'i Bill of Rights. The court argued that the bar against same-sex marriage was discriminatory on this basis (*Baehr* 1993: 15ff) and, in so doing, according to Peggy Pascoe, "the Hawai'i Supreme Court went further than any other American court had ever gone toward declaring 'sex' a fully suspect legal category" (2000: 105). In the court's reasoning, because sex is a ground for suspect class status as defined in the Hawai'ian constitution's equal rights amendment and because the Hawai'i marriage statute restricted access to the rights and benefits of marriage based on sex, the statute required strict scrutiny (*Baehr* 1993: 15ff; see Strasser 1997: 44–46; Dupuis 2002: 52; Andersen 2005: 178–183).[6] The court stated that "[t]he result we reach today is in complete harmony with the *Loving* Court's observation that any state's powers to regulate marriage are subject to the constraints imposed by the constitutional right to the equal protection of the laws" (*Baehr* 1993: 22). In other words, the ruling made a clear comparison between same-sex marriage and the constitutional challenges to the legal bars on interracial marriage which were struck down in the *Loving* case (see also Buseck 2004; Kristen 1999).

As a result of the decision by the Hawai'i Supreme Court, the case was remanded for hearing to a lower court, where the state now had the burden of proving that there was a compelling state interest in restricting marriage to opposite-sex couples (*Baehr v. Miike* 1996). The state of Hawai'i (now represented by Miike) altered the case from the one presented at the earlier stage. According to Miike's arguments, the denial of same-sex marriage rested on three main points: the fact that the legal marriage of heterosexuals was the best possible environment for the raising of children; that the restriction of marriage to opposite-sex couples was necessary to ensure that Hawai'i's marriage laws would be recognized in other jurisdictions; and that the state was concerned with the financial implications of recognizing same-sex couples (*Baehr* 1996: III). Most of the case was taken up with the hearing of evidence on the health and development of children raised in homes with same-sex parents. The court denied the state's claims that granting same-sex marriage would undermine the well-being of children, given that three-quarters of the state's own witnesses gave evidence that same-sex parenting did not undermine child welfare and that, in fact, extending the legal recognition of marriage to same-sex partners would assist the children raised in such families (Ryan 2000: 14–20). The court concluded that the state had not proved its case and ruled in favor of Ninia Baehr and Genora Dancel and the other applicant couples on the ground of sex-based discrimination. As we will see later in this chapter, unlike the rulings in favor of same-sex marriage in Canada, this court decision did not lead to happy and legal nuptials for the applicant couples.

The second same-sex marriage case in the U.S. over this period was *Brause v. Bureau of Vital Statistics* (1998) in Alaska, filed by Jay Brause and Gene Dugan. They raised very similar claims to those brought forward in Hawai'i, namely, that the ban on same-sex marriage violated their right to privacy and their right to equal protection under the law. Once again, these arguments were made under the constitution of Alaska, which, like Hawai'i's, explicitly recognized the right to privacy. As in Hawai'i, the Alaska Court agreed that the bar on same-sex marriage constituted sex discrimination and that the state had to demonstrate a compelling purpose for engaging in such discrimination. Just as the Hawai'i court had taken note of the *Loving* precedent on interracial marriage, so too Judge Peter A. Michalski of the Superior Court of Alaska repeatedly cited *Loving* and alluded to racial segregation in the U.S. in developing an analogy to same-sex marriage, arguing that there was a strong relationship between the right to marry and equal protection doctrine. Unlike the *Baehr* rulings, he argued that the right to same-sex marriage also entailed fundamental privacy rights and that, while same-sex marriage was not deeply rooted in the nation's history, the right to choose an intimate partner was deeply rooted and must be considered a component of the right to privacy (*Brause*: V). In addition, he ruled that banning same-sex marriage constituted a sex-based classification that required strict scrutiny under equal protection doctrine. Hence, on both counts, he accepted the arguments of the plaintiffs and stated that:

> It is not enough to say that "marriage is marriage" and accept without any scrutiny the law before the court. It is the duty of the court to do more than merely assume that marriage is only, and must only be, what most are familiar with. In some parts of our nation mere acceptance of the familiar would have left segregation in place. In light of Brause and Dugan's challenge to the constitutionality of the relevant statutes, this court cannot defer to the legislature or familiar notions when addressing this issue (*Brause*: V).

The third case of this period was *Baker*, filed in Vermont in 1997. As in the *Baehr* and *Brause* cases, the applicant couples in *Baker* drew on provisions of the state constitution, including Vermont's equal protection clause as well as its common benefits clause, which states that benefits provided by the state must be made available to all citizens. Again, the plaintiffs argued their case on the basis of equal protection and the fundamental right to marry in state law, contesting the link drawn by the state of Vermont between procreation and marriage (Bonauto, Murray and Robinson 1999). While the plaintiffs lost at the first stage in the trial court, they were successful in winning their case on appeal to the Vermont Supreme Court, which ruled in 1999 that the exclusion of same-sex couples from legal marriage violated the common benefits clause of the Vermont constitution (*Baker v. State of Vermont* 1999). The Vermont Supreme Court did not order the lower court to reconsider the case in light of its finding in order to evaluate whether or not the state had a compelling interest in maintaining a distinction between opposite sex and same-sex couples; instead, the Supreme Court simply decided that the state had not justified the discrimination given the evidence that was presented (Andersen 2005: 184–185).

The Vermont constitution's common benefits clause played an important role in the case. The majority decision compared the clause of the Vermont Constitution to federal equal protection doctrine and argued that the purpose of the common benefits clause was different than the federal equal protection provisions because the Vermont constitution aimed to ensure access to common benefits for the whole community rather than simply protecting the rights of minorities. The majority in *Baker* favored a "balancing" approach to the common benefits clause in which the court would evaluate the extent to which citizens were denied the benefit of Vermont law and how this denial was related to the government's stated purpose. In undertaking this analysis, the court could consider the nature and importance of the benefits. The court found that, indeed same-sex couples and, especially, their children were denied common benefits and that this denial was, in fact, the opposite of the state's own stated objective of protecting the family. The trial court had dismissed the case by stating that procreation distinguishes same-sex and heterosexual relationships. Yet the Vermont Supreme Court held that procreation did not provide a ground to distinguish relationships and highlighted the harm to the children of same-sex couples caused by their parents' exclusion from the right of legal marriage.

The ruling in *Baker* also used the "deeply rooted" test, which, as we have already seen, was given contradictory interpretations in *Baehr* and *Brause*. While the judge in *Baehr v. Miike* stated that the recognition of same-sex relationships was not deeply rooted in the nation's history, the judge in *Brause*, while recognizing this historical reality, stated that the right of intimate association did meet the deeply rooted test. The state of Vermont tried to make its case against same-sex marriage by arguing that the "deeply rooted" rights of intimate association and privacy could not encompass the recognition of same-sex relationships. Further, the government argued that same-sex marriage was not permitted in other states. However, the majority of the Court in *Baker* rejected the argument that past discrimination would justify current discrimination (Blandin 1999/2000).

Thus, the rights of applicant same-sex couples in three states were recognized by state courts over the course of the 1990s. This recognition posed a constitutional problem for those who opposed same-sex marriage. Fortunately for same-sex marriage opponents and unfortunately for the applicant couples, the U.S. political system provided many opportunities for opponents to limit the effects of these court decisions and these opportunities were successfully exploited to block same-sex marriage in the three states whose courts had issued the pioneering decisions of the 1990s.

COUNTERMOBILIZATION AT THE FEDERAL
AND STATE LEVELS IN THE U.S.

Countermobilization against same-sex marriage litigation in the U.S. began in the early 1990s when the *Baehr* case was first filed. It picked up in the post-1994 Republican Congress, which reacted strongly to the first Hawai'i ruling in 1993. As Paul Frymer argues, lesbian and gay political interests had been largely ignored in national party politics until the Clinton era (Frymer 1999: 187–189). As we have seen, while Bill Clinton himself took a pro-lesbian and gay rights stance during his first presidential campaign, promising to lift the ban on lesbians and gays in the military, to increase funding for AIDS research and to appoint lesbians and gays in his adminis-tration (Vaid 1995), early in his administration he retreated from his pledge to allow gays and lesbians to serve in the military and sanctioned the adop-tion of the "don't ask, don't tell" policy. While the Clinton administration might have wanted to close the door on the contentious issue of gay rights after the debate on discrimination in the military, the issue was reactivated by the litigation in state courts. The Christian Right and other conserva-tives demanded the passage of "defense of marriage" legislation, as they termed it, which would deny the recognition of same-sex marriages by the federal government and by other states. The Republican victory in the 1994 mid-term elections led to demands for the passage of the Defense of Mar-riage Act (DOMA), which was signed by President Clinton (Frymer 1999; Wilcox 2006: 90–95). The virulent opposition to lesbian and gay rights that had been sparked over the "gays in the military" issue provided the backdrop for the Clinton administration's decision in the aftermath of the Hawai'i marriage case to support the adoption of the federal DOMA. The legislation provided that marriage would only be recognized in federal law as the union of one man and one woman, even if same-sex marriages were recognized in one or more of the states and, furthermore, it provided that states did not have to recognize same-sex marriages performed in other states.

The legislation was an attempt to stop same-sex marriage from "spread-ing" to other states, once it had been legalized in one state; however, although DOMA created an institutional hurdle to the legalization of same-sex marriage, legal commentators considered that it might be struck down as unconstitutional on a broad range of grounds. It was argued that the legislation created an invidious distinction between same-sex and opposite-sex married couples; that it constituted an unconstitutional inter-vention in state jurisdiction over marriage; that, like the infamous and unconstitutional Colorado Amendment 2, it was based solely on publicly expressed animus and hatred toward gays and lesbians; and, most impor-tantly, that it was unconstitutional under the "full faith and credit" clause of the U.S. constitution in which states must recognize the laws of other states (Eskridge 1999:1099–1100; see also Strasser 1997). Nonetheless, the signing of DOMA by President Clinton reinforced the centrist Democratic commitment to "family," work and responsibility and explicitly linked these themes at the same time that the administration was pursuing a welfare reform that was in part sold as a means to solidify putatively heterosexual families (Soss et al. 2003b).

Institutional opportunities at the federal level for same-sex marriage opponents were complemented by opportunities at the state level, which limited the effect of pro-marriage decisions in all three states while providing different policy solutions in each: weak provisions for domestic partner benefits in Hawai'i; the banning of same-sex marriage in Alaska through constitutional amendment, and the passage of civil union legislation in Vermont. In the case of Hawai'i, there was interplay between the legislature and the courts over the issue of marriage in which both arenas were the object of struggle by same-sex marriage opponents and supporters. After the 1993 and 1996 decisions, same-sex marriage opponents mobilized behind the idea of passing a state constitutional amendment to ensure that same-sex marriage would be banned, despite the decisions of the courts. The Hawai'i debate was a foreshadowing of later developments as legislators fought over how best to protect heterosexual marriage. In the 1996 ruling, the judge had stayed his decision to provide an opportunity for legislative or constitutional response. A proposed constitutional amendment was devised, which declared that the existing definition of marriage was constitutional; this proposed amendment sought to reassert the legislature's right to make the law of marriage (Coolidge 2000). However, at the same time, a reciprocal beneficiaries bill was introduced, which enabled interdependent partners to register as reciprocal beneficiaries, entitling them to some of the rights and protections of marriage (Hull 2006: 155). The purpose of this bill was to ensure that the legislature could continue to prohibit same-sex marriage or to uphold a ban on legal marriage for same-sex couples through providing access to benefits for same-sex couples, short of legal marriage.

A battle ensued between the House and the Senate over which version of the bill would prevail. In the Senate's strong version of the bill, substantial benefits would have been conferred on same-sex couples at the state level and, in addition, the proposed amendment stated that the burden would be on the state to show why these benefits should be restricted. However, the House opposed this strong version of the bill. The Senate then compromised with the House of Representatives and proposed an amendment that would reserve to the legislature the right to regulate the issuing of marriage licenses. There was also debate over the relationship of this amendment to the equal protection clause of the Hawai'i constitution because, if the amendment was placed within equal protection as an exception, this would have precluded equal protection for lesbians and gays under the Hawai'i constitution. In the end, the amendment was placed in the equal protection clause as a new section. The amendment passed the Hawai'i Congress in 1997, was placed on the ballot for 1998 and passed. It clearly stated that the opposite-sex definition of legal marriage in Hawai'i did not violate the Hawai'i Bill of Rights and that the power to regulate marriage was reserved to the legislature (Coolidge 2000).

In addition to the pressure exerted through the legislature and through a large-scale and well-financed campaign against same-sex marriage, opponents also took advantage of the state constitution to organize a constitutional convention on same-sex marriage. The ballot measure to hold the constitutional convention—which undoubtedly would have taken an even firmer line on same-sex marriage than the proposed amendment—failed while the proposed amendment reserving the right to define marriage to the legislature passed. Yet, the threat of the organization of a state constitutional convention on same-sex marriage clearly played a role in influencing the Hawai'i debate, adding a further lever in the hands of same-sex marriage opponents.

The Christian Right spent large sums of money in the Hawai'i battle and organized a number of front line organizations that diluted the impact of direct church involvement in the political debate. Kathleen Hull's account of the Hawai'i debate on the 1998 amendment makes it clear that the Roman Catholic Church and the Church of Latter Day Saints (Mormons) were the main supporters of Save Traditional Marriage '98. Groups such as the Alliance for Traditional Family and the Hawai'i Family Forum were associated with Focus on the Family while Hawai'i's Christian Coalition was also involved in the campaign. On the other side, the Human Rights Campaign as well as groups from the women's movement, the ACLU and Japanese American groups organized in favor of same-sex marriage recognition (Hull 2006: 156–157; see also Goldberg-Hiller 2002). It has been estimated that gay and lesbian groups spent about $1.4 million on the campaign against the constitutional amendment, while the religious right spent $2.2 million, with the Mormon Church adding $500,000 at the last minute (Kristen 1999: 112). The attendant media coverage of the same-sex marriage issue provided an important platform to the Christian Right to buy advertising and to engage in large-scale political mobilization.

In the wake of these developments, same-sex marriage supporters in the U.S. had to regroup as the reach of the courts in Hawai'i had been limited by the amendment. From the perspective of the lesbian and gay movement in the U.S., the religious right had financed the campaign to overturn the Hawai'i courts' decisions in favor of equal protection for lesbian and gay couples. This seemed to vitiate the purpose of judicial review and to allow the legislature and the political mobilization of citizens to enforce discrimination against a minority group, a group that was not only denied the symbolic affirmation of the recognition of their relationships through marriage but, in social policy terms, were deemed second-class citizens in terms of the benefits of legal coupledom.

While the reciprocal benefits bill initially provided some rights for same-sex couples, it was also deeply problematic. For one thing, the bill did not recognize the spousal relationship of same-sex couples. Instead, it also recognized the rights of any interdependent parties who wished to register as a couple for the purpose of accessing benefits. This characteristic of the legislation can be seen as a disadvantage for same-sex couples because it means that their relationships were not seen as fully equivalent to heterosexual marriage but, rather, were lumped with non-spousal relationships. A second problem with the provision for reciprocal benefits was that the bill was designed so that the benefits would erode over time. Same-sex marriage opponents wanted to use the reciprocal benefits legislation as part of a policy package with the constitutional amendment to forestall the full legal recognition of same-sex couples as might have resulted from the next then-pending round of the *Baehr* case. This was especially the case given that the 1993 and 1996 court rulings had been particularly clear and sweeping on the subject of equal protection. The *Baehr* court rulings had promised to have important implications for the litigation of same-sex marriage throughout the U.S. and the Hawai'i courts had clearly and unequivocally brought lesbians and gay men into the ambit of equal protection. Therefore, opponents of same-sex marriage were careful to design reciprocal benefits with a sunset clause in which some of the benefits had to be renewed through action of the legislature, therefore opening up the possibility for the benefits to be eroded within a limited time period. The legislation was passed in 1997 with health, pension, insurance and other benefits but, when the bill was renewed in 1999, these benefits were not included (Cahill et al. 2002).

Finally, after the passage of the 1998 constitutional amendment, the last stage of the *Baehr* case was a legal inevitability. Because the 1998 state constitutional amendment reserved to the legislature the right to define marriage as heterosexual, the Supreme Court of Hawai'i ruled that the case was moot in *Baehr v. Miike* in 1999. Similarly, in Alaska, the effects of the *Brause* decisions were immediately vitiated by the passage of a state constitutional amendment banning same-sex marriage in Alaska.

Vermont provided yet another battleground for lesbian and gay rights opponents on the same-sex marriage issue after the court's ruling in *Baker*. The ruling did not order the immediate remedy of same-sex marriage. Rather, the court indicated that it was up to the legislature to provide the benefits of marriage to same-sex couples. In this ruling, the court made specific reference to the case of Hawai'i, anticipating that a ruling in favor of same-sex marriage, if not stayed, would unleash a backlash that would result in a state constitutional amendment to ban same-sex marriage (*Baker*: II). In response to this, a number of possibilities were canvassed in the legislature running the gamut from a mini-DOMA for Vermont to the full extension of legal marriage (Andersen 2005: 186). However, in the end, the Vermont legislature decided to pass a civil union bill that provided some of the benefits of marriage without going all the way to full same-sex marriage. In this way, the Vermont legislature met the requirements set out by the *Baker* ruling because the civil union legislation provided that same-sex couples and opposite-sex couples were treated in the same way. Yet, because civil union was not recognized in federal law and because it was not necessarily recognized by other states, the rights of couples who are civilly joined in Vermont are far less than the rights of couples who are legally married in Vermont (Andersen 2005: 186).

Therefore, despite three rulings in favor of applicant couples at the state level over the course of the 1990s, same-sex marriage was forestalled through the mechanism of state constitutional amendment in two cases (Hawai'i and Alaska) and through the deference of the court to the legislature, in the case of Vermont. The effects of key rulings in state courts were limited through concerted political action of same-sex marriage opponents, using measures of direct democracy and exploiting the political opportunities provided by the separation of powers system.

RELATIONSHIP RECOGNITION IN CANADA: *ROSENBERG* AND *M v. H*

As the same-sex marriage cases were brought to American state courts over the course of the 1990s, a series of key decisions in Canadian courts expanded the definition of discrimination from the individual to the same-sex couple, setting the stage for the same-sex marriage cases of the early 2000s. As we have seen, the *Egan* and *Vriend* cases were critically important in establishing sexual orientation as analogous to the other named grounds of discrimination in section 15 (equality rights) of the Charter. *Egan* (1995) was the first case on same-sex relationship recognition to reach the Supreme Court of Canada and the first occasion on which the Court considered the issue of defining sexual orientation as an analogous ground of discrimination to the other grounds named in section 15. While the Court agreed that sexual orientation was analogous to the other grounds, the Court ruled against Egan and Nesbitt's claim to be treated like spouses under Old Age Security (one of two federal pension programs) on the grounds that the limitation on same-sex spousal claims was a reasonable limitation under section 1 of the Charter. This section—the balancing clause of the Charter—stated that Charter rights were subject to "such reasonable limits as may be prescribed by law in a free and democratic society." The ruling in *Egan* was a matter of grave concern to other stakeholders in section 15 of the Charter such as ethnocultural groups and the women's movement. That the Court was willing to casually deploy section 1, general limitation clause, to exclude same-sex couples from pension benefits suggested that section 1 might be used systematically by the Court to circumscribe the reach of section 15. While U.S. equal protection doctrine had evolved for the purpose of ensuring African American citizenship and had placed "race" at the high point of the classificatory system (as requiring strict scrutiny and as having suspect class status under equal protection), section 15 of the Canadian Charter was in flux in this early stage of litigation. As we have seen, the section was written in a way that named most of the grounds of discrimination in an open-ended way, but excluded sexual orientation. While the *Egan* case was positive for lesbian and gay rights claimants in placing sexual orientation on an equal footing with the other named grounds of discrimination in the clause, it also undermined the power of this protection by suggesting that it could be set aside by the Court on section 1 grounds ("reasonable limits"). Egale's executive director, lawyer John Fisher, was quick to build alliances with other section 15 stakeholders in pointing to the danger that this decision might pose for all (Fisher 2001; Go and Fisher 1998). In this way, at a key juncture, the different groups who were affected by section 15 worked together to ensure that section 1 would not be used to diminish the impact of section 15.

In *Rosenberg v. Canada* (1998), the Supreme Court of Canada sent different signals about the reading of section 15. This was brought by the Canadian Union of Public Employees (CUPE) on behalf of Nancy Rosenberg and Margaret Evans, lawyers working with the CUPE national office, who claimed pension benefits from CUPE as an employer. While CUPE was willing to recognize same-sex partner benefits, it was unable to permit Rosenberg to claim her partner under federal income tax legislation, which defined a spouse as a person of the opposite sex for the purposes of the tax rules governing company pension plans. CUPE could not allocate spousal pension rights to Rosenberg without jeopardizing the tax status of its own contributions and that of all other employees. Therefore, CUPE brought a Charter challenge against the federal government. At the first stage of the case, in 1995, a lower Court ruled that the precedent of *Egan* had to be applied to the case of Rosenberg and that, although the Court agreed that the exclusion of same-sex partners from pension legislation was a violation of the equality guarantees of the Charter, this exclusion was reasonable and justified under section 1 of the Charter as a limit that could be "reasonably justified in a free and democratic society" in the pursuit of a worthwhile objective (*Rosenberg v. Attorney General* 1995). This validated the fears of Egale and other groups that the *Egan* decision would be used as a precedent for using section 1 to trump the equality rights guaranteed in section 15.

The 1995 lower court decision was appealed to the Ontario Court of Appeal, which ruled in favor of CUPE (for Rosenberg and Evans) and against the federal government (*Rosenberg* 1998). The Court took on the Supreme Court's ruling in *Egan* and argued that, in other cases, the Supreme Court had defined section 1 of the Charter as requiring the government to defend the limitations on Charter rights in terms of specific government goals, goals that could only be reached by permitting the specified limitations. In this case, this would have meant that the government would have had to have explained how the exclusion of same-sex couples from pension legislation undermined the government's objectives in the pension legislation. Yet, in *Egan*, the Supreme Court had ruled that the goal of the pension legislation was to protect women and, therefore, that it was not required to include same-sex couples. In contrast, the Ontario Court of Appeal stated that, even if the objective of the pension legislation at issue was to protect the income of women in their senior years, the government was not required to limit section 15 equality rights by excluding same-sex couples from the legislation in order to achieve this policy objective. The Court of Appeal also cited the decision in *Vriend* (1998), which the Canadian Supreme Court had issued since *Egan*. Given the Supreme Court's strong statement about section 15 equality rights in *Vriend* and given that there was no valid objective to the pension legislation that would be undermined by including same-sex benefits, the Court of Appeal stated that the limitation on section 1 rights that was used in *Egan* was not justified and ruled in favor of CUPE (on behalf of Rosenberg and Evans).

Compared to the U.S., the government itself did not make a strong case against same-sex couples. In fact, the government's arguments in *Egan* and *Rosenberg* centered in part on the idea that the government wanted to reserve to itself the right to proceed incrementally, in recognizing benefits and obligations for same-sex couples, rather than arguing against benefits for same-sex couples. In neither case did the government take on the question of homosexuality or argue that the state had an interest in promoting heterosexuality or security for children and families. Hence, the government's presentation of the case differed very substantially from what we have seen in the U.S. Therefore, the evolution of lesbian and gay rights policies in Canada depended not only on the decisions of courts, but also on the broad political support for these rights and the reluctance of governments to challenge "Charter values," given their association with (English) Canadian nationalism. Moreover, as we shall see, gay rights opponents were shut out of the centralized and elite-driven dynamics of policy change in this area.

These factors can be seen at play in the single most important lesbian and gay rights case heard by the Supreme Court of Canada, the case that opened the way for same-sex marriage—*M v. H* (1999). This case concerned the right of spousal support upon the breakup of a same-sex relationship where the two partners were living together. M sued H for spousal support upon the breakup of their relationship, arguing that she had helped build H's business and that she was financially dependent on H. H. denied M's claim and argued that requirements of spousal support were not part of lesbian culture or same-sex relationships. The Supreme Court issued its decision in 1999. Not only did the majority of the Court rule in favor of M's right to spousal support, the Court's reasons, and even the dissents in the case, made it clear that the Court would not countenance any inequality in the treatment of same-sex relationships. Justice Lamer wrote on behalf of the majority that consideration of equality rights under section 15 of the Charter must take into account the extent to which public policy was discriminatory in imposing burdens or withholding benefits "in a manner that reflects the stereotypical application of presumed group or personal characteristics, or which otherwise has the effect of perpetuating or promoting the view that the individual is less capable or worthy of recognition or value as a human being or as a member of Canadian society, equally deserving of concern, respect, and consideration" (*M v. H*: I).

While this was different from the specific method by which the Hawai'i, Alaska and Vermont state courts reached their results (each drawing on their own state constitutions), this construction shares with those rulings the fundamental idea that lesbians and gays—and their relationships—are worthy of "concern, respect, and consideration." The majority in *M v. H* goes on to argue that in excluding same-sex couples from spousal benefits Ontario family law implies that such couples are "incapable of forming intimate relationships of economic interdependence as compared to opposite-sex couples" and that, therefore, "[s]uch exclusion perpetuates the disadvantages suffered by individuals in same-sex relationships and contributes to the erasure of their existence" (*M v. H*: I). Further, the Court did not offer any comment on the immutability debate. It stated simply that the evaluation of differential treatment entailed a "purposive and contextual" understanding of "the stereotypical application of presumed group or personal characteristics."

This was consistent with the developing jurisprudence on section 15 which, from the first case on sexual orientation—the 1995 *Egan* decision— had not substantially ventured into the question of immutability. While the Court had to consider how sexual orientation was analogous to other grounds, it only rarely mentioned the issue of the mutability or immutability of sexual orientation (e.g., briefly in *Egan* 1995). Once the analogous status of sexual orientation had been established in *Egan*, the Court did not revisit that question. Rather, the Court drew from early section 15 jurisprudence (*Andrews* 1989) in which the Court had been concerned with distinctions based on deeply felt personal characteristics, especially for groups that had suffered historic disadvantage. The Court also based its approach on its previous decision in *Law* (1999), namely, that the government must not violate human dignity through the imposition of burdens, stereotyping or disadvantage. Further, section 15 jurisprudence as epitomized by *Law* also stated that, in making comparisons between groups, the analysis should begin with the claimant's perspective and then it should be tested with reference to the judgment of "any reasonable person" in circumstances similar to the claimant, in light of the context. Context was defined to include elements such as pre-existing vulnerability of the group or the law's ameliorative purpose (*M v. H* I; see also *Law* 1999).

Another noteworthy difference from U.S. jurisprudence that can be seen in the *M v. H* case is that there is no Antonin Scalia on the Supreme Court of Canada. Rather than arguing in favor of the constitutional legitimacy of discrimination against lesbians and gays as did Scalia in *Romer* (and as he would later in *Lawrence* 2003), the dissent in this case made a case against same-sex relationship recognition by invoking equality of the sexes. Rather than arguing that the promotion of heterosexuality was a legitimate end and objective of the state's actions, Justice Gonthier, who dissented, suggested that it was legitimate for the state to distinguish same-sex from heterosexual couples on the grounds of the actual circumstances of same-sex couples without engaging in stereotyping. Gonthier rested the distinction between the two types of couples on what he termed "their specific, unique role." In his view, women were more likely to be economically dependent in heterosexual relationships due to the fact that they take on the predominant share of child care. The legislation mandating support obligations for separating couples was designed to provide for women in this circumstance. Gonthier was careful to state that what might be termed in American legal terms as "animus" against homosexuals was not at the root of his dissent. In fact, despite his dissent, he stated that homosexuals and their relationships were worthy of dignity and respect: "the state is not barred from recognizing that some relationships fulfill different social roles and have specific needs, and responding to this reality with positive measures to address those differences" (*M v. H:* I). Gonthier recognized that homosexuals suffered historical and structural disadvantage in Canadian society, as had women as a group; however, in his view, following H's presentation of her position as the partner from whom the spousal support was claimed, this disadvantage did not apply in the specific circumstances of spousal obligations for same-sex couples. While Gonthier's presentation of the "different social roles" of same-sex and opposite-sex couples might be viewed as discriminatory, the emphasis in his dissent was on the idea that "different social roles" should not entail a lack of recognition of social worth or a stigmatization of certain "social roles" as less than others.

The Court's decision striking down the opposite sex provisions of the family law statute of Canada's most populous province was by far the most important Canadian court decision on lesbian and gay rights and paved the way for the same-sex marriage cases. Given the Court's view of equality in this case, it was very difficult to see how the Court could have maintained the distinction between marriage for heterosexuals and some other conjugal status for same-sex relationships that would not have offended the bar of equality established in this decision. As the U.S. Supreme Court would do later on in *Lawrence* decision, with *M v. H.*, the Supreme Court of Canada opened the way for claims on same-sex marriage.

COUNTERMOBILIZATION IN CANADA

Just as opponents of lesbian and gay rights in the U.S. mobilized over this period in response to the same-sex marriage cases, so too in Canada, the Christian Right and other opponents of lesbian and gay rights were concerned about the rising political and legal success of "the homosexual agenda" (e.g., Morton 2000). As in the U.S., the evangelical political right in Canada fretted over the expansion of women's rights and access to abortion as well as the pending specter of "gay rights" throughout the decade. As we have seen in the previous chapter, the breakup of the governing Progressive Conservative Party and the establishment of the Western-based Reform Party in 1987 was in part motivated by concerns over social conservatism and the dominant social moderation of the governing Progressive Conservative Party during the Mulroney era, including its early commitment to the effective implementation of section 15 of the Charter (Harrison 1995). Conservative groups in Alberta and British Columbia were actively involved in opposing the *Vriend* decision as well as in running candidates for school boards, especially in British Columbia. The evangelical movement opposed the inclusion of queer-positive materials in the public school system in B.C. and this local level activism led to a battle between gay teachers and evangelicals in the B.C. school system (Smith 2004; McKenzie 2005). In addition, the evangelical movement in B.C. repeatedly targeted gay Member of Parliament (MP) Svend Robinson for defeat even before he became Canada's first openly gay MP on the grounds that he supported women's right to abortion. In addition, evangelical groups such as Focus on the Family Canada and the Evangelical Fellowship of Canada played an active role as interveners in court cases and in presenting evangelical and conservative views to government and to courts (Evangelical Fellowship of Canada 2000).

Over this period, public opinion on lesbian and gay rights in Canada changed substantially. Matthews' (2005) analysis of Canadian public opinion on same-sex marriage fits well with the analysis presented here. Canadians were divided on the extent to which they wished to recognize lesbian and gay rights, and opposition to such recognition has been quite substantial over time. Matthews argues that court decisions cued Canadian public opinion to extend a greater recognition and tolerance of lesbian and gay rights than might have been the case otherwise. However, it was not only the courts that cued public opinion. The evangelical movement, along with the motivated and mobilized opponents of lesbian and gay rights, were disadvantaged by the structure of Canadian political institutions, just as their U.S. counterparts were privileged by the structure of U.S. political institutions. In Canada, lesbian and gay rights opponents had much less opportunity to bring pressure to bear against the legal mobilization of the movement compared to the U.S. The dominance of the executive in Canada meant that legislatures lack the independent role that the legislature played in the debate in the Hawai'i, Alaska, and Vermont and that it would later play in Massachusetts and other states. The response to lesbian and gay rights recognition was in the hands of the political executive, dominated over this period by the Liberal Party at the federal level. While the Liberal government held hearings on various aspects of lesbian and gay rights recognition over the years and held several non-binding votes in the House of Commons in order to reassert the traditional definition of marriage, government lawyers in the Department of Justice had difficulty mounting a convincing jurisprudential case against the expansion and recognition of lesbian and gay rights, given the terms set by the equality rights clause of the Charter. In *Rosenberg* and *M v. H*, the federal government embraced statements about the key role of the heterosexual couple and family in relation to procreation and other key assertions used against lesbian and gay couples' recognition in the U.S. only reluctantly and mounted a half-hearted case that seemed to indicate that the government was bowing to what it saw as the inevitable outcome of the litigation, namely, the recognition of lesbian and gay rights (Smith 1998, 2002).

For lesbian and gay rights opponents, the options were very limited. Opponents could use their status as interveners to speak to the Court regarding the legal issues. Of course, the lesbian and gay rights movement mounted extensive organization on the other side to ensure that the views of the religious right were countered by the views of mainline liberal churches and denominations such as the United Church of Canada and Metropolitan Community Church of Toronto. The opponents mounted expert witnesses to testify in defense of the traditional family but the lesbian and gay movement also had full access to third party (*amici*) intervention before courts and brought a train of witnesses to bear to testify about lesbian and gay family relationships (*M v. H* 1999: I).[7] Opponents of lesbian and gay rights could pressure the federal government to circumvent the rulings of courts, as opponents were successful in doing in the U.S. However, unlike the U.S., opponents did not have the option of constitutional amendment at the sub-national or national levels, they did not have the option of citizen-initiated political action through initiative and referenda, and they were not able to pressure legislators as effectively as they could do in the U.S. because of the operation of party discipline, which substantially raised the costs of dissension for individual MPs. The only institutional mechanism for circumventing the decisions of courts on equality rights issues was the notwithstanding clause, which allows governments to override certain of the Charter's provisions, including the equality rights of section 15. However, this power had never been used by the federal government and only rarely by the provinces (Hiebert 2002, 2007). The optics of using the clause to set aside the court-sanctioned equality rights of lesbians and gay men was not something that the Liberal Party wanted to undertake and there was reason to doubt that even the right-wing parties would exercise the unpopular clause, given that this would open them up to accusations from the Liberals that they were undermining the Charter rights of Canadians. The best means for the countermovement to have stopped the recognition of lesbian and gay rights at this stage would have been for a majority government of the right to have deployed the notwithstanding clause against the courts' decision, sending the clear signal that the recognition of lesbian and gay rights by the courts had gone beyond what was defined as socially acceptable to the majority of Canadians. However, the conservative parties did not win a federal election during this period.

CONCLUSIONS

In a short burst of litigation beginning with *Baehr* and ending with *Baker* (1999) and *M v. H* (1999), the U.S. and Canada took important steps toward the recognition of same-sex relationships and, in doing so, pushed the discussion of lesbian and gay rights into new territory. In the U.S., the *Baehr* case upended the traditional wisdom in the lesbian and gay rights movement that same-sex marriage was an impossible goal, while the Canadian decision in *M v. H* indicated that Canada's highest court clearly embraced the idea that same-sex relationships should receive the same constitutional recognition as heterosexual conjugal relationships. In doing so, the *M v. H* decision put Canada on the path toward same-sex marriage because there was no remaining legal or constitutional reason to bar equality for same-sex couples, according to the Supreme Court's own jurisprudence. Indeed, as we will see in the next chapter, Canadian courts moved very quickly from the *M v. H* decision to the full recognition of same-sex marriage in the early 2000s.

In contrast, the fragmentation of the U.S. political system generated uneven policy outcomes across state and federal jurisdictions. While federal jurisdiction remained blocked for lesbian and gay rights advocates during this period, most potently and poignantly symbolized by Bill Clinton's signature on DOMA, state courts were policy innovators and sparked fresh debates on lesbian and gay rights recognition across the U.S. and beyond. The 1993 decision in the *Baehr* case was particularly important in breaking down judicial barriers to the legal recognition of same-sex marriage and inspired others across the U.S., Canada and internationally to believe in the possibility of same-sex marriage.

When we seek to understand how policy outcomes turned out differently in these two societies on this issue over this time period, it is impossible to argue that factors such as religiosity or public opinion explain the sequence of events. U.S. state courts were leaders in same-sex marriage jurisprudence and yet their decisions resulted in the passage of state constitutional amendments against same-sex marriage. These considerations demonstrate the importance of considering the wider institutional context in which judicial behavior occurs. U.S. courts face a different set of institutional relationships than Canadian courts, a context that can be defined in relation to the two major axes of institutional differences: differences in the operation of federalism and differences in the separation of powers vs. Westminster parliamentary system. The role of judicial federalism in the U.S. system and the fact that the states have jurisdiction over same-sex marriage meant that plaintiffs could use the provisions of state constitutions to strengthen their legal claims. Several of the states in which the initial cases occurred had amended their constitutions to include the ERA or to explicitly provide for the right to privacy. However, the impact of progressive judges in states like Hawai'i, Alaska, and Vermont was mitigated by the role of the legislature in balancing the decisions of courts in determining policy outcomes. In Canada, the decisions of courts were not vulnerable to limitation or circumvention by the governments and legislatures.

6 Policy Divergence and Policy Diffusion: Same-Sex Marriage in the 2000s

The early 2000s was a period of profound policy divergence between the U.S. and Canada, especially because of the court decisions in Canada that led to the legalization of same-sex marriage in 2005, contrasted with the diffusion of DOMAs and constitutional marriage bans throughout the U.S. as states moved to change their marriage laws to forestall the development of same-sex marriage. This backlash accelerated when the Massachusetts Supreme Judicial Court, the highest state court in Massachusetts, ruled in favor of same-sex marriage in the *Goodridge* decision, which led to the legalization of same-sex marriage in Massachusetts in 2004. At the same time, the U.S. also saw the development of a marriage movement—outbursts of civil disobedience in New Paltz (New York), Portland, San Francisco, and Sandoval, New Mexico—in which straight political leaders at the local level permitted, licensed or officiated at the marriages of same-sex couples. This marriage movement was evidenced by spontaneous demonstrations by same-sex couples and their supporters in New York City and other locations across the U.S. and small-scale acts of civil disobedience in claiming legality for same-sex marriages, especially through ceremonies performed by clergy from Unitarian, liberal Protestant and reform Jewish faiths (see Pinello 2006). While the assertion and claiming of legality for same-sex relationships (especially through the use of religious ceremonies) also occurred in Canada, the decisions of the courts and the lack of challenge from the federal government to these decisions, led to a relatively quick passage of same-sex marriage legislation. As this chapter will show, these cross-national differences in public policy were facilitated by political institutional differences and shaped by the policy legacies of past experiences with lesbian and gay human rights issues.

These events occurred during an intensely conservative period of U.S. politics, one that contrasts with the middling and centrist liberalism of Canada's dominant Liberal Party on social issues. The historical timing of the lesbian and gay movement relative to the partisan politics of the post-1960s epoch privileged the movement in Canada and penalized the movement in the U.S. This is exemplified in the presidency of George W. Bush, which epitomized the hard right politics of the backlash against the Great

Society, the civil rights movement, and the women's movement. For these conservative party leaders, opposition to lesbian and gay rights was one of the symbolic markers of the political project. Bush continued the Clinton-era policies of using social policies such as welfare to promote the nuclear family based on the foundation of legal heterosexual marriage, denying the right of legal marriage to same-sex couples, and encouraging gays and lesbians in the military to live their lives in the closet without "telling." When he was governor of Texas, Bush opposed the repeal of Texas's anti-sodomy laws, opposed adding sexual orientation to hate crime laws in Texas, opposed allowing lesbians and gays to become adoptive partners and opposed any measures which would prohibit discrimination based on sexual orientation as "special rights." Upon becoming President, he imple-mented an AIDS funding policy in the U.S. and abroad that focuses on sex education through abstinence (Ota 2001). While evangelical Christians might have been disappointed in Bush's failure to roll back abortion rights as well as his lack of action on other conservative issues, Bush's policies clearly signaled that lesbians and gays would remain outsiders. Moreover, until the 2006 midterm elections, the Democrats were politically weak and did not mount a systematic opposition to the Bush Administration.

In contrast to this situation, during the early 2000s, Canada was gov-erned by the centrist Liberal Party, the party that had authored the Charter as a means of solidifying Canadian nationalism in the wake of the sover-eignist threat from Quebec. In the course of crafting, authoring and sup-porting the passage of the Charter in the constitutional crisis of 1980–1981, the Liberals had increasingly defined Canadian values as Charter values and identified the defense of Charter rights with the Liberal Party. While in the U.S., the Democrats were weak and divided, during most of this period, in Canada, it was the conservatives who were weak and divided. While Republicans in the U.S. made opposition to lesbian and gay rights one of their hallmark policies, in Canada, the Liberals eventually made support for the Charter (and, *inter alia*, tolerance of "gay rights") one of their hallmark policies. Just as Democrats hesitated to challenge the Republican discursive and political hegemony, so too conservatives in Canada were hesitant to openly challenge the Liberals on lesbian and gay rights policies.

This chapter surveys this key period, beginning with an account of the *Lawrence* case, in which, at long last, the U.S. Supreme Court struck down sodomy laws as unconstitutional. Then the chapter discusses the pivotal *Goodridge* ruling, which resulted in same-sex marriage in Massa-chusetts. After discussing American developments, the chapter describes the three main Canadian same-sex marriage cases of this period and the developments that led to the passage of same-sex civil marriage legisla-tion in June 2005. I also consider the question of policy diffusion among the states in the U.S., considering how the recognition of same-sex rela-tionships is incrementally disseminated. The period from 1999 to 2004 saw dramatic developments in the U.S., which, after thirty years, finally moved past the question of the criminality of sodomy with the Supreme Court's decision in *Lawrence*. During the same period, Canadian policy-makers were responding to the *M v. H* decision with a raft of legislative changes that brought co-habiting same-sex partners into virtual equality with co-habiting heterosexual couples.

THE U.S. SUPREME COURT'S DECISION IN *LAWRENCE*

The *Lawrence* case, decided by the U.S. Supreme Court in 2003, con-cerned the constitutionality of a provision of the Texas penal code that outlawed homosexual sodomy. At the time of the *Lawrence* ruling in 2003, four states retained sodomy laws that applied solely to same-sex couples while nine states had laws on the books that applied to both same-sex and opposite-sex couples (Lambda Legal 2003). After the *Bowers* decision, struggles had taken place in a number of states to overturn sodomy laws. Courts in states such as Tennessee and Kentucky struck down state sod-omy laws in the 1990s, rejecting the logic of *Bowers*. Generally, attempts to change the sodomy laws through the legislature alone without litigation were not successful (Pierceson 2005: 62–98). In 2003, a second sodomy case reached the U.S. Supreme Court. This case, brought on behalf of John Geddes Lawrence and Tyron Garner, explicitly invited the Court to rule on whether their criminal convictions under the Texas penal code violated the Fourteenth Amendment, particularly given that the Texas law criminalized sodomy for same-sex couples but not for opposite-sex couples. In addition, the petitioners asked the Court to rule on whether the criminalization of sodomy violated their rights to liberty and privacy under due process and invited the Court to rule on the validity of *Bowers* (Harlow 2002).

As set out by lawyers from Lambda Legal, the plaintiffs' case empha-sized that the Texas Penal Code contained a specific section on "homo-sexual conduct" and that this section prohibited sexual behavior in private that was not prohibited for opposite-sex couples. Lambda emphasized that these laws were different from the general prohibition on sodomy that had concerned the Court in *Bowers*. Laws such as the one in Texas had been specifically adopted to penalize homosexual behavior, even as general pro-hibitions on sexual behavior for opposite-sex couples had been lifted. Law-rence and Garner argued that the Texas Penal Code discriminated based on sexual orientation and, specifically, claimed that such discrimination could not be justified because it violated the Fourteenth Amendment's equal pro-tection provision (Harlow 2002: 3–7). Further, by criminalizing private behavior in the home, the Texas Penal Code "sends a powerful signal from the State condemning homosexuals" (Harlow 2002: 8) and thus justified discrimination against gays and lesbians. Lawrence and Garner argued that this was a "glaring affront to the Constitution's guarantee of equal protection" (Harlow 2002: 9) and that there was a clear conflict between the decision of the Court in *Bowers* and the decision of the Court in *Romer v. Evans*. As *Romer* made clear, animus toward a group could not justify discriminatory classification. On behalf of the plaintiffs, the brief argued that "[t]he State's inability to put forth even a rational and legitimate basis is fatal under any level of scrutiny" (Harlow 2002: 21). In other words, the plaintiffs argued that, even if the Court did not recognize policy differences based on sexual orientation as requiring strict scrutiny and even if the Court did not recognize lesbians and gay men as a suspect class under the Fourteenth Amendment, at the very least, the Court should recognize that the sodomy statute requires a "rational basis," the weakest of the three levels of scrutiny of state action.

Moreover, Lawrence and Garner made clear that their equal protection claim was separate from their right to privacy claim (Harlow 2002: 9–10). This was an important distinction because the Court could have responded by stating that the Texas law was unconstitutional in distinguishing same-sex from opposite-sex sexual activity when, in fact, the plaintiffs wanted to argue that any form of criminal regulation of sodomy in private between consenting adults—even if applied equally to same-sex and opposite-sex couples—would stigmatize homosexuals (especially because experience had shown that same-sex couples were much more likely to be prosecuted under such laws than opposite-sex couples). With regard to privacy claims, Lawrence and Garner argued that it was an American tradition to respect privacy and intimacy in the home, that three-quarters of states had already done away with their sodomy laws, and that "both law and society now widely recognize the connection between same-sex intimacy and committed relationships, families with children, and households fundamentally like those inhabited by heterosexuals" (Harlow 2002: 10). The plaintiffs discussed the ways in which the criminalization of same-sex sexual activity reinforced and perpetuated other forms of discrimination against lesbians and gay men in such areas as child custody and access as well as the passage of measures outlawing discrimination based on sexual orientation (Harlow 2002: 14–16). Further, they argued that *Bowers* had not been taken to heart in the U.S. as other key decisions of the Court had been, that the *Bowers* decision was out of step with the trend toward protection and recognition of the importance of privacy in sexual and intimate matters, and that lesbian and gay couples, parents and families were increasingly accepted in all walks of American life (Harlow 2002: 22–30; in general, see also Harlow 2003).

In reply, the District Attorney for Harris County, Texas, on behalf of the state of Texas (as respondent) baldly stated that the sodomy provision in the Texas Penal Code did not violate the Fourteenth Amendment of the federal constitution or the equal rights provisions of the Texas constitution, which guarantee the equal protection of the law on grounds including sex. Texas argued that the prohibition on homosexual sodomy "does not implicate fundamental rights or a suspect class, and it has a rational basis in the

Legislature's determination that homosexual sodomy is immoral" (Rosenthal et al. 2001: 3). In the respondent's view, there could be no fundamental right (under the concepts of the right to privacy or the right to intimate association) to engage in homosexual sodomy since this activity had long been criminalized, a view that had been upheld by the Court in *Bowers* and that could not be held to have changed in the few years since *Bowers* was decided (Rosenthal et al. 2001: 4–5). Further, Texas argued that the fact that other state courts had struck down their sodomy laws on the grounds of equal protection had no bearing on federal equal protection analysis and that those cases had been decided based on state constitutional provisions and not on federal constitutional provisions. Texas held that the criminal law was not aimed at homosexuals but at homosexual conduct that might be engaged in by homosexuals, bisexuals or heterosexuals (e.g., in prison) and that, moreover, even if it was assumed that the statute represented "a legislative classification involving sexual orientation, the use of the deferential 'rational basis' standard of review would still be appropriate, since it is well established that individuals of homosexual orientation do not constitute a suspect class for the purpose of equal protection analysis" (Rosenthal et al. 2001: 12–13; see similar arguments in Rosenthal et al. 2003).

The Supreme Court's ruling in *Lawrence* was its most important lesbian and gay rights decision; in it, the Court overturned *Bowers*. The majority ruled that the case should be decided on the basis of the due process rights of Lawrence and Garner, ruling that *Bowers* had erred in a number of specific ways, most notably, by defining the question in terms of the fundamental right to engage in sodomy. In contrast, the Court in *Lawrence* stated that the question was not one of sexual behavior, but of the right to engage in intimate relationships (*Lawrence*: 3). The Court cited the line of cases beginning with *Griswold* on contraception and continuing through *Roe* on abortion rights in relation to the right to privacy in intimate relationships and in decisions related to sexuality and childbearing. The Court also disagreed with the *Bowers* characterization of sodomy as a practice that had long been condemned in law and society, using briefs filed by historians and other expert witnesses to argue that sodomy was not specifically criminalized between men but, rather was criminalized in general, and that sodomy laws were most often applied and enforced in cases of rape or child abuse (*Lawrence*: 6–9). For these reasons, according to the majority ruling, the *Bowers* ruling was wrong to interpret these laws as specifically aimed at same-sex behavior any more than they were aimed at non-procreative sex in general. Sodomy laws in the U.S. were most often enforced against men having sex in public and it was not until the 1970s that sodomy laws were passed that specifically targeted same-sex behavior and, even then, only nine states passed such laws (*Lawrence*: 9–10). The Court acknowledged that same-sex behavior was broadly condemned throughout history and that there might be many in the U.S. who might still want to condemn it. However, the Court cited the *Casey* (1992) ruling in which the majority had stated that "Our obligation is to define the liberty of all, not to mandate our own moral code" (cited in *Lawrence*: 10). Furthermore, the Court argued that, even at the time of *Bowers*, views on homosexuality were changing. Even at that time, sodomy laws were rarely enforced, even in Georgia where Bowers was arrested. Moreover, the American Law Institute's model penal code had recommended removing these laws in 1955, Britain's Wolfenden Report had recommended the same in 1957 (changes that were implemented in Britain in 1967) and the European Court of Justice had struck down Northern Ireland's sodomy laws in 1981 under the European Convention on Human Rights. Justice Kennedy, writing for the majority, went on to cite even more precedents established beyond the U.S. in the "values we share with a larger civilization" and pointed to decisions in U.K. and European courts and courts of other countries regarding the issue (*Lawrence*: 16). As for the acceptance of *Bowers* in the U.S., although there had been twenty-five states with anti-sodomy laws in 1986 when *Bowers* was decided, there were only thirteen remaining at the time of the *Lawrence* decision, of which only four specifically prohibited same-sex activity and, even then, without enforcing this prohibition in private behavior (*Lawrence*: 12–13). *Bowers* had been roundly condemned by legal and political opinion in the U.S. and five lower courts had simply refused to follow it. In addition, the majority ruling pointed out that other cases decided since *Bowers* such as *Casey* and *Romer* pointed to the need to overturn it, *Casey* on grounds of the right to privacy and intimate association and *Romer* on grounds of animus directed against homosexuals.

Importantly, the majority declined to decide *Lawrence* on the basis of equal protection as that would have left the door open for laws that condemned sexual behavior in private by both opposite-sex and same-sex couples. That is, the equal protection claim would have struck down legal distinctions between opposite-sex and same-sex couples but it would not have protected the liberty and privacy interests of individuals under due process. The Court argued that striking down sodomy laws as unconstitutional under due process would assist the equal protection claims of homosexuals since "[i]f protected conduct is made criminal and the law which does so remains unexamined for its substantive validity, its stigma might remain even if it were not enforceable as drawn for equal protection reasons. When homosexual conduct is made criminal by the law of the State, that declaration in and of itself is an invitation to subject homosexual persons to discrimination both in the public and in the private spheres" (*Lawrence*: 14; see also 16–17).

In contrast, Antonin Scalia's dissent, supported by Justices Rehnquist and Thomas, linked *Bowers* with *Roe* and asked why, if *Bowers* could be overturned, *Roe* could not be overturned as well. The dissent argued that there was a long line of jurisprudence regulating sexual behavior in the name of public morality and that this jurisprudence should not be set aside. Scalia called the overturning of *Bowers*, "a massive disruption of the current social order" (Scalia in *Lawrence*: 7), while the overturning of *Roe* would only return the situation to what it was prior to 1973. Throughout the dissent, Scalia compared every step in the reasoning of the majority to the reasoning of the Court in *Roe* and in subsequent cases on abortion rights. Scalia rejected the idea that there was an "emerging awareness" in favor of sexual freedom and condemned the majority's reliance on decisions made in "foreign" courts as irrelevant to the definition of fundamental rights and historical traditions in the U.S., although he did invoke his own international examples in pointing out that sodomy is illegal in many countries (Scalia in *Lawrence*: 13–14).

Further, Scalia framed lesbian and gay rights issues as a "culture war" rather than a question of fundamental social, political and economic equality. He claimed that there would be no way for the Court to rule against same-sex marriage once it had asserted that the morality of the majority could not be used to infringe the liberty interests of the minority. Scalia argued that many Americans in what he terms "the mainstream" wanted to have the right to discriminate against homosexuals and, in fact, as he pointed out, discriminating against homosexuals was perfectly legal in many states and in federal jurisdiction. Scalia pointed out that legislatures, including Congress, had declined to protect lesbians and gays from discrimination and had even mandated discrimination (e.g., gays in the military). Therefore, Scalia argued, the Court was out of step with mainstream opinion and the Court should leave it to the states, the legislatures, and the people to decide where to draw the line with regard to homosexuality. In fact, he suggested the line might well be drawn at the point at which sodomy was not criminalized and in which same-sex marriage was prohibited. Nonetheless, he argued that this line should be drawn by legislatures through the political process and not by judges. Citing *Halpern*, he pointed out that, once public morality was no longer a rational basis for the state's action, there would be no basis on which to deny a constitutional claim for same-sex marriage: "[t]oday's opinion dismantles the structure of constitutional law that has permitted a distinction to be made between heterosexual and homosexual unions, insofar as formal recognition in marriage is concerned" (Scalia in *Lawrence*: 20–21).

As Laurence Tribe commented, Scalia's dissent "made the majority's point" (2004: 1907) by stating that the criminalization of sodomy stigmatized lesbians and gay men and justified discrimination (see also Feigan 2004). Tribe, who was lead counsel for the plaintiffs in *Bowers*, argued that the essence of *Lawrence* was that the Court refused to reduce relationships to sex acts and that the Court identified the ideas of stigmatization and respect for lesbians and gays as central to its decision in *Lawrence*. In other words, the Court singled out the idea of the oppression and stigma created for lesbians and gays by the sodomy prohibition (Tribe 2004: 1948). Mark Strasser interpreted *Lawrence* in a similar way, stating that it would lead to same-sex marriage (Strasser 2004; in support of this view, see Hassel

2004; Peterson 2004; for another interpretation, see Eskridge 2004). Others argue that the Court did not retreat from the question of morality as posed by Scalia because it had shied away from the question of ruling on the status of gays and lesbians under equal protection (McGowan, 2004; see also Mohr 2005; Richards 2005; Stein 2004).

By striking down the Texas sodomy provisions as unconstitutional, the Court brought the U.S. in line with other developed democracies such as Canada, the U.K. and, indeed, other European countries. An issue that had been resolved in the 1960s in Canada was finally resolved many years later in the U.S., removing a huge burden of energy, money and effort from the U.S. lesbian and gay movement, which had fought these laws state-by-state for thirty-five years. The decision symbolically removed the stigma of criminalization from homosexual behavior, and forestalled the further deployment of criminal law against other lesbian and gay rights claims, most notably anti-discrimination laws and in civil suits. At the same time, the case of sodomy laws demonstrates the limits of arguments based on the effects of policy change in one period and policy change in a subsequent time period. The existence of sodomy laws had a chilling effect on the litigation of other lesbian and gay rights issues. At the same time, however, social movements also mobilize against policy legacies; the existence of policy obstacles such as the sodomy laws galvanizes social movements to seek their eradication. Whether policy legacies will spark feedback effects that reinforce existing pathways or whether they will spark countermovements that cycle against existing policies, the fact of the existence of sodomy laws over this thirty-five year period constituted a major policy divergence between Canada and the U.S., one that hampered the efforts of the U.S. movement in other critically important arenas of public policy, especially the two other major areas discussed in this book: anti-discrimination law and same-sex relationship recognition.

Further, the state-by-state fight to change sodomy laws in the U.S. required coordinated organization in the lesbian and gay movement as well as the ability to mount campaigns locally. While the litigation effort was organized at the national level through organizations such as Lambda Legal and through legal networks, there were also grassroots campaigns at the local level to reform sodomy laws in the states. In Canada, there were campaigns to change human rights legislation in the provinces during the 1970s; however, with the advent of the Charter, battles over lesbian and gay rights in these policy areas were centralized because of the paramountcy of the Charter over other laws and because of the relatively unified nature of the Canadian court system compared to the U.S. system of judicial federalism. While the supremacy clause of the U.S. constitution and the application of the U.S. Bill of Rights subordinate state constitutions and state laws to federal authority, judicial federalism in the U.S. combined with state jurisdiction over many key policy areas such as criminal law and marriage gave state courts a more important role in the evolution of lesbian and gay litigation. The close comparison of the U.S. and Canada shows the complex effects of the fragmented and decentralized U.S. political system and, in particular, how policy change in the U.S. is often slow moving, compared to the rapidity of policy change in the Canadian case.

CANADIAN LEGAL CHANGE AFTER *M v. H*

As discussed in Chapter 5, *M v. H* was a critically important lesbian and gay rights case in Canadian jurisprudence. While *Egan* held that sexual orientation constituted a prohibited ground of discrimination under the equality rights section of the Charter, *M v. H* was important in delineating the legal view that same-sex couples were no different from opposite-sex couples in terms of rights under the common law for partners that lived together. The strong wording used in *M v. H* and the clear enunciation of the idea that same-sex relationships should not be stigmatized or treated as if they were less worthy of dignity and respect than opposite-sex couples led to the inexorable conclusion that, as Scalia would argue in *Lawrence*, there would no principled constitutional grounds on which to distinguish same-sex and opposite-sex couples with regard to marriage. More immediately, the Supreme Court's strong message and the clear victory for M in her fight to obtain spousal support from H led to a raft of legislative changes across Canada, to bring provincial and federal laws into conformity with the decision. In most provinces, it was not necessary for lesbian and gay couples to litigate to obtain equality in the treatment of same-sex relationships from provincial and federal governments. With a Supreme Court ruling on the table, lower courts would have been obligated to follow the Supreme Court's direction and, in most jurisdictions, legislation was passed to forestall further litigation from same-sex couples. In Ontario, the right-wing government of Mike Harris had been given six months by the Court to amend the province's family law statute in light of the *M v. H* ruling and, in response, passed a bill whose title clearly indicated the provincial government's view of the Supreme Court's having struck down the province's family law: An Act to Amend Certain Statutes Because of the Supreme Court of Canada Decision in *M. v. H*.[1] British Columbia had already undertaken an extensive revision of provincial legislation under the NDP governments of the 1990s, including adoption, relationship recognition, health care consent, and pensions. Following *M v. H*, B.C. removed the last vestiges of inequality in the treatment of same-sex couples in provincial jurisdiction.

Other provinces also acted to ensure that, in matters ranging from the provision of drivers' licenses to provincial pension plans, same-sex couples were treated in the same way as opposite-sex couples. Some provinces such as Nova Scotia and Quebec enacted civil union legislation while, in contrast, Alberta made it clear by amending its law regulating marriage in the province that it would only recognize a marriage between partners of the opposite sex and, in doing so, it invoked the notwithstanding clause of the Canadian Charter, as well as Alberta's human rights legislation (Alberta 2000).[2] Alberta's amendment to its marriage statute was viewed as unconstitutional at the time it was passed, because of the lack of provincial jurisdiction over the determination of the capacity to marry, although the law was never challenged in court (Casswell 2001). The Klein government continued to state that it would oppose same-sex marriage and that it would implement a scheme of civil partnerships in order to recognize the legal reality of *M v. H*. In fact, the Klein government did pass the Adult Interdependent Act (2002),[3] which recognized relationships of emotional and financial attachment between two adults living together outside of a legal civil marriage. As of 2002, this excluded same-sex couples. Unlike domestic partner or civil union provisions in other jurisdictions such as Vermont, which recognized the spousal nature of same-sex relationships, the Alberta legislation deliberately broadened the application of the Act to any two people living together and specified that a conjugal relationship was only one of the grounds that might provide the definition of such a relationship. Notably, the Alberta Act forced the recognition of such relationships after three years of cohabitation for those who met the standard set by the Act. This was yet another attempt to circumvent same-sex marriage on the part of the Klein government, and the heterosexual nature of marriage was explicitly affirmed in its preamble (Bailey 2004a). However, the notwithstanding clause expires after five years and, therefore, the use of the clause in the Marriage Act 2000 expired in 2005. By that time, the Klein government accepted the redefinition of marriage by the federal government, recognizing that there was little point in continuing to fight a continued legal battle against the jurisdiction of the federal government (Larocque 2006: 110–115). Alberta's restrictive approach can be contrasted with the civil union legislation in Quebec, which was passed along with extensive recognition of same-sex parenting rights in 2002 (Nicol 2005). This change built upon Quebec's previous amendments of 1999, which had extended recognition to same-sex couples in some areas of provincial law. The 2002 changes were more extensive and provided for legal protection for same-sex couples and the option of civil union for both same-sex and opposite-sex partners (Bailey 2004a).

Early in 2000, the federal government passed the Modernization of Benefits and Obligations Act (MBOA),[4] which comprehensively amended many federal laws and regulations to bring them into conformity with *M v. H*. In stark contrast to the 1996 federal DOMA in the U.S., this change explicitly recognized the rights and obligations of same-sex couples in all areas of federal law and policy, short of full legal marriage. Once the bill was passed, there were very few areas in which same-sex couples were not treated in the same way as opposite-sex legally married couples. Aside from the symbolic use of the term "marriage," these remaining areas of inequality concerned immigration, where opposite-sex married couples enjoyed stronger protections in terms of their right to immigrate to Canada and to sponsor their spouse for immigration, entry and citizenship as well as the right of immunity from testifying against a spouse in criminal law. In addition, of course, same-sex couples did not benefit from the recognition of their relationship in other legal jurisdictions (M. Bailey 2004a; see also Smith 2002). Nonetheless, it is important to note that the federal government would have faced a long course of litigation if it had chosen to maintain the exclusion of same-sex couples from these rights and obligations, given the *M v. H* decision. At the same time, the federal government ensured that the preface to the Modernization of Benefits and Obligations Act (MBOA) clearly ruled out same-sex marriage. This "interpretation clause" or preamble of the MBOA states that "[f]or greater certainty, the amendments made by this Act do not affect the meaning of the word 'marriage', that is, the lawful union of one man and one woman to the exclusion of all others" (Canada, MBOA, 2000, section 1.1). Therefore, governments passed the hot potato of the gay rights issue to courts and allowed the courts to tread where they feared to go (Smith 2002). The federal government wanted to make clear that it would draw the line on same-sex marriage and, hence, inserted Canada's very own DOMA into the preface of the Act. This symbolic statement in protection of opposite-sex marriage had been made each time the Liberals had extended recognition to lesbians and gays. Just a few years earlier, when the Liberals formally amended the Canadian Human Rights Act to include sexual orientation protection (which had already been recognized by the courts), they were careful to make a similar DOMA-type statement regarding the sanctity of heterosexual marriage (Smith 1998; for an overview of developments in each jurisdiction, see Hurley 2005).

The impact of *M v. H* then, was substantial in terms of bringing about policy change. The Supreme Court had clear jurisdiction to strike down provincial legislation as unconstitutional under the federal Charter which, as we have seen, applies to provincial and federal governments alike. As in *Vriend*, the centralizing effect of the Charter was clear in this decision. Recalcitrant provinces, such as Alberta, were not able to circumvent the *M v. H* decision without using the notwithstanding clause. Furthermore, Alberta and other provinces were only able to use the notwithstanding clause on the issues that fell under their own jurisdiction. While family law and spousal support in common law relationships fell under provincial jurisdiction, the area of defining the capacity to marry did not. Hence, Alberta and other provinces would not be able to use the notwithstanding clause to stop same-sex marriage. Further, the *M v. H* decision did not run into problems of implementation. On the contrary, most provinces, like the federal government itself, preferred to have the Court blaze the trail in this area because neither the federal Liberal government nor the provincial governments themselves wanted to take a clear position against gay rights or step out ahead of public opinion by embracing positions on gay rights that might be repudiated by the public.

The reaction of governments in Canada to the *M v. H* decision was very different from the reaction of legislatures in the U.S. to the same-sex marriage litigation, and these reactions are influenced by the structural-institutional factors which are emphasized in this analysis. First, with respect to policy legacies, it is difficult to see how the Supreme Court in *M v. H* could have reached the conclusions it reached if it had still been debating the criminality of sodomy. Throughout the judges' discussions in the judgment of *M v. H*, there is nothing akin to the comments of the dissent in *Lawrence* regarding the constitutional legitimacy of discriminating in the criminal regulation of homosexual sexual conduct, let alone the legitimacy of discrimination with regard to the broad range of other issues that are mentioned by Scalia in *Lawrence*. The contrast in the jurisprudential discussion of the constitutionality of discrimination is very different in the decisions of *M v. H* in 1999 and the decision in *Lawrence* in 2003. In the *Lawrence* case, the U.S. Supreme Court is dealing with evidence and legal debates from the 1950s and 1960s on the purpose and application of sodomy laws while this issue had long been removed from the policy and legal agenda in Canada. Discrimination against lesbians and gays is constitutionally thinkable and permissible for Scalia and his constituency. Treating same-sex relationships as less valuable than opposite-sex relationships was not something that even the dissenting judge on the Supreme Court of Canada wanted to condemn as his dissent was framed on wholly other grounds.

Second, jurisdictional differences in the operation of federalism between the two countries and across different issues provide different institutional levers for supporters and opponents of same-sex relationship recognition. In Canada, the recognition of unmarried partners falls under provincial jurisdiction along with other areas of family law, although it is governed by the federal Charter, yet the determination of the capacity to marry is in federal jurisdiction. The fact that family law falls under provincial jurisdiction gave Alberta the opportunity to use the notwithstanding clause to regulate relationships of adult interdependency, while the fact that the capacity to marry was assigned to federal jurisdiction, meant that only the federal government could circumvent the court rulings by this means. In contrast, in the U.S., family law, civil marriage and criminal law are issues that belong to the states. Thus, policy change is more challenging in the U.S., in the absence of clear direction from the Supreme Court that would bind the states on a point of federal law or under the provisions of the Bill of Rights, as in *Lawrence* with respect to the constitutionality of criminalizing sodomy.

Third, in addition to federalism, the difference in the separation of powers is also important in shaping political debates over these issues as is the relationship between courts and legislatures. These two institutional features are closely connected. The fusion of legislative and executive authority in the parliamentary system, especially strong in situations of majority government, acts to stifle debate among legislators in contrast to the U.S. system where the separation of powers and concomitant lack of party discipline opens up legislators to lobbying from interest groups and to the multiplication of points of views, logrolling, legislative compromises and coalition building. Much of this is obviated in the Canadian system by party discipline; although internal dissent in the party caucus occurs, MPs are not subjected to the barrage of lobbying and the requirements of coalition-building that precede the passage of legislation in the U.S. system. Rather, the majority government puts forth the legislation it wants and is able to pass it, mustering the support of its disciplined party supporters in the legislature. This also concentrates blame and the responsibility on the political executive in Canada and encourages the executive to pass the responsibility for contentious political issues to the courts (Pal and Weaver 2003). Furthermore, in the Canadian system, the legislature is not accustomed to replying to the courts in an adversarial way. The ethos of the Charter permeates Canadian political institutions, including the legislatures (see Hiebert 2002; J. Kelly 2005); however, this rights consciousness and debates about the application and implementation of rights are not constructed in an adversarial context simply because Canadian legislatures have only one institutional weapon with which to counter a court decision—the notwithstanding clause. In contrast, legislatures in the U.S. can, among other things, propose to amend the constitution—including a state constitution—which opens up yet another option and lever for opponents of court decisions and for their mobilized supporters. While the notwithstanding clause became defined as an illegitimate institutional lever very soon after the passage of the Charter in 1982, the state constitutional amendment and its concomitant measures of popular democracy such as the ballot initiative are longstanding features of the American system and are legitimate and commonly used levers for the legislatures to circumvent court decisions in the states (Tarr 1998). Therefore, legislatures in Canada did not have the means of reply to *M v. H*, even if they had the political will to oppose lesbian and gay rights. From the full recognition of same-sex spousal rights in common law relationships, it would be a short step to same-sex marriage.

SAME-SEX MARRIAGE CASES IN CANADA AND THE U.S., 2000–2003

In the U.S., same-sex marriage cases occurred concurrently with the challenge to the constitutionality of sodomy laws. Many of the cases drew on state law and state constitutions and avoided making claims under federal equal protection in part because of the *Bowers* precedent. Even after *Lawrence*, there was no clear direction from the Supreme Court on equal protection even if, as Scalia and some legal commentators argued, the Court had opened the door to same-sex marriage through the *Lawrence* decision. At the same time, the decision in *M v. H* opened the floodgates of same-sex litigation in Canada and there was little doubt about where this litigation would end up, assuming that lowers courts and, eventually, the Supreme Court of Canada itself, held true to the precedent of *M v. H*.

U.S. Developments

At the same time as *Lawrence* was decided in 2003, the historic *Goodridge* ruling in Massachusetts brought the issue of same-sex marriage to the fore in the U.S. as never before. As in Hawai'i, Alaska and Vermont, the plaintiffs raised fundamental issues of civil rights and equality under state constitutions. Indeed, the central legal argument in *Goodridge* focused on the equality provisions of the Massachusetts constitution. The plaintiffs in *Goodridge* sought to bypass constitutional argument by pointing out that existing marriage law in Massachusetts did not specifically mention gender. However, recognizing that such a literal reading of the law would likely not suffice to win the Court's support for same-sex marriage, the plaintiffs argued that the Massachusetts constitution guarantees the right to marry the person of one's choice, that the plaintiffs were harmed by their exclusion from civil marriage and that the constitution was designed to change with the times. The plaintiffs defined lesbians and gays as a suspect class, meaning that any discrimination against the suspect class would have to be rationally related and narrowly tailored to a compelling state interest (Bonauto 2001; Bonauto et al. 2002: 2–12; see also Loewy 2004).

Moreover, the plaintiffs also argued there was profound harm in excluding same-sex couples from marriage (Bonauto 2002: 109) and recalled the legal struggles around civil rights from *Plessy* to *Brown* (Bonauto 2002: 12–14). The plaintiffs provided a substantial history of the constitutional right to marry, arguing that it was a fundamental right in the Massachusetts constitution and that marriage rights fell into the zone of the right to privacy and autonomy for the individual. Thus, the plaintiffs tied the issue of same-sex marriage to the project of personal liberty and drew on a long history of cases regarding marriage choice, most critically with regard to interracial marriage (Bonauto 2002: 30–40). By framing the issue as one of liberty and choice for the individual within the concept of the right to privacy, the plaintiffs provided a response to those who viewed homosexuality and same-sex marriage as moral wrongs and threats to family values. By recalling an era in which interracial marriage was considered illegal and immoral, the plaintiffs in *Goodridge* sought to counter the framing of heterosexual marriage as natural and inevitable.

The majority in *Goodridge* agreed with this, citing the cases of *Perez* and *Loving* in which interracial marriage was found to violate due process and equality guarantees. Justice Marshall, writing for the majority, argued that the Massachusetts Constitution prohibited the creation of second-class citizens and pointed to both the tangible and intangible benefits that flow from marriage (*Goodridge*: 1, 12). Liberty and due process rights were strongly protected by the Massachusetts Constitution, according to the majority in *Goodridge*, even more so than in the federal constitution (*Goodridge*: 15).

In addition, the central position of children was affirmed in the Court's decision. The Supreme Judicial Court argued that, by upholding the "marriage ban," the Court would be discriminating against children on the grounds of sexual orientation by preventing children of same-sex couples "from enjoying the immeasurable advantages that flow from the assurance of a stable family structure in which children will be reared, educated, and socialized" (*Goodridge*: 2). By rejecting arguments based on procreation and arguments based on the idea that the heterosexual family unit was better for children than families headed by same-sex couples, the majority in *Goodridge* rejected the rational basis of the state's discrimination against same-sex couples (see Friedman 2006; Loewey 2004; Mohr 2004).

The decision was stayed by the court for 180 days, during which frenetic activity took place by same-sex marriage opponents to forestall the implementation of the decision, set for May 2004. Massachusetts's Governor at the time, Mitt Romney, stated that he would direct the Department of Public Health (responsible for issuing marriage licenses in the state) to bar same-sex couples from marrying in Massachusetts, using the provisions of a 1913 Massachusetts law (still on the books but no longer enforced) that had been passed to prevent out-of-state interracial couples from marrying in Massachusetts. In addition, there was an attempt in the legislature to organize a "Vermont" solution to the *Goodridge* decision by passing a civil union bill, which would deny the right to marry to same-sex couples. The proposed legislation was referred to the Supreme Judicial Court under the provisions of the Massachusetts constitution that permit either branch of the legislature or the governor to request an advisory opinion from the high court. However, the civil union solution was rejected by the court, which likened the creation of a separate category of civil unions for same-sex couples to segregation:

> Because the proposed law by its express terms forbids same-sex couples' entry into civil marriage, it continues to relegate same-sex couples to a different status. The holding in *Goodridge*, by which we are bound, is that group classifications based on unsupportable distinctions, such as that embodied in the proposed bill, are invalid under the Massachusetts Constitution. The history of our nation has demonstrated that separate is seldom, if ever, equal (*Opinion* 2004: 1).

In reaction to this decision, Massachusetts began issuing marriage licenses to same-sex couples in May 2004.

In Massachusetts, as in the other states, an organized campaign against same-sex marriage in the state had already been galvanized in the 1990s as same-sex marriage emerged as a legal and political issue. The court rulings in Hawai'i and the subsequent attempts to pass DOMAs (either by statute or by constitutional amendment) had led the Massachusetts Family Institute and other conservative groups to attempt to ward off same-sex marriage in the state, before the *Goodridge* ruling. One of the main conservative organizations, the Massachusetts Family Institute (an affiliate of Focus on the Family), had begun organizing in favor of a defense of marriage act in Massachusetts in 1998 (Pinello 2006: 35). In reply, lesbian and gay rights supporters in Massachusetts organized their own campaign through Mass Equality, in alliance with the litigators in the *Goodridge* case from the New England-based litigation fund, Gay and Lesbian Advocates and Defenders (GLAD). In order to amend the Massachusetts state constitution, the legislature, meeting in constitutional convention, would have had to approve the amendment in two successive sessions after which it would have been submitted to the voters in a ballot. Alternatively, the constitution could have been amended through citizen initiative in which, after gathering a specified number of signatures, the amendment would have had to have obtained 25% approval in two successive constitutional conventions, prior to being placed on the ballot. Conservative opponents of same-sex marriage succeeded in obtaining signatures sufficient to trigger a first constitutional convention in 2002, which was adjourned prior to a vote and same-sex marriage opponents were focusing on a legislative strategy at the time that *Goodridge* was decided in 2003. In the 2004 election cycle, supporters of same-sex marriage were re-elected and a plan to ban same-sex marriages while creating a civil union scheme failed to pass a 2005 constitutional convention. However, same-sex marriage opponents returned to the strategy of citizen initiative in order to place the question on the ballot for the 2008 election. This initiative was defeated, although the question may recur again in the future (Belluck 2007; in general, see Pinello 2006: 33–72).

The structure of Massachusetts's political institutions provided same-sex marriage opponents with multiple political opportunities for mobilization and activism. Because of this, same-sex marriage opponents could reopen the issue using the means at their disposal for amending the state constitution. The separation of powers system at the state level meant that Massachusetts's legislators were open to lobbying and political pressure from anti-same-sex marriage groups and, as Pinello (2006: 45–47) points out, the lesbian and gay movement in Massachusetts had less leverage than same-sex marriage opponents until the Court ruled in *Goodridge*. The decentralized political parties in Massachusetts and the openness of the legislature to public pressure made it more challenging for the party leadership to undertake the strategic calculus made by the party leadership in Canada.

In the separation of powers systems, the electoral calculus of politicians is expressed by the individual legislator while, in the disciplined party system of the Westminster model, it is expressed by the political party and, even more precisely, by the party leadership because of the fact that individual legislators rarely deviate from party policy. Institutional factors such as the separation of powers system, the consequent lack of disciplined political parties, and the jurisdictional divisions of federalism that allocate the regulation of marriage to state jurisdiction played an important role in shaping the politics of the same-sex marriage debate in Massachusetts as in other states. And, importantly, the fact of the existence of state constitutions and the mechanisms they provide for constitutional amendment provide means by which same-sex marriage opponents could seek to circumvent or forestall decisions made by courts. Although these mechanisms vary from state to state, even in states in which it is very difficult to amend the state constitution, as in Massachusetts, there is more political opportunity than exists in Canada where there are no constitutions at the sub-state level.

The *Goodridge* decision had a profound effect on the same-sex marriage debate in the U.S. and its consequences are still being felt. This decision, coming as it did after the decisions in Hawai'i, Alaska and Vermont, made it more difficult for state courts to rule against same-sex marriage on the grounds that such couples were completely undeserving of any constitutional recognition. Furthermore, the decision (and the anticipation of the decision), along with the emergence of a grassroots marriage movement supported by and even initiated by straight political leaders, led to a shift in strategy among same-sex marriage opponents. During the 1990s, the main goal of the anti-marriage movement had been to pass state laws banning same-sex marriage. However, in the 2000s, the issue of same-sex marriage was increasingly constitutionalized as opponents sought to bar the door on same-sex rights, undercut the legitimacy of same-sex marriage, and forestall the "spread" of such marriages across the states. While the 1996 federal DOMA had sufficed in the 1990s, the experiences of Vermont and Massachusetts indicated that constitutional weapons were needed to limit the scope and spread of same-sex marriage.

This led to the spate of constitutional marriage bans in the 2004 election cycle and to the escalating discussion of a federal constitutional ban. In the wake of *Goodridge*, George Bush indicated that he supported a constitutional amendment to reassert the heterosexual definition of marriage. A Federal Marriage Amendment (FMA) had been introduced prior to *Goodridge* by Bush supporters; following *Goodridge*, hearings were held on the proposed amendment in 2004 in both the House and the Senate. The amendment would have built on earlier DOMAs by enshrining the opposite-sex definition of marriage in federal policy and by preventing any state constitution from permitting same-sex marriage. The exact wording of the proposed amendment introduced in the Senate in 2004 purported to tell the courts how to interpret the constitution by stating that "Neither this Constitution, nor the constitution of any State, shall be construed to require that marriage or the legal incidents thereof be conferred upon any union other than the union of a man and a woman" (U.S. Senate 2004). As the political director of the Log Cabin Republicans noted, "[t]he Bush proposal runs roughshod over principles of federalism, state autonomy, and individual liberty that the Republican Party is supposed to represent" (Barron 2004: 28). In addition, the amendment in this form clearly attempted to forestall a federal decision on the constitutionality of DOMA as well as further decisions such as *Goodridge* in state courts (Bossin 2005). The proposed FMA would make it impossible for courts to use any part of the federal or state constitutions or federal or state law to sanction same-sex marriage or even to sanction limited forms of recognition such as second-parent adoption and domestic partner benefits. In 2004, the FMA was softened somewhat to restrict the scope to same-sex marriage and common law protection for unmarried heterosexuals (Cahill 2004: 11). In July 2004, the Republican-dominated House passed the *Marriage Protection Act*, which would have banned courts from hearing same-sex marriage cases, a measure that was very likely unconstitutional, but, at the same time, expressed the mounting ire of same-sex marriage opponents.[5] Supporters of the proposed legislation argued that the federal courts should not be allowed to rule on the constitutionality of the federal DOMA. As Representative Sue Myrick, Republican of North Carolina, stated, "[l]ifetime appointed federal judges must not be allowed to rewrite marriage policy for the states" (Fitzgerald and Cooperman 2004). As of 2007, the Marriage Protection Act and the Federal Marriage Amendment have not been passed by Congress.

In reaction to these events, a campaign of civil disobedience began in some states in order to push for same-sex marriage. In reaction to Bush's 2004 State of the Union address, the mayors and other local officials in San Francisco, Portland, Sandoval (New Mexico) and New Paltz (New York) performed same-sex marriages, despite the fact that these marriages were not official or legal while, in New York City, public weddings were held on the steps of City Hall in defiance of city officials who refused to issue marriage licenses. This wave of demonstrations and civil disobedience led to major court cases in California as well as to criminal charges in New York State against the mayor of New Paltz and against some of the Unitarian Universalist ministers who assisted in performing marriage ceremonies for same-sex couples (Nicol and Smith 2007; see also Pinello 2006; 90–93). This movement generated a wave of new legal challenges on same-sex marriage and directly challenged same-sex marriage opponents with the specter of grass roots civil disobedience in favor of same-sex marriage by local authorities and straight political leaders.

At the state level, DOMAs and state constitutional amendments spread throughout the states. As of 2004, thirty-nine states had passed some form of DOMA (whether statutory or constitutional; Cahill 2004: 7–9).

While DOMAs themselves prohibit same-sex marriage within the state or the recognition of same-sex marriages performed in other jurisdictions, super-DOMAs prohibit any form of recognition of same-sex relationships, including civil union or domestic partnership and may put into jeopardy private sector arrangements and benefits that recognize same-sex domestic partners (Cahill 2004: 9). As of 2006, twenty-one states have passed super-DOMA statutes or, more commonly, constitutional amendments (Task Force 2006).

The same-sex marriage debate also resuscitated the discussion of federal discrimination protection on the basis of sexual orientation and gender identity. Unsurprisingly, the federal Employment Non-Discrimination Act (ENDA) failed to pass in the Republican-dominated Congress. The Human Rights Campaign, the main LGBT group working on ENDA, wanted the proposed legislation to include gender identity in order to ensure that trans people, as well as lesbians, bisexuals and gay men, would be protected by the legislation. The idea of including gender identity made the bill even more unpopular in Congress (Carpenter 2004). Even after the victories in *Lawrence* and *Goodridge*, only seventeen states and the District of Columbia ban sexual orientation discrimination as of January 2007 (Task Force 2007b). In the fall of 2007, there was a new push to pass ENDA in the more favorable political climate following the 2006 midterm elections. Yet, despite broad support in U.S. public opinion for banning employment discrimination against gays and lesbians (Lofton and Haider-Markel 2007), policy change has been painfully slow.

Canadian Developments

On the Canadian side, beginning in 1998, there were three important same-sex marriage cases that unfolded in the three most populous provinces—Quebec, B.C. and Ontario. As we have seen, the lesbian and gay legal network in Canada had discouraged an appeal of the 1993 decision in *Layland*. However, the issue of same-sex marriage continued to simmer and, in 1997, Egale held a consultation exercise in Ottawa to discuss the issue with lawyers and potential litigants from across Canada. As a result of this consultation, at least one couple was persuaded not to go ahead with legal action for fear of a loss (Fisher 2001). However, despite this decision and the opinion of the lawyers who were most familiar with the most recent rounds of litigation in the cases of the time such as *Egan, Vriend,* and *Rosenberg*, in 1998, a gay couple in Montreal decided to challenge the marriage law. Michael Hendricks and René Leboeuf, who had long been active in the AIDS movement in Montreal, went to Montreal City Hall and attempted to obtain a marriage license in full view of the media, whom they invited to witness their rejection. They filed a marriage case which, in the first instance, argued against the Quebec government's definition of marriage in the provincial Civil Code. Neither the couple nor their original lawyer was connected to the legal networks in English-speaking Canada, which, up to this point, had led the way in Charter litigation. For Hendricks and Lebouef, their decision to pursue the right of legal marriage was in part connected to their experience in AIDS organizing in which they saw the costs of the lack of legal recognition of same-sex relationships (Nicol 2006).

Legal networks in Quebec and English-speaking Canada are highly segmented in certain areas of law, especially those touching on civil matters, because of the different legal training required for practice with the civil code compared to the common law in the other provinces and territories. In addition, the linguistic barrier between English-speaking and French-speaking lawyers also impeded networking among lawyers (as among other groups) at the pan-Canadian level (Fisher 2001). Quebec activists had been less interested in the Canadian Charter, in part because of the political illegitimacy of the constitutional patriation of 1982, which had enacted the Charter. Like other provinces, Quebec had its own provincial human rights code as well as its own civil code for matters defined under common law in the English-speaking provinces. In the first instance, Hendricks and Leboeuf cast their case in terms that challenged the Civil Code exclusion of same-sex marriage on the grounds that it violated the Quebec Charter of Rights (the provincial human rights code), not the Canadian Charter of Rights. Soon after their case got underway, however, they linked up with the pan-Canadian legal and political network on same-sex marriage litigation, which was coordinated by Egale and, eventually, by a spinoff organization called the Canadians for Equal Marriage, which was founded in 2003 (Munter 2005).

Meanwhile, the decisions in *Vriend*, *Rosenberg* and *M v. H* spurred litigants in Ontario and B.C. to go forward with same-sex marriage challenges. Given the *M v. H* precedent, litigants came forward in other provinces and were coordinated by Egale and by the pan-Canadian legal network that had grown up around gay and lesbian litigation under the Charter. In B.C., lawyer and activist barbara findlay[6] brought together three couples who wanted to challenge the law in that province; in addition, Egale also sought out litigants who would present a diverse picture of lesbian and gay life to the courts and brought a case based on five applicant couples. The litigants organized by findlay came forward first and filed at the end of 1998, after the *Vriend* and *Rosenberg* decisions but before the *M v. H* decision. By 2000, nine couples had been denied licenses to marry by the Director of Vital Statistics for B.C. The initial reaction of the NDP government of B.C. had been to seek an order from the B.C. Supreme Court to ask if marriage commissioners in B.C. could issue licenses to same-sex couples. The NDP in B.C. had long supported gay rights and had implemented legislation to recognize the right of same-sex parents to second parent adoption as well as to the naming of two same-sex parents on birth certificates in B.C. However, this petition was withdrawn when the Liberals were elected in B.C. in 2001. Unlike the federal Liberals, the provincial Liberals in B.C. are a right-wing party, more akin to the federal Conservatives. At the initial stage, the B.C. couples were turned down by the lower court (see the procedural background outlined in *Barbeau v. British Columbia* 2003; on party politics in B.C., see Carty, Cross and Young 2000).

At the same time, in Toronto, couples had also come forward requesting marriage licenses from city hall and after a series of applications by the couples and by the clerks themselves, the case was constituted and filed in 2000 by sixteen applicant couples supported by Egale and by the Metropolitan Community Church of Toronto (MCCT). In January 2001, two couples were married following the reading of banns of marriage in the MCCT. By reading the banns, the couples, the church and Egale circumvented the process of requesting a marriage license from city hall. Rather, they went ahead and held the marriages in MCCT in January, 2001. Following this, the couples and their lawyers attempted to register their marriages but were denied. The couples and MCCT then brought suit against the city for refusing to register the marriages that had taken place in the church. MCCT argued that its religious freedom under the Charter was abridged by the city's denial of a marriage that had taken place in the church by an official authorized to perform marriages and following the reading of banns. These two cases were joined and became the *Halpern* case (Bourassa and Varnell 2002; Elliott 2002).

The first decision of this trio of cases came from the Supreme Court of B.C., which ruled against the applicant couples in October 2001, arguing that, although the exclusion of lesbians and gays from marriage was discriminatory under the equality rights provision of the Charter (section 15), discrimination was reasonable under the Charter's section 1 (reasonable limits) clause (*Egale v. Canada* 2001). Thus, the court employed a logic similar to that of the 1995 *Egan* decision. The applicant couples and Egale, which was directly involved in the litigation, immediately appealed the decision. The next decision occurred in Ontario where the ruling from the Ontario Superior Court of Justice (Divisional Court) favored the applicant couples; the court ruled that the common law ban on same-sex marriage could not survive a Charter challenge under section 15, nor could it be saved under the Charter's section 1 "reasonable limits" (*Halpern* 2002). In the case of Hendricks and Leboeuf, decided by the Superior Court of Quebec in 2002, the court ruled that the ban on same-sex marriage in the Federal Law—Civil Law Harmonization Act (the act that ensures recognition and harmonization of Quebec civil law provisions with federal law), the preamble to the Modernization of Benefits and Obligations Act, and the Quebec Civil Code were all unconstitutional under section 15 of the Charter (*Hendricks v. Quebec* 2002), because they defined marriage in opposite-sex terms. In 2003, the B.C. Court of Appeal overturned the decision of the lower court and ruled that the ban on same-sex marriage was unconstitutional (*Barbeau v. British Columbia* 2003). In all three provinces, the courts left the federal and provincial governments with a two-year period to bring their legislation into line with the constitutional requirements of the Charter. By this time, the idea of legalizing same-sex marriage throughout Canada was being openly debated in Liberal Party circles and the Research Branch of the party had written a report endorsing legalization (Larocque 2006: 112).

In the Ontario case, the couples were dissatisfied with the two-year stay that had been provided as part of the remedy by the court and they decided to appeal to the Ontario Court of Appeal, one of the most progressive courts in Canada. In June 2003, the Court released its decision in the *Halpern* appeal, ordering the City of Toronto to issue marriage licenses and the provinces to register the marriages that had taken place at the Metropolitan Community Church, Toronto in 2001 (*Halpern* 2003). This decision and a similar decision on appeal in B.C., which occurred soon after, opened the door to legal same-sex marriage in Canada. The federal government was faced with a near-unanimous set of rulings from lower courts and, in the face of these decisions, a number of other same-sex marriage challenges in other provinces had also started to go forward as couples in every province began to seek lawyers to bring cases in order to change the law in their jurisdiction. This led to a patchwork quilt, as, in some provinces, same-sex marriages were permitted by court rulings (e.g., Ontario and B.C.) while, in other provinces, they were not, although it could be inferred that the legal challenges of couples in Nova Scotia, Manitoba and other provinces were highly likely to be successful. There was near-consensus from lower courts—only one lower court (B.C. Supreme Court) had ruled against the same-sex couples since the *Layland* decision of 1993.

Because the Ontario and other rulings in lower courts challenged the federal law on marriage, the federal government had the right to continue to appeal these cases to the Supreme Court of Canada. However, the government decided not to appeal in light of the overwhelming response of lower courts and in light of its own estimation of the likely outcome in the Supreme Court of Canada (Larocque 2006; see also Canadian Press 2007). Marriage laws had become uneven across the country as same-sex marriage was legal in some provinces but not in others. This uneven pattern required the government to ensure that, at least as far as the question of legal marriage, which was clearly under the jurisdiction of the federal government, the legal playing field was level across Canada, that marriages contracted in provinces in which same-sex marriage was legal would be recognized in other provinces, and that same-sex couples would not have to undertake myriad legal challenges throughout Canada. Across Canada, there were applicant couples and lawyers who wanted to come forward and lawyers from across Canada who were involved in these cases attempted to manage the pacing and order of the cases by networking among lawyers (Elliott 2002; Foreman 2006; Nicol 2006). In Quebec, a subsequent challenge to the *Hendricks* ruling by a religious organization failed when the Quebec Court of Appeal denied standing to the group and lifted the suspension of the remedy that had been put into place by the lower court in *Hendricks*, thus enabling same-sex couples to marry legally in Quebec immediately, as in Ontario and B.C. (*Ligue catholique pour les droits de l'homme c. Hendricks* 2004). By June 2005, eight provinces and one territory had recognized the right to same-sex marriage through litigation (for an overview of developments in each jurisdiction, see Hurley 2007). It is important to note that these are very different from decisions in U.S. state courts regarding same-sex marriage. In the Canadian cases, the federal government was either the main respondent in most of these cases or was an intervener or potential intervener in cases that were brought against the provincial or municipal authority's failure to issue the marriage license. Litigation in each court followed the precedents set by the pioneering decisions in B.C., Ontario and Quebec, especially the decision from the Ontario Court of Appeal. Because of the unified court structure, these decisions would all end in the same final court of appeal—the Supreme Court of Canada—and decisions in one province had direct implications for constitutional law in other provinces as all the cases were litigated under the pan-Canadian Charter of Rights.

As these cases developed and in light of the fact that same-sex marriage was legal in some provinces and territories, but not others, the federal government decided to craft legislation to recognize same-sex marriage and, at the same time, to ensure that the legislation was constitutional by undertaking a reference case on its constitutionality to the Supreme Court of Canada. Like the advisory opinion procedure in Massachusetts, the reference case procedure allows the government to query the Court on a constitutional issue in the absence of a specific dispute or appeal. During the period that the case was under consideration at the Supreme Court of Canada, the Prime Minister, Jean Chrétien, resigned and Paul Martin became Prime Minister. The Martin government added an additional question to the reference process. In addition to asking the Court to rule on the constitutionality of the legislation (both under the Charter and in terms of the federal government's jurisdiction) and on whether or not the legislation contravened religious freedom under the Charter, the Martin government specifically asked the Court if the legislation was constitutionally required (see *Reference*: 1–7). During this period, the government did not oppose same-sex couples who challenged their exclusion from civil legal marriage in other provinces and territories; the government either refrained from opposing the plaintiffs' applications or intervened in these cases by asking courts to await the Supreme Court's decision in the reference case before ruling. However, courts in other provinces and in one territory declined to wait for the Supreme Court decision in the reference case; instead, they ruled that the exclusion of same-sex couples from civil marriage was unconstitutional and ordered the immediate issuing of marriage licenses (for example, *Boutilier v. Nova Scotia* 2004; see Hurley 2007 for an overview of these cases).

In December 2004, the Supreme Court of Canada issued its ruling in the reference case (*Reference re Same-Sex Marriage* 2004). According to the Court, the government's proposed same-sex marriage legislation was constitutional under the Charter, it fell within the jurisdiction of the federal Parliament, it did not violate the provisions on freedom of religion in the Charter, and it would not require religious organizations to perform same-sex marriages. The Court refused to answer the question on whether or not same-sex marriage was constitutionally required. On the question of jurisdiction, the Court stated that it was "trite law" to say that the federal government regulated the capacity to marry and confirmed that, indeed, the Liberal government's proposed bill on same-sex marriage was within the authority and jurisdiction of the federal Parliament. Despite the Court's rebuke to the government's question, it was politically useful for the federal government and for provincial governments to have this point confirmed because of Alberta's threats to employ the notwithstanding clause and because of the fact that Alberta had already used the notwithstanding clause to pass its Adult Interdependent Relationships Act, as we have seen. By stating that the capacity to marry was within the sole authority of the federal Parliament while the provinces were responsible for the performance of marriages for those who have the capacity to marry under federal law, the Court made it clear that Alberta would not be able to stop same-sex marriage using the notwithstanding clause nor would it be constitutional for a province to refuse to implement federal same-sex marriage.[7]

The idea that recognizing the right to marry for same-sex couples would violate the rights of religious groups or the rights of opposite-sex married couples was clearly rejected by the Supreme Court. The Court commented that "[the] mere recognition of the equality rights of one group cannot, in itself, constitute a violation of the rights of another" (*Reference*: 46) and, with regard to religious rights, the Court observed that, since the legislation regulated the capacity for civil marriage, it did not compel religious officials to perform same-sex marriages. Further, the Court stated that, if it did, it would clearly violate religious freedom guaranteed in the Charter (*Reference*: 55–56). The Court accepted the facts on the ground that had been created by the decision by the Ontario Court of Appeal in *Halpern* and the acceptance of the *Halpern* ruling by the federal Attorney General as well as the fact that, at the time of the litigation of the reference case, the opposite-sex requirement for marriage had been struck down by courts not only in the three most populous provinces but also in Manitoba, Nova Scotia, Saskatchewan and the Yukon Territory (*Reference*: 66). Given the government's determination to proceed with legislation to provide for uniformity of the law throughout Canada, a power that was clearly within its jurisdiction, the Court ruled that there was no purpose in answering the question as to the constitutional obligation to provide for same-sex marriage (*Reference*: 67–71).

In the debate in Parliament in which the bill to legalize same-sex marriage was proposed by the government for its second reading, Paul Martin, Liberal Prime Minister of the time, made a speech in the House of Commons that well encapsulated the Liberal government's identification of Charter values with Canadian values. Recalling the Progressive Conservative Prime Minister, John Diefenbaker, who had introduced the federal Bill of Rights in 1960 and his own predecessor as Liberal Prime Minister, Pierre Trudeau, who had introduced the Charter in 1982, Martin stated:

> This is an important day. The attention of our nation is focused on this chamber in which John Diefenbaker introduced the Bill of Rights, and in which Pierre Trudeau fought to establish the Charter of Rights and Freedoms. Our deliberations will not be merely about a piece of legislation or sections of legal text. More deeply they will be about the kind of nation we are today and the nation we want to be. This bill protects minority rights. This bill affirms the Charter guarantee of religious freedom. It is that straightforward and it is that important. That is why I stand before members here today and before the people of our country to say that I believe in and I will fight for the Charter of Rights. I believe in and I will fight for a Canada that respects the foresight and the vision of those who created and entrenched the Charter. I believe in and I will fight for a future in which generations of Canadians to come, Canadians born here and abroad, have the opportunity to value the Charter as we do today, as an essential pillar of our democratic freedom (Martin in Canada 2005: 1520).

Martin went on to explain that his government would not use the notwithstanding clause to set aside the decisions of the court on same-sex marriage, even though he admitted that he had voted in favor of the maintenance of the traditional definition of marriage in Parliament only four years earlier, influenced by his personal Roman Catholic faith. Martin's stance on the use of the notwithstanding clause reflected the meta-constitutional norms of Canadian practice, in which the clause is viewed as a constitutional taboo in practical terms by federal politicians. In Martin's words: "We cannot exalt the Charter as a fundamental aspect of our national character and then use the notwithstanding clause to reject the protections that it would extend. Our rights must be eternal, not subject to political whim" (Martin in Canada 2005: 1521). This speech, made at a time when the government was in a minority position, demonstrates the ways in which the government was prepared to use the Charter and to use the issue of same-sex marriage to make an electoral appeal. As Martin explained, "[i]f the Charter is not there today to protect the rights of one minority, then how can we as a nation of minorities ever hope, ever believe, and ever trust that it will be there to protect us tomorrow?" (Canada 2005: 1521). Thus, in a "nation of minorities," same-sex partners are not only recognized as citizens, the recognition of their rights is defined as a point of nationalist pride and the Charter has acquired a quasi-sacred status in political debate.

Yet, in the early 2000s, as the same-sex marriage issue was litigated, 46% of Canadians *opposed* same-sex marriage (Matthews 2005: 841). In this light, the Prime Minister's statement cannot be viewed as the straight-forward translation of public opinion and political cultural values into pub-lic policy. Nonetheless, it can be read as a strategic decision by the Liberal Party leadership to define the party's electoral interests in an attempt to distinguish itself from social conservatives in the opposition Conservative Party. The Conservatives opposed the civil marriage bill and called for the government to leave the traditional definition of marriage and to allow civil union and domestic partner arrangements as had already been recognized in the provinces in the wake of *M v. H* (Harper in Canada 2005: 1540). Ralph Klein, the Progressive Conservative premier of Alberta, along with Focus on the Family Canada, an evangelical offshoot of the U.S. Focus on the Family, called for a national referendum to be held by the govern-ment on the use of the notwithstanding clause to oppose gay marriage, and social conservative opponents of same-sex marriage within the federal liberal Caucus also suggested this strategy (O'Malley 2003; see also CTV News 2004; Gulliver 2004). Polling evidence commissioned by the conser-vative newspaper, the *National Post*, suggested that there was support for a referendum on or opting for civil union or other forms of recognition of same-sex relationships at this time (Compas 2005). Despite this pressure, the Martin government passed the bill over the opposition of the Conserva-tive Party, supported by the Quebec-based Bloc Québécois and the social democratic New Democratic Party.

COMPARATIVE RESPONSES TO COURT DECISIONS

Political institutions and policy legacies are the unseen structures behind the vociferous battle between same-sex marriage advocates and defenders. In both the U.S. and Canada, there are social movements for and against same-sex marriage and, by any measure, the Christian Right organizations in both countries are able to outspend and outresource lesbian and gay organizations in both countries. U.S. lesbian and gay organizations are much stronger than similar Canadian organizations. Organizations such as the Human Rights Campaign and the Task Force in the U.S. have well developed professional capacity compared to the two or three employees of the main Canadian lesbian and gay rights group, Egale, during this period. When the Campaign for Equal Families spun off from Egale to focus on the same-sex marriage issue, it built political support for same-sex marriage among churches, trade unions, women's groups and other movement allies and coordinated the campaign among those groups to take a pro-same-sex marriage position to the public and to politicians. However, this was a temporary campaign and not a permanent lesbian and gay organization. The 2003 budgets of the main lesbian and gay organizations in the U.S. ranged from $5 million to $17 million (Cahill 2004). In Canada, the budget of Egale, the main gay and lesbian group favoring same-sex marriage in Canada, was less than $350,000 in 2004 at the height of the same-sex marriage campaign. Given that Canada's population is one-tenth that of the U.S., the entire budget of Egale was only about two-thirds of the budget of the smallest U.S. lesbian and gay organization, and less than one-third of the budget of the best-resourced American organization. While there were other groups working for same-sex marriage in trade unions, churches, and through the media campaign coordinated by Canadians for Equal Marriage, there was no Canadian lesbian and gay organization that had access to the money and organization of the large U.S. lesbian and gay groups such as the Task Force or the Human Rights Campaign on a per capita basis (Munter 2005; Hickey 2006, Fisher 2001). Therefore, the financial resources of these two sets of social movement organizations tell us very little about the outcome of the same-sex marriage battle.

Moreover, political culture, at least as measured in the values and beliefs that are expressed in public opinion, cannot explain why Canada adopted same-sex marriage in 2005. As we have seen, about half of Canadians opposed same-sex marriage and yet the government adopted the policy unimpeded by the opposition. Within the dominant Liberal party, behind the nationalist speech made by the prime minister, there was a substantial group of MPs who opposed same-sex marriage (Larocque 2006: 167ff). Yet, this group, which in the U.S. would have been the vehicle for the anti-same-sex marriage campaign and which would have been lobbied hard by Christian Right and conservative groups, was not able to exercise influence in the Canadian party system. Same-sex marriage opponents, including evangelicals, were outflanked by party leaders and because of the system of party discipline, they were not able to exercise influence. In addition, the logic of the Charter was the logic of the Liberal Party, which created a conflict between Charter values and religious values in the case of some MPs, almost certainly including Prime Minister Jean Chrétien and his successor, Paul Martin. In the face of the conflict between the Roman Catholic religion in which they had been raised and the logic of the Charter rights and values which they saw as central to the success of the Liberal Party and as attributes of Canadian nationhood, religion lost and the Charter won (on politicians' personal views, see Larocque 2006; Canadian Press 2007). This outcome makes sense in light of an historical institutionalist analysis that considers the structure of political institutions, the role of courts and the role of historical pacing in policy development.

Developments in Massachusetts provide a striking contrast to Canada. While both Massachusetts and Canada arrived at a similar policy result—legalization of same-sex marriage—they did so by different routes (and, because of the lack of recognition of same-sex marriage in U.S. federal

law, with less than full legal equality for Massachusetts couples, compared to Canadian couples). In Massachusetts, in 2006–2007, a majority
of citizens supported the same-sex marriages that were constitutionally
required by the state's highest court in the *Goodridge* ruling in 2003 and
again in the court's rejection of civil unions in its 2004 advisory opinion to the state Senate. As we have seen, advocacy groups on both sides
of the issue waged a furious campaign in Massachusetts from the late
1990s when same-sex marriage opponents began organizing to obtain a
same-sex marriage amendment. The demonstration effect of the Hawai'i,
Alaska, and Vermont decisions in Massachusetts encouraged conservative
groups to try to close the door on same-sex marriage before courts had
ruled. Groups on each side of the issue mobilized using every means possible, from lobbying legislators, working in election campaigns to ensure
that supporters of same-sex marriage were elected and re-elected, and
using grass roots campaigns to bring the diverse faces of same-sex couples
and their children to the attention of the media and other citizens, unlike
the Canadian campaign, which occurred almost entirely through litigation with very few demonstrations and less lobbying of legislators. Given
that most legislators were bound to follow the party leadership, pressure
on legislatures in Canada occurred behind closed doors as individual MPs
made the case for or against same-sex marriage within their own party
caucus in confidential meetings, rather than through public statements
and legislative activity as in the case of individual legislators in Massachusetts' separation of powers system.

While political actors have choices and agency in relation to political
institutions, the close comparison of American and Canadian developments demonstrates the extent to which the strategies used by advocacy
groups and social movement organizations were structured by the institutional openings available to them. In the U.S., there are powerful litigation
funds that coordinate the state-by-state battle, reflecting the decentralized
jurisdiction of lesbian and gay rights issues as well as the power and influence of courts in the U.S. political system. These funds were often allied
with broad advocacy groups that concentrate on lobbying legislators in
order to protect judicial gains from rollback through constitutional amendments and citizen initiative. Similarly, in Canada, the strong role of courts
and the centralized and closed nature of parliamentary institutions, especially when combined with exclusive federal jurisdiction in a particular
policy area (as in these cases) encouraged an elite-driven process, focused
on litigation and legal networks but without the associated organizational
structure of allies and advocacy groups found in the U.S. system. The alliance between GLAD and Mass Equality in Massachusetts or the division
of labor between Lambda Legal and other national lesbian and gay organizations in the U.S. such as the Human Rights Campaign and the Task
Force was not replicated in Canada. Instead, Canada's same-sex marriage
drive was spearheaded through one small litigation-focused organization

operating in Ottawa, along with a spin-off group that temporarily coordinated a media-based campaign to secure support from other groups such
as churches and trade unions. The role of litigation funds such as GLAD
and Lambda Legal in the U.S. was mainly taken by informal networks of
lawyers, operating with some organizational infrastructure provided by
Egale. However, in contrast to Lambda Legal and other litigation organizations in the U.S., Egale did not have its own project or staff lawyers
but, rather, relied on hiring outside counsel or tapped into *pro bono* contributions from the pan-Canadian litigation networks (Fisher 2001; Elliott
2002; Marchildon 2005). These organizational differences can be directly
linked to the structure of political institutions, including the operation
of the federal division of powers in relation to important lesbian and gay
issues such as marriage.

POLICY DIFFUSION

As scholars of federalism have long noted, the decentralized jurisdictions
of federalism may provide laboratories for policy experimentation as well
as functioning as impediments to policy change (Rose-Ackerman 1980; see
also Trudeau 1968; Leman 1977; Krane 2007). When policies are made in
sub-national units, substantial policy differences may arise among states,
creating legal and political challenges for the recognition of one state or
province's laws by another state or province. The fact that Vermont and
Massachusetts moved ahead with the recognition of same-sex relationships
has caused policy diffusion as well as policy backlash. Couples who are
married in Massachusetts or who have entered into a Vermont civil union
may challenge the law of other states when they move across state lines
and seek recognition of the legal status of their relationships. In addition,
couples married in Canada or other jurisdictions that permit same-sex marriage may also pose legal challenges in other jurisdictions when they migrate
and seek recognition of their marriage or civil union. Canadian marriages
have already sparked the first recognition of same-sex marriage in the state
of Israel after a High Court case in which five gay couples who had been
married in Toronto successfully claimed the right to have their marriages
recognized by the state (Yoaz 2006). In the U.K., a lesbian couple married in
Canada challenged the U.K. 2004 Civil Partnership Act on the grounds that
it was in violation of the European Convention on Human Rights and the
U.K. Human Rights Act (Wilkinson 2006; see also BBC News 2006; Scherpe
2007). In addition, at least one unsuccessful case has been brought in the
U.S. by a couple married in Canada and challenging the federal DOMA (*In
re Kandu* 2004; in general, see M. Bailey 2004b). Through these means,
other jurisdictions are forced to react—legally and politically—to same-sex
couples and in this way, both policies and policy debates are diffused across
state lines and across the borders of the nation-state.

In the U.S., it is evident that policy diffusion is a major fear of same-sex marriage opponents and, so far, we have seen that constitutional marriage bans and statutory DOMAs are widespread in the U.S. However, the story is more complicated than that. There are signs that the fact of the existence of same-sex marriage in Massachusetts, civil union in Vermont, Connecticut, and New Jersey (with other states pending as of 2007), and domestic partner laws in other states, are sparking new and complex challenges in state law. With regard to recognition by states within the U.S., only residents of Massachusetts may marry in Massachusetts; residents of other states may not contract these marriages if they are not legal in their home states (see Koppelman 2006: 102103). However, this does not solve the problem of recognizing the marriages that have occurred in Massachusetts. Some states have clearly stated that they will not recognize Massachusetts' marriages while others have made this statement through the passage of statutes or constitutional amendments banning the recognition of same-sex marriage. However, some of the states that do not have DOMAs, such as Connecticut and Rhode Island, have stated that they may recognize Massachusetts' marriages (Koppelman 2006: 103). As Koppelman discusses, similar problems arise with migratory marriages, where couples who have married abroad come to the U.S. While states that have implemented civil union such as Vermont and Connecticut may recognize such marriages, these benefits are far short of the benefits of marriage and may eventually spark litigation, challenging the non-recognition of such foreign marriages.

Same-sex marriage opponents are concerned about any form of recognition that may be provided to same sex marriages or civil unions and this can sometimes lead to absurd situations. For example, in Iowa, in 2003, a district court dissolved a same-sex (Vermont) civil union and same-sex marriage opponents sought standing in the Iowa Supreme Court to deny the dissolution of the civil union in district court, arguing that the dissolution constituted recognition of same-sex civil unions. Interestingly, the judge who had crossed out "termination of marriage" on the form and wrote in "dissolution of Vermont same-sex civil union" survived an attempt to oust him by anti-same-sex marriage groups in a retention election in 2004 (Brandenburg 2005: 323–324). In another standing case in Nebraska, Citizens for Equal Protection challenged the constitutionality of an amendment to the Nebraska constitution that would have prevented the recognition of same-sex marriage or civil union in any form. The plaintiffs argued that they had standing to challenge this because such standing derives from "injury in fact" and a denial of equal protection constitutes an injury in fact sufficient to justify standing. In the case of a clerk who did not want to perform a same-sex civil union in Vermont, a standing case brought by a group failed because members of the groups were either politicians or taxpayers without injuries "in fact" and that clerk was permitted to accommodate his/her religious beliefs by delegating the job of performing same-sex unions to another clerk (Brandenburg 2005: 332–333). Status claims are made very directly here through the process of heterosexual legal mobilization. For example, the plaintiffs in *Alons* in Iowa argued that they were married and that they had "a substantial interest in the promotion of traditional marriage" (cited in Brandenburg.: 335). They further argued that, as they are married, they are entitled to "certain rights and privileges not granted to others" and that the recognition of same-sex relationships "would dilute the value of traditional marriage" (cited in Brandenburg: 335). Hence, same-sex marriage opponents attempted to claim status losses (see also Cruz 2001, 2002). One of the individuals was a minister who argued that his religious rights would be violated if he was presented with a marriage license in which one of the parties had been party to a Vermont civil union.

In the Iowa case, the district judge gave application to the Vermont civil union by dissolving it as an equitable union. Other courts have also recognized the right within their states to dissolve same-sex civil unions including courts in Connecticut, Georgia, New York and Massachusetts (Ibid.: 341–345). As Koppelman points out, although full faith and credit does not require the recognition of same-sex marriages contracted in other states, the existence of the federal DOMA does create problems in the recognition of the decisions of courts outside the states in which the decisions were made, effectively withdrawing full faith and credit from any court judgment that recognizes a same-sex marriage (Koppelman 2006: 123ff). As Koppelman states, "for the first time in American history, DOMA creates a class of second-class marriages, which are valid under state law but void for federal purposes" (2006: 131). Even under state DOMAs, Koppelman finds eleven scenarios in which these state laws and constitutional provisions could be challenged in court by plaintiffs such as married same-sex couples passing through the state or as parties to litigation in the state or migrating to the state and so forth (Ibid.: 139–140). Koppelman argues that many of these laws are overly broad and, for example, as in the case of Michigan's, might ban any contract between any two people of the same-sex. These laws might run into constitutional problems on these grounds or on the grounds that they express animus against lesbians and gays (Harvard Law Review 2004).

Institutional factors such as state control over marriage, judicial federalism and the separation of powers thwart policy change in the U.S.; nonetheless, policy changes do "spread" from state to state in more ways than one. Following *Baehr*, DOMAs spread from state to state but at the same time, progressive court decisions that recognized lesbian and gay rights at the state level have also "spread" from one state court to the next. Even in more recent cases in which courts in New York, Washington and Maryland were less inclined to rule in favor of same-sex marriage, state courts found substantial grounds for lesbian and gay rights claims to equality in the treatment of conjugal relationships and parenting rights. While these cases were setbacks for the lesbian and gay marriage movement, the reactions of politicians suggested that the effect of the ongoing litigation campaign and of decisions such as *Baehr, Brause, Baker* and *Goodridge* had begun to fundamentally alter the conversation about same-sex relationships in the U.S. Eliot Spitzer, while a candidate for Governor of New York, indicated very clearly that the law should be changed and, subsequently, a vote in favor of same-sex marriage was carried in the New York State Assembly (see Karlin 2007; Goldstein 2006). In New Jersey's same-sex marriage case in the fall of 2006, the state's highest court ruled that the unequal benefits and obligations for same-sex and opposite-sex couples could not be tolerated under the state constitution. This particularly strong statement in favor of equality for same sex couples was made in a unanimous ruling; the judges differed on the appropriate remedy for this constitutional violation with a majority opting to send the issue for resolution to the legislature and a dissenting minority arguing for the full legalization of same-sex marriage (*Lewis v. Harris* 2006). In the wake of this decision, New Jersey instituted a civil union policy. In 2007, an Iowa District court ruled in favor of same-sex couples' application for a marriage license (*Varnum v. Brien* 2007) and a New York court ruled in favor of recognizing Canadian same-sex marriages in New York state (*Godfrey v. Spano* 2007).

Recent cases on same-sex marriage in the states have demonstrated that courts in the U.S. are taking the claims of same-sex couples seriously and that courts that wish to rule against same-sex marriage are facing challenges in locating a principled legal ground on which to do so. Reviewing recent cases in Arizona and Indiana, Evan Gertsmann (2005) argues that, in these cases, the sole ground on which the courts could make distinctions between opposite-sex and same-sex couples was on the means by which they procreated and, in the Indiana case, there was an extensive discussion by the court of the stability of same-sex couples and their parenting relationships, with the court arguing that, since same-sex couples had gone to such trouble to have children by artificial means, they were more likely to have invested heavily in their parenting; thus, it was opposite-sex couples who need the protections afforded by legal marriage (*Morrison v. Sadler* 2005). A similar line was followed in the New York State same-sex marriage case (*Hernandez v. Robles* 2006). Although the case went against the applicant couples, the court's judgment argued that the issue was best left to the legislature. The court commented that the legislature might conclude that heterosexuals required the bonds of legal marriage and the material incentives it provided in order to maintain stable households while same-sex couples were likely to have made a greater investment in parenting, given that special measures were necessary in order to achieve it. This case also included a very strong dissent in support of same-sex marriage. Therefore, it is clear that same-sex marriage is gaining legal momentum among judges at the state court level.

Furthermore, there are signs that the spread of marriage bans may have been halted and that these state measures—especially the so-called super-DOMAS—may have reached their political and legal limits. In the

2006 election, for the first time, a same-sex marriage ban failed to pass in an election in a "red state"—Arizona—in part because of the fears of unmarried heterosexual partners that they would lose legal rights under the sweeping wording of the proposed measure (Davey 2006; see also Johnson 2006). Sweeping marriage bans in the states have raised serious legal problems, especially through the creation of unintended consequences. For example, in Ohio, a man attempted to use the state's constitutional ban on same-sex marriage to shield himself from prosecution on domestic violence charges. He argued that the denial of recognition to unmarried partners under the state's same-sex marriage ban voided the application of domestic violence laws to unmarried opposite-sex couples. This claim was put to rest after three years of litigation in *State v. Carswell* (2007) when the Ohio Supreme Court ruled that the state's constitutional same-sex marriage ban did not apply to the state's criminal law on domestic violence. And, in the twilight of the Bush era, the evangelical community is reportedly moving away from its focus on "moral" issues and may move in different and more diverse political directions (Kirkpatrick 2007).

Given these developments, it is conceivable that the U.S. will eventually arrive at full civil marriage rights for same-sex couples, although the path to achieving this policy result—like the thirty-five-year battle to change sodomy laws—will proceed state-by-state, full of swings and misses, with intense conflict between movements and countermovements which will exploit multiple institutional opportunities to push forward and roll back lesbian and gay rights in a drawn-out process of incremental policy change. At some point in this cycle of swings and misses, it is likely that an increasingly conservative U.S. Supreme Court will be called upon to rule on the constitutionality of the 1996 federal DOMA. Whether the U.S. Supreme Court will turn down same-sex marriage with a *Bowers*-like decision or whether it will follow the logic of *Lawrence* remains to be seen. Even if the Court declines to strike down the federal DOMA, the strength of the marriage movement, the pattern of decisions in state courts that have recognized the constitutional validity of its claims under state constitutions, and the growing legitimacy of options such as civil union as an alternatives to marriage all suggest that even a Supreme Court decision against same-sex marriage could end up as little more than a discredited *Bowers*-type ruling.

CONCLUSIONS

The close comparison of U.S. and Canadian legal and political develop-ments on lesbian and gay rights over this period highlights the contrast between the ease and rapidity of policy change in Canada compared to the relatively slow pace of policy change in the U.S. Political institutional factors play a major role in explaining the outcomes but also in explaining the process and timing of policy change. That is, a focus on the structuring influence of political institutional factors on policy change helps to explain not only the policy outcomes, as observed or measured in a particular time period, but also the *process* by which policy change is achieved and the *timing* of such change. The ease of policy change in Canada for lesbian and gay rights claimants was facilitated by the institutional factors that have been highlighted throughout this analysis: the jurisdictional divisions of the federal system that place criminal law and the determination of capacity to marry within federal jurisdiction, the lack of judicial federalism and the relatively unified court system, and the concentration of power in the parliamentary system in the hands of the executive, which is able to make decisions unhindered by considerations of direct legislative influence. In contrast, in the U.S., policy change is blocked by state control over the jurisdictions of criminal law and marriage; by judicial federalism, which creates conflicts among states over recognition of policy changes such as marriage; by the role of state constitutions with provisions for direct democracy and provisions for amendment which open up multiple opportunities for pre-emptive action or rollback by lesbian and gay rights opponents; and by the separation of powers system which gives legitimacy and weight to legislative solutions to policy problems. The thirty-five-year campaign for repeal of the sodomy laws that culminated in *Lawrence* may well provide a model for the pattern and the ultimate result to be expected from a long-term, state-by-state litigation and lobbying campaign by the U.S. marriage movement and by lesbian and gay social movement organizations on the issue of same-sex relationship recognition and same-sex marriage. We might well consider whether U.S. political culture and public opinion (and even the extent of American religiosity) are at least in part the products of a set of political institutions in which the Christian Right and other traditional religious groups have a broad array of institutional weapons with which to build and mobilize a mass political base. By considering the process and pace of political change as well as the macro-historical timing of social movement politics relative to the broad political context in which such movements arise, the enduring strength of political institutions as deep structures that set parameters for social movement strategies, claims and impact, is highlighted. With a comparative perspective, the distinctive features of U.S. political institutions are emphasized and their role in influencing social and political change in the U.S. is brought to light.

7 Conclusions: Historical Institutionalism and Lesbian and Gay Rights

In the summer of 2006, a group of LGBT scholars and activists in the U.S. issued a statement calling on the LGBT movement in the U.S. to move "beyond marriage." This statement, signed by scholarly luminaries such as Wendy Brown, Judith Butler, Lisa Duggan, John D'Emilio, and Jonathan Katz, among others, as well as by activists from some grassroots queer organizations, argued for an alternative vision of the role of the state in relationship recognition and called attention to a broad "pro-family" policy agenda that encompasses not only same-sex marriage but also abortion, contraception, the active promotion of heterosexual marriage, the moral regulation of single mothers, and attacks on the welfare state. The statement argued that the pursuit of same-sex marriage as a "stand-alone" issue permitted right-wing politicians and the Christian Right to exploit marriage as an issue of backlash politics, strengthening the attack on alternative forms of family, including not only the LGBT communities but also single parents and others living outside of conventional family structures. From a political standpoint, the authors of the statement pointed out that existing same-sex partner and parenting benefits had been rolled back in the backlash against same-sex marriage and, therefore, they argued that the movement should push for a much broader set of policy goals including: "[l]egal recognition for a wide range of relationships, households and families—regardless of kinship or conjugal status; [a]ccess for all, regardless of marital or citizenship status, to vital government support programs including but not limited to health care, housing, Social Security and pension plans, disaster recovery assistance, unemployment insurance, and welfare assistance; [s]eparation of church and state in all matters, including regulation and recognition of relationships, households and families; [and] [f]reedom from state regulation of our sexual lives and gender choices, identities and expression" (Beyond Marriage 2006).

As a "moral hot button," same-sex marriage has been used to signify a broader attack on gender and racial equality. While critiques of same-sex marriage are heard in Canada regarding the privileging of conjugal relationships in social policy, these critiques focus on the protection of queer cultures, especially of cultures based on resistance to sexual regulation by the state and on traditional lesbian feminist critiques of marriage (Herman 1989; Brown 2001; Cossman 2002; Kirby 2001; Boyd and Young 2003). Generally, criticisms of same-sex marriage in Canada from within the LGBT communities have not sought to link same-sex marriage with the politics of social inequality, let alone to unemployment, welfare, health care, disaster recovery, or immigration status, as in the U.S. statement. Suggestions to move Canadian social policy "beyond conjugality" have been principally circulated among legal academics and have found little currency outside legal circles (Law Commission 2001). The longstanding proposals by the Coalition for Lesbian and Gay Rights in Ontario (CLGRO) to move away from conjugal status in social policy have also received very little political support (CLGRO 2000). Even these cases form a marked contrast with Beyond Marriage because they do not link the issue of "gay rights" as a component of a right-wing morality attack on women, the poor, racial minorities, non-citizens, and other groups but focus solely on alternative family forms and the rights of single people without reference to broader issues of social and economic inequality, let alone race, gender, and immigration status.

These debates illustrate differences in the way that sexuality, race and gender are situated in partisan political debates in the U.S. and Canada and how the legacies of previous policies and the historical timing of the rise of the lesbian and gay movements in the two countries shaped the subsequent politics and policy evolution in the lesbian and gay area. Rather than defining lesbian and gay politics as a "moral hot button" that must be analyzed according to particular theories especially designed to explain "moral" issues, this book has interpreted lesbian and gay politics using the ordinary tools of comparative politics, especially the historical institutionalist approach. The historical institutionalist approach moves beyond a focus on policy discourse or the role of ideas in policy debates to situating policy outcomes within a long-term sweep of historical change.

The approach taken in this book is based on the view that all policy choices might be defined as having moral dimensions and that the label of "moral hot button" when applied to questions of capital punishment, abortion or gay rights, reflects a particular framing and definition of policy options. The framing of these issues as questions of conscience in itself reflects the gendered and racialized organization of knowledge in the academy, in which the study of marginalized peoples—women, racial minorities and queers—has often provoked battles over "political correctness" and over the very scholarly legitimacy of these topics. If different factors are indeed at work in explaining policy outcomes on "moral" issues, then this finding should be of interest to scholars of comparative public policy. If "issues of conscience" can be explained using the same sorts of theory we use to explain social and fiscal policy, then there is no need to frame these policy questions differently than we would frame our research questions concerning other types of policy outcomes. Public opinion studies show that the public defines same-sex marriage as a "moral" issue, meaning that the issue is not considered to be complicated and it is one about which ordinary people feel confident expressing an opinion about its "rightness" or "wrongness" (e.g., Lofton and Haider-Merkel 2007). Although this may be quite true, if we confine our analysis to treating religions and moral beliefs as static features of the political landscape, we are missing part of the story. Political cultural beliefs are produced through political conflict and struggle and, as this book has argued, these conflicts and struggles play out within particular institutional structures. Just as an historical institutionalist approach provides explanation of government spending or the evolution of the welfare state in the U.S., so too it is a fruitful approach for understanding conflicts on so-called "cultural issues." This study shows that the factors that have been used to explain the evolution of other types of policy outcomes, especially social policy outcomes, also apply in the area of lesbian and gay rights. By setting up a classic cross-national comparative analysis of similar systems, this study confirms longstanding conclusions about American political institutions—their built-in resistance to policy change, especially because of the separation of powers; the premium placed on incremental change and the resulting drift in the evolution of American public policy; the limits of judicial review in a system of multiple veto points; and the importance of the jurisdictional divisions of federalism in shaping the process of policy change and political mobilization in particular policy sectors. These conclusions, which reflect accumulated knowledge across a broad range of policy sectors including health, labour market, and social policy (Weir 1988; Maioni 1998; Hacker 2004; Pierson 2007), also apply in the area of lesbian and gay rights. The comparative and longitudinal analysis of policy change highlights the big and slow-moving processes (Pierson 2004: 54ff) and the influence of the less visible structural factors in producing policy change.

At the same time, by treating lesbian and gay politics as a subject of ordinary policy analysis rather than as a special "hot button" topic, this study also shows the links between sexuality and social policy development. In this sense, this study is inspired by and builds on the work of scholars such as Anna Marie Smith (2001), Cathy Cohen (1999) and others who have highlighted the intersections among race, gender and sexuality in political organizing and public policy. In particular, it does so by emphasizing the role of political parties and partisan conflict in framing debates on public policy, the differences between parties that, in part, are shaped by institutional differences and the role of the historical timing of social movements in relation to other social movements and other areas of policy change. The lesbian and gay movement arose in the U.S. and Canada in the same historical period, fuelled by similar sociological changes in the two very similar North American societies. However, the historical timing of the lesbian and gay movement intersected with a partisan backlash against the two most important social movement precursors to the lesbian and gay movement, namely, the civil rights movement and the women's movement. The lesbian and gay movement was the third in the sequence of these in the U.S. and was greatly affected by the outcome of the political battles that had already been fought or that were already in train at the time of arrival of the movement in the late 1960s and early 1970s. This is not simply a question of one social movement spinning off from another movement; rather, it is a question of the ways in which the gains and losses of other movements have shaped partisan conflict, electoral coalitions, policy discourse and configurations of public policy. As we have seen, U.S. criminal law and civil rights policies created unique obstacles for the lesbian and gay movement in the U.S.

By using the historical institutionalist approach the analysis points to the ways in which policy changes in the lesbian and gay area must be placed within the long-term historical context and considered in light of other social movements that have mobilized to achieve policy change through courts. The racialization of American politics has an important effect on lesbian and gay politics and creates barriers to public policy changes that would recognize lesbian and gay rights while, in Canadian politics, the processes of racialization have played out in a different way, solidifying the policy and partisan discourse of "Charter values" in ways that have strengthened lesbian and gay rights claims rather than undermining them. In the U.S., the legal legacy of chattel slavery and its aftermath resulted in a legal structure of equal protection into which lesbian and gay equality claimants must fit; in contrast, Canada's laggard status in the constitutional codification of its bill of rights ironically provided an easier legal pathway in the battle for lesbian and gay legal and political recognition. In turn, gender is linked to racialization because of the importance of the regulation of women's presumptively heterosexual sexuality in relation to racialized social policy provision. Debates over poverty and welfare reform in the U.S. since the 1960s have linked welfare dependency to family forms, and policies designed to shore up the heterosexual nuclear family have formed part of the most recent rounds of welfare reform in the U.S. The African American family has been a battleground for these social policy debates (Quadagno 2000; Reese 2001); in these debates, the existence of lesbian and gay people of color has been marginalized and erased, especially in the case of lesbians, parenting children as "single" parents (although, far from being "single," they may be living in same-sex relationships that are unrecognized by law and policy; Cahill and Tobias 2007). To the extent that queer sexuality challenges the heterosexual family, it is cast in this debate as a threat to family, social and even national stability. In contrast, in Canadian debates, lesbians and gays are embraced as emblematic of Canadian national identity, and same-sex marriage is treated as a marker of Canada's supposed tolerance and embrace of diversity (for example, Canada 2007).

The lesbian and gay rights movement arose in the U.S. and Canada during the same historical time period and, in fact, the spark for the gay liberation movement in English-speaking Canada was certainly provided by the example of Stonewall and the role of early radical liberation groups such as New York's Gay Liberation Front. The social movements were quite similar in the two countries during the early period as the radical forms of urban, grassroots organizing as well as the liberationist and/or (lesbian) feminist ideologies and goals were broadly similar. As we have seen, the lesbian and gay movement in the U.S. has been less successful than the Canadian movement, at least as measured by the three very important public policy goals that have long dominated the politics of the movement(s) in both countries: (de)criminalization of sexuality; anti-discrimination protection on the basis of sexual orientation; and legal recognition of same-sex relationships. While these three policy goals do not exhaust the policy repertoire of the gay liberation and lesbian feminist movements in the two countries, they are certainly very important goals for movement organizations over the time period covered in this book.

POLICY LEGACIES: SODOMY LAWS AND EQUAL PROTECTION DOCTRINE

The concept of the policy legacy has been used to refer to the ways in which policies make politics (see Pierson 2006). Past policies are institutionalized in ways that influence current debates. As Orloff (2005) has emphasized, policy legacies certainly do not dictate outcomes but, rather, create a number of different possibilities and pathways for political action and policy development. In particular, policy legacies and policy feedback can lead to social movement cycling, in which policies arouse and galvanize political opposition. This cycling is centrally important in explaining movements for political and legal recognition of marginalized and stigmatized groups because, as we have seen in other policy areas, when such groups obtain policy gains, this often sparks a countermovement, just as each policy move to recognize the rights of the marginalized has sparked a counterrevolution. However, unlike the pluralist approach, which emphasized the possibility that overly strong groups may arouse opposition, thus leading to a balance of forces over the long run (see LaVaque-Manty 2006), historical institutionalism calls attention to the idea that, once countermovements arise, their form, impact and influence will be shaped by the structure of existing policies and institutions. From this perspective, historical institutionalism explains stability more effectively than it explains change. This is certainly true of the concept of the policy legacy, which calls attention to the ways in which the past frames the present, but without shedding much light on the extent to which this occurs, how policy legacies are overcome, and how policy change occurs. As Weir, Orloff and Skocpol (1988) pointed out with regard to the idea of policy feedback, there is more than one possible reaction to a past policy (see the discussion in Orloff 2005). That is, while some policy legacies may generate feedback loops akin to those created by technological innovations, others may not. As Orloff puts it, citing Thelen's (1999) work, "most things political are not contingent at the outset, nor are decisions, once made, protected in perpetuity against recontestation as losers do not typically disappear" (Orloff 2005: 213). The analysis of this volume exemplifies this as social movement actors strongly contest lesbian and gay policy issues. Each step in the making of policy in this area is contested. Existing policy exerts a powerful inertial force but social movements contest these policies. As change occurs, backlash against new politics happens immediately, as the Christian Right and its conservative allies mobilize against lesbian and gay gains. Two key policy legacies, which have exerted an important inertial force on policymaking in this field, are the U.S. sodomy laws which existed at the time of the arrival of the lesbian and gay movement on the political scene in 1971 (but which did not exist in Canada during the same time period) and differences in legal doctrine between Canada and the U.S. Specifically, the Fourteenth Amendment constitutes a higher hurdle for the recognition of lesbian and gay rights in the U.S. than does section 15 of the Canadian Charter.

First, the fact that sodomy laws remained on the books in the U.S. created substantial obstacles to the recognition of lesbian and gay rights throughout the first long period of lesbian and gay organizing in the U.S. and Canada, a period that spans the transformation of the homophile movement into the modern lesbian and gay rights movement, signified by the Stonewall riots of 1969, through to the *Lawrence* decision in 2003. The state-by-state battle to reform sodomy laws in the U.S. took up the resources of the U.S. lesbian and gay movement; however, as Tina Fetner's (forthcoming) work highlights, the process of cycling against the sodomy laws also led to the establishment of strong national organizations, which could coordinate state-by-state campaigns. The ongoing stigma of the criminalization of homosexual sex in many states made it more difficult for the lesbian and gay movement in the U.S. to claim rights across a broad range of areas ranging from anti-discrimination laws to education to parenting. The criminal stigma reinforced the distinction between the evangelical discourse of "hating the sin" but "loving the sinner," reinforced in American legal doctrine through the distinction between conduct and status. By distinguishing conduct and status, American law and policy attempted to carve out a space for lesbian and gay rights in a context in which the defining characteristic of lesbian and gay identity—sexuality—was included as potentially criminal behavior, at least in some states. To assert that discrimination should be unconstitutional against a class that—by definition—engaged in conduct deemed criminal was a challenge. While the sodomy laws left a policy legacy in which social movement actors cycled against law in order to change it and eventually succeeded in doing so, they also left a very strong legacy in legal and policy discourse in the U.S. of the conduct/status distinction. By distinguishing conduct and status, there was more political space in the U.S. for the view that homosexuals may be tolerated but that homosexual relationships and families could still be considered inferior to heterosexual families and for the view that rights cannot be recognized for people who engage in criminal conduct (hence, demands for "special rights"). Given the criminal stigma of the sodomy laws, it was clearly legitimate to promote the heterosexual nuclear family in law and policy and to express concern over the public expression of homosexuality, which might be defined as promoting criminal behavior. Therefore, in U.S. policy, it is more legitimate to tolerate homosexuals while openly holding that homosexuality is inferior to heterosexuality. As Wendy Brown (2006) has argued, tolerance can be a means by which superiority is asserted. In the lesbian and gay area in the U.S., this form of tolerance as a means of asserting superiority was reinforced by the criminal stigma of the sodomy laws.

These dynamics can be seen at work in many of the events, cases and debates discussed in this book. As discussed in Chapter 2, the initial proposals for law reform in both the U.S. and Canada emphasized the importance of separating law and morality. In the proposals for criminal law reform made by legal elites in both Canada and the U.S. and in the British Wolfenden Report that was so influential in defining the legal terrain, especially for Canadian lawmakers, there was no endorsement of homosexuality. It was clear that homosexuality was a behavior to be tolerated in private and there was no suggestion that it would be viewed as equivalent to heterosexuality and family as it was defined in the 1950s and 1960s. However, the reform of the Criminal Code in Canada facilitated the claims-making of the lesbian and gay movement, which, especially in the strategies of the gay liberation movement of the 1970s, precisely claimed that "gay is good," attempting to reverse the stigma and to reclaim and proclaim queer identities. Although there were many attempts to police the public identities and communities of gays and lesbians in the 1970s and 1980s in Canada— the bath raids in Toronto, the charges against *The Body Politic* and other examples—these attempts to police public sex and to reinforce the zone of privacy for the tolerance of homosexuality were burdened by the fact that there was nothing "wrong" with homosexual behavior in private and it was widely known that it was perfectly "legal." This opening in the political and legal system provided the leverage for the gay and lesbian rights claims of the 1970s, which began the process of creating the Canadian lesbian and gay community as a rights-seeking and rights-claiming community. This effort was to flower in the 1980s and 1990s, a period in which the U.S. lesbian and gay community continued to battle against the sodomy laws and devoted its energies and resources to a state-by-state campaign to repeal the laws through legislative means and to locate and pursue cases that might lead to the repeal of the *Bowers* decision. This effort, which took almost thirty-five years, finally reached its fruition in *Lawrence* in 2003.

Second, the concept of the policy legacy also plays out through legal doctrine and jurisprudence. The idea that the past decisions of courts influence the current decisions of courts is nothing new to students of judicial behavior. In fact, much of the study of judicial behavior has concerned itself with moving away from this positive view of law, in which judges are expected to apply the general principles of law to specific situations, toward a view of judicial behavior in which judges are understood to be influenced by their attitudes, policy preferences, or audiences (Baum 2006). The realist view of judicial behavior distinguishes norms such as *stare decisis* in common law, in which the judges follow past decisions and jurisprudence develops incrementally over a long period of time, from what the realists view as a more accurate depiction in which legal doctrines are not the sole explanation of judicial behavior but merely provide the justification for policy preferences, judicial performance, or strategic behavior. In contrast, this work suggests that the law itself and legal doctrines used by the courts to interpret and apply it are important in understanding the process of legal mobilization by social movements and countermovements and to understanding the political claims and clamor, policy discourse, and partisan conflict over the public policy issues that reach the courts. Legal doctrine constitutes a specific type of policy legacy, in which past policies that have been encoded in rules of legal interpretation that set the parameters of contemporary policy debates and frame the policy narratives in which political actors, including social movement claimants, must cast their claims.

In the U.S./Canada comparison, the differences between the equal protection doctrine of the Fourteenth Amendment and section 15 of the Charter are particularly important. American equal protection doctrine is inveterately connected to the question of race, as the very purpose of the Fourteenth Amendment was to provide for equal protection for blacks in the postbellum era. From the outset, this forms a stark contrast with the Canadian Charter, which was written a century after the Fourteenth Amendment and two centuries after the U.S. Bill of Rights. While the Bill of Rights provided for individual rights for an agricultural society under limited government, the Canadian Charter was designed for a postindustrial society with a developed welfare state. Whatever the intentions of the framers of the Fourteenth Amendment and whatever the debates that occurred in initially defining the meaning of the Amendment during and after the Reconstruction era, the provision evolved in the contemporary era into a threefold classification in which, for obvious historical reasons, race was defined as a suspect class, requiring strict scrutiny. As cases on the basis of sex and sexual orientation were litigated, sex was defined as a quasi-suspect class requiring intermediate scrutiny and other classifications (such as sexual orientation) invoked at most the weakest level of protection. The Canadian Charter and the Canadian constitution in general might be understood to have similar hierarchies of rights and constitutional recognition, and the interplay of factors such as language and nation have been central for the evolution of the Canadian approach to equality rights as race has been for the American approach to civil rights. Language and education rights for official language minority communities have a special place in the Canadian constitutional order. However, section 15 of the Charter, which is analogous to the Fourteenth Amendment, includes each ground of discrimination on the same footing and provides for equal protection and equal benefit of the law for all without discrimination on a list of named grounds, including race and sex. By leaving the list of grounds open-ended, the Charter's framers admitted the possibility that additional grounds could be added on the same footing with the named grounds and, indeed, this is how sexual orientation came to be included in the Charter.

For lesbians and gays in the U.S., it has been much more challenging to gain entry to the Fourteenth Amendment given the hierarchical classification system. The fact that strict scrutiny has been reserved for race-based classification has privileged a discourse of legal claims-making in which every other group must cast their claims in terms of analogies to race. This encourages politically explosive analogies between race and sexual orientation as categories, encourages claims based on the supposed "immutability" of sexual orientation, and reifies and reinforces the boundary lines between race, sex, and sexual orientation, rather than opening up conversations on intersectionality. The Fourteenth Amendment was passed at a time when basic legal and political equality for African Americans was in doubt and aimed to ensure that gross violations of civil rights such as the denial of the right to vote did not occur. In contrast, the Canadian Charter was passed during a historical period in which legal and political citizenship rights for minority groups were no longer in question. The historical analogies that are entwined in the jurisprudence of the Fourteenth Amendment inevitably encounter the legal roots of widespread chattel slavery in the U.S. while, in contrast, the Canadian Charter does not encounter this legal legacy.

In this respect, it is noteworthy that almost every legal case on same-sex marriage in the U.S. makes reference to the civil rights struggle and almost every issue that touches lesbian and gay rights has some link to struggles for racial equality. For example, marriage cases in the U.S. almost always refer to interracial marriage. The right to marry or the right to intimate association, which are important in same-sex marriage litigation in the U.S., do not play the same role in Canadian law and, to the extent that the zone of privacy is recognized, it does not receive the constitutional protection of the "right to privacy" doctrine in the U.S. More broadly, the analogy between gay and lesbian struggles and civil rights struggles is politically challenging for the LGBT movement in the U.S. in a number of ways, making it difficult to form alliances with African Americans and difficult to politically mobilize LGBT people of color, especially African Americans, in political struggles which deploy the analogy or language of the civil rights struggle (for example, references to lesbian and gay "civil rights"). These struggles do not exist in the same form in Canada. In Canadian litigation on same-sex marriage, relationship recognition and other aspects of lesbian and gay rights, there is very little reference to the debate on the origins of homosexuality or to the immutability question. In contrast, in the U.S., the immutability of race, as it has been jurisprudentially understood, is apparently central to the claims for justice and equality. In contrast, Canadian litigation on section 15 issues reflects a different understanding of rights and diversity. There is no need to demonstrate that homosexuality is something that is biologically determined or immutable or somehow not the "fault" of the person who is "different" from the mainstream. The discourse of immutability seems to suggest that claims to racial equality (or gender equality) are legitimate because, after all, being black or female is a matter of biology, not a "lifestyle" choice. In this highly racialized and gendered construction, claims to justice and equality are based on the fact that people cannot help being somehow deviant or different from the white heterosexual male norm.

Furthermore, the application of the Fourteenth Amendment to the states and the eventual application of equal protection doctrine in areas of private discrimination such as employment was a long political struggle in the U.S. While Title VII of the Civil Rights Act of 1964 prohibits discrimination in employment as well as other areas, the grounding for the regulation of private discrimination has taken place through a highly racialized discussion of affirmative action, one that has solidified and reinforced the partisan attack on "liberalism" and "big government." U.S. policies on affirmative action open up the charge that such measures provide special rights for minorities at the expense of whites and are part of a partisan package of backlash politics that constructs crime and welfare as racialized urban problems. Rather than building racial solidarities, U.S. social policies have reflected and contributed to the racialization of U.S. politics. In this way, the regulation of private discrimination in the U.S. is a perilous political and legal project and the fragile protections against private discrimination in the U.S. for all groups constitute a powerful policy legacy for lesbian and gay citizens. Demands for protection against discrimination for lesbian and gay citizens are thrown into the cauldron of racially coded "special rights" and the Christian Right has cleverly appealed to white Americans by stating that civil rights are for those who "really" need it—namely, African Americans—and not for "specially privileged" groups such as rich gay (white) men. Yet, despite the professed concern of the Christian Right for "real" civil rights, the partisan attacks of the right-wing political machine in the U.S. over welfare, crime, affirmative action, abortion, and the traditional family constitutes a white backlash against the gains of the civil rights movement as well as a reassertion of traditional male patriarchal authority against the gains of the women's movement. The policy legacies of these conflicts in the U.S. has meant that claims for anti-discrimination measures in the U.S. for lesbians and gays face obstacles that do not exist in the Canadian case. The development of independent human rights commissions and human rights legislation across the Canadian provinces helped to shape the debate on human rights conversation in Canada and provided the institutional and discursive grounding for the advent of the Charter. The Charter governs the operation of human rights legislation in every Canadian jurisdiction and ensures that protections against private discrimination are systematically implemented in every jurisdiction, providing institutional openings for claims of redress from discrimination, despite the defects in its implementation and despite ongoing problems of racism in Canadian society (Howe and Johnston 2000).

Policy legacies are not cast in stone. In the U.S., the lesbian and gay movement has developed specialized and professional organizations ranging from Lambda Legal as a litigation fund to broad human rights organizations such as the Task Force and the Human Rights Campaign. These organizations represent social movement cycling against policy legacies. However, as such organizations mobilize in the U.S. political systm, they face a unique set of barriers which do not exist in Canada. These barriers shape the politics of political mobilization by social movement organizations as they confront the legacy of previous policies.

FEDERALISM: JURISDICTIONAL DIFFERENCES AND SUB-STATE CONSTITUTIONS

While courts have captured most of the attention in discussions of lesbian and gay rights in the U.S., federalism plays a surprisingly important role in explaining cross-national policy difference in this area, and federal structure of political institutions in the U.S. and Canada must be considered in conjunction with the role of the executive, the legislature and political parties in evaluating the impact of court decisions on the evolution of public policy. The analysis here has emphasized several important aspects of federalism as a political institutional structure in the lesbian and gay rights policy area. To begin, the jurisdictional division of powers between the federal and sub-state governments in this policy area favors the federal government in the Canadian system, while at the same time it favors state governments in the U.S. system. Thus, although we might generally consider American federalism to be more centralized than Canadian federalism, in this area, American federalism constantly shows its confederal origins and the influence of states' rights doctrine. In particular, the states have jurisdiction over criminal law, which, in itself, vastly complicates the process of achieving criminal law reform throughout the U.S. In order to change the sodomy laws, a state-by-state battle was necessary, given the jurisdictional division of powers whereas, in Canada, the criminal law could be changed through the action of the federal government. In the area of same-sex marriage and relationship recognition, the question of who has the right to marry lies within federal jurisdiction in Canada and in state jurisdiction in the U.S. This jurisdictional difference eased the path to same-sex marriage in Canada, given that there was no need for a province-by-province battle, once the federal government had decided to act. At the same time, the assignment of jurisdiction to the federal level in Canada combined with the concentration of power in the Westminster parliamentary system also generated blame-avoiding behavior by governments of Canada in the case of the same-sex marriage cases. While in the case of criminal law reform, the federal government under the dynamic leadership of Pierre Trudeau was able to lead in the area of law reform, packaging the legalization of homosexuality along with no-fault divorce as a reflection of the changing era of the 1960s, Liberal governments of the 2000s were pushed into action by the decisions of courts, which made lesbian and gay rights into a quintessential Charter issue. In this way, the role of federalism intersected with the role of courts.

The jurisdictional division of powers in the federal system affects the influence of courts. Judicial federalism in the U.S. gives lesbian and gay plaintiffs a choice of venue; however, the same dynamics also raise the costs of achieving a floor for lesbian and gay rights that will prevail throughout the U.S. The role and relative power of state courts in the U.S. has facilitated the conversation on lesbian and gay rights in the U.S. as, especially on the marriage issue, state courts have been in the forefront of litigation and have rendered important decisions not only with regard to the right to marry but on the recognition of same-sex civil unions and marriages. The federal structure of U.S. courts (compared to the unitary structure of Canadian courts) and the state jurisdiction over same-sex marriage (compared to the federal jurisdiction in Canada) has made this possible. The jurisdictional divisions on two of the major policy areas for lesbian and gay rights—criminal law and marriage law—demonstrate the two sides of the arguments on the impact of federalism on policy development—that federalism retards policy change by creating multiple obstacles to change and that federalism spreads policy innovation by permitting one state to innovate while others follow suit through policy 'spread' and policy diffusion. When the jurisdictional division of powers permits policy spread and diffusion in a federal system, this can produce policy outcomes that would not otherwise come through concerted federal action. In this sense, states can circumvent laggard national governments and produce policy innovation from below. However, this process of diffusion and spread is incremental and slow-moving in the U.S., especially because of the multiple access points of the separation of powers system. Battles are fought in each state and, within each state there are multiple veto points as social movement organizations compete to influence state courts and legislatures. In contrast, in Canada, provincial governments are organized on the Westminster parliamentary model so that, as in the federal government, power is concentrated in the executive. In addition, provincial courts in Canada are not organized in a separate judicial system as they are in the U.S. Policy spread can take place quickly in the Canadian federal system where provincial governments have more institutional capacity for concerted political action. In the U.S., policy diffusion through the states is a slow process because of multiple institutional barriers and jurisdictional divisions. Just as the policy change in sodomy laws took over thirty years, so too with same-sex marriage, we may expect the same time frame in producing policy changes in the U.S. federal system.

State constitutions similarly provide obstacles and opportunities, although each of these has its own distinctive pacing during the period under consideration here. State constitutions are amended much more frequently than the federal constitution, in part the result of the fact that the amending process is much simpler at the state level, usually involving fewer veto points and, in some cases, occurring in a smaller and more homogeneous political environment (Tarr 1998). The ease of state amendment has been a boon and a bane to the lesbian and gay movement in the U.S. Because of the ease of amendment, many states have adopted expansive bills of rights that recognize specific forms of civil rights and have been fruitfully used by the lesbian and gay movement such as explicit right-to-privacy provisions or equal rights amendments in the era of new judicial federalism. Further, state courts have located lesbians and gays within specific and sometimes unique provisions of state constitutions and have used the lever of state constitutional protections of various types to recognize lesbian and gay rights. As we have seen in this book, this occurred in the key same-sex marriage cases in Hawai'i, Vermont, and Massachusetts. In Hawai'i, the state's ERA opened up arguments about equality based on sex, which could be deemed to include sexual orientation. In Vermont, the equal benefits clause of the state constitution was used to argue that same-sex couples could not be denied the benefits of marriage under the state constitution. In *Goodridge*, the equal protection provisions of the Massachusetts constitution provided a lever for the plaintiffs. In this way, the existence of state constitutions affords an additional layer of potential political opportunity for advocates of lesbian and gay rights in state courts.

On the other side, however, state constitutions also create long-term barriers to policy success for lesbian and gay rights advocates. As we have seen, direct democracy in many state constitutions provides critically important openings for the Christian Right and other opponents of lesbian and gay rights. Many studies of the political process of claims-making for lesbian and gay citizens have emphasized that, for this group, as for women and racial minorities in the U.S., majority rule through the institutions of the legislature is inimical to effective rights protections, while a strong system of judicial review and executive political leadership (sometimes working in tandem) are the most effective institutional mechanisms for policy change (Werum and Winders 2001). The direct democracy that is built into many state constitutions is inimical to lesbian and gay rights because it provides political openings for well-resourced and well-organized Christian Right movement organizations to mobilize to roll-back decisions that have been made by courts or, in some cases, by executive order. This has taken place along a number of different policy pathways. In some cases, ballot initiatives were undertaken to pass state laws that forestalled anti-discrimination protection for lesbians and gays, in others to repeal anti-discrimination ordinances that had already been passed (Anita Bryant's campaign in Dade County in the 1970s). In other cases, state constitutional amendments were proposed and passed to forestall anti-discrimination protections (Colorado's Amendment 2), same-sex marriage and other forms of relationship recognition for same-sex partners. The waves of DOMAs and state marriage bans around the time of the federal DOMA in 1996 and again after the *Goodridge* decision were facilitated by state constitutional provisions. All of these countermeasures depended on the existence of state constitutions, either because state constitutional amendment was the institutional mechanism used to strike down, repeal, or prevent the legal recognition of lesbian and gay rights claims or because state constitutions provided for measures of direct democracy such as ballot initiatives. In contrast, in Canada, there are no freestanding provincial constitutions and there are no institutional mechanisms for ballot initiatives, referenda or provincial constitutional conventions.

With regard to the impact of federalism, it is particularly important to note the differences in pacing that affect the balance of opportunity and obstacle that are provided in federal systems. If we view the issue of same-sex marriage in the U.S. over the longer time span such as the fifty-year period beginning with the first *Baehr* decision in 1993, it is quite conceivable that same-sex marriage will slowly spread throughout the states through a process of policy diffusion, pushed by the movement of married couples from Massachusetts to other states and the process of constant legal challenge posed by couples who are married outside the U.S. and who challenge U.S. law for legal recognition of their relationships. While civil union may provide an in-between policy option in some states, whether it is called civil union or marriage, at some point there will be a federal case to challenge the exclusion of same-sex partnerships from recognition in federal law as such exclusion clearly creates an explicit and material inequality between opposite-sex and same-sex relationships, one that cannot be easily defended in constitutional terms under existing state constitutions or under federal equal protection. The prospect of such diffusion through the states inspired the 1996 DOMA and the proposed Federal Marriage Amendment, which are attempts to lock in the exclusion of same-sex couples from family rights. As more children make their home in families with same-sex parents, whether through adoption or through the use of new reproductive technologies and as more opposite-sex partners and single women undertake reproduction using new technologies rather than traditional biological means, the idea of discriminating against such children on the basis of their adopted status or their biological origin will eventually become constitutionally problematic. The children raised in these families have shown every sign of mobilizing themselves as a new social movement and children of new reproductive technologies have also begun pushing for the right to know their biological fathers; these new movements will push the frontiers in legal recognition of new forms of family that move away from the opposite-sex "biological"[1] model of parents and children (see Colage 2007; Scherpe 2007). As this occurs, the legal and material inequalities in these family forms will have to be addressed in law.

Federalism provides "multiple cracks" at policy influence (Grodzins 1982) and the marriage movement among U.S. lesbians and gays is powerful and well resourced. Despite the seeming successes of the Christian Right in the Bush era, public opinion in the U.S. is moving in the direction of recognizing lesbian and gay rights claims and this trend has occurred despite the resources and political power of the Christian Right in American politics since the 1970s (Craig et al. 2005). However, the process of policy diffusion of lesbian and gay rights recognition is slow-moving and invisible, in Pierson's (1994) terms, while the processes of policy blockage in the states are small, fast-paced and highly visible in electoral politics. The quick passage of DOMAs and other anti-gay and lesbian initiatives following the *Goodridge* decision shows how the institutional mechanisms of the system favor the short-term victories of the Christian Right while the slower and less visible diffusion of the same-sex marriage debate throughout the U.S. from the time of the initial *Baehr* decision in 1993 has been a longer term process of change on a state-by-state level. Similarly, the changes to the sodomy laws in the U.S. occurred state-by-state in a process of gradual policy change, beginning in the 1970s and ending with the *Lawrence* decision in 2003. We may expect the same gradual diffusion of lesbian and gay rights recognition across the U.S. states as a longer term, gradual, and incremental process, stopped and started, periodically, by Christian Right and conservative exploitation of ballot initiatives, state constitutional amendment, and other institutional mechanisms, but, fundamentally driven by the a very large number of small cases in which individual lesbians and gays push for legal recognition throughout all the points of access of the U.S. legal system and across a broad range of areas of claim.

SEPARATION OF POWERS: ACCESS AND AVENUES

The differences between parliamentary and separation of powers systems play a key role as in other policy areas (Pal and Weaver 2003). The lines of accountability in the parliamentary system may also make the executive cautious of offending extremes. The concentration of accountability in the parliamentary system also concentrates blame. As the executive is clearly responsible for having undertaken a given measure, the executive will receive the political backlash and will be held accountable by political opponents. In the Canadian federal system, majority governments usually circumvent this problem by exploiting the two limitations on the executive's authority: federalism and judicial review. A determined executive that wishes to avoid blame may design policies that download blame to provinces or, alternatively, take action after having been forced to act through court decisions. In the case of lesbian and gay human rights, the courts play a key role in re-framing the issue in terms of human rights and in forcing majority governments to act in reaction to court decisions, allowing majority governments to deflect the blame by stating, "the courts made us do it." Similarly, in the U.S., the separation of powers system, checks and balances, and limitations and roadblocks to policy change offer innumerable opportunities for lesbian and gay rights opponents to stop policy change. As discussions of divided government in the U.S. have made clear, the separation of powers does not stop policy innovation when there is a broad agreement on policy goals; however, when there is division and disagreement, divided government impedes concerted action (Mayhew 2005: 139).

Political institutions in the parliamentary system concentrate the political blame for politicians at the centre in responding to courts, forcing politicians, especially government leaders, to take responsibility for their reactions to the decisions of courts. Successive Liberal governments engaged in just such blame-avoidance behavior in response to the same-sex marriage cases. In a 1999 motion in the House and again in 2000 when the Liberal government passed the Modernization of Benefits and Obligations Act (MBOA) to equalize the benefits and obligations of common law same-sex partners, the Liberals agreed with a heterosexual definition of marriage. In a preamble to MBOA, the government asserted that nothing in the bill would affect the definition of marriage. And, indeed, the Liberal government chose to present a strong case against same-sex marriage in the Ontario and B.C. same-sex marriage cases, although it ultimately decided not to appeal those cases.

When the Liberal government referred the question of the constitutionality of same-sex marriage to the Supreme Court of Canada in 2004, the Liberals were following a longstanding pattern—a pattern they had followed throughout the Chrétien era—of consistently referring this question to the court and acting only in response to court decisions. Early on, back in the mid-1990s, the government had not even wanted to add sexual orientation to federal human rights legislation and did so only after a pattern of lower court decisions made it clear that the Supreme Court would inevitably force the government to do so (Smith 1998). This pattern of blame-avoidance behavior that was designed to defuse the issue of same-sex marriage within the Liberal caucus—shifted the responsibility back to the court and enabled Chrétien to manage his caucus. This interaction between the Liberal government and the courts demonstrates that exploring the relationship between courts and legislatures by focusing on the role of Parliament or the role of "legislatures" (in the abstract) misses the fact that, of course, it is the government of the day that dominates the legislature. The dialogue is not between the legislature and the courts in the most meaningful sense but between the government of the day and the courts. Political parties and partisan conflict play an important role, as different political parties will deal with court decisions differently, according to their electoral calculus. In the U.S., the executive's authority is more limited and the legislature is wide open to compromise proposals, log rolling, coalition building and lobbying, all of which defuse the responsibility for policy decisions and provide multiple openings for opponents of court rulings to influence policy and the framing of policy issues.

The organization of political parties is also linked to the structure of political institutions. In the separation of powers system, political parties are undisciplined and reasonably weak as autonomous organizations. In particular, political parties do not have strong control over the positions taken by individual candidates or over the votes of their caucus members in Congress. Because of campaign financing laws in the U.S., candidates are independent of the party apparatus and are able to raise money from a wide range of sources. Individual candidates act as independent entrepreneurs who seek electoral support and financing on their own and who take positions in direct response to lobbying and electoral/financial pressure from powerful backers. Until recently, this system has strongly favored the Christian Right, which has been able to mobilize the money, organization and political strategies to pressure candidates and which has profited from its association with a broad range of right-wing think tanks and lobby groups with deep pockets. In contrast, lesbian and gay organizations, while highly organized, well funded, and professionalized compared to such organizations in other countries, including Canada, have not been able to exercise the same level of political, financial, and electoral pressure on individual candidates and have been disadvantaged by the relative financial and strategic weaknesses of progressive nonprofits, lobby groups, and think tanks in the Bush era. The polarization of American politics has penalized the groups that have been traditionally excluded such as lesbians and gays, minorities, women, and the poor. The independence of the candidate from the party in the U.S. separation of powers system has enabled the Christian Right and other conservatives to intervene very forcefully in the electoral process and to influence primary campaigns. As have other right-wing groups, the Christian Right has threatened candidates in the Republican primary who do not agree with its views, contributing to the demise of moderate Republicans in the Bush era (Hacker and Pierson 2005). In contrast, in Canada, the Westminster system creates incentives for disciplined party behavior. Because Canadian voter volatility is very high, parties tend to be even more disciplined than political parties in other Westminster systems as they seek to sing with one voice in order to capture a fickle and constantly shifting electorate (Carty, Cross and Young 2000). Therefore, there are far fewer chances for any organized groups from the outside to influence the development of party policy or candidate positions, let alone the behavior of parties in the legislature.

COURTS AS POLICY ACTORS

In the area of lesbian and gay rights, courts have played a critically important role in shaping policy. This study drives home the point that courts are more likely to recognize lesbian and gay rights than other political actors. In the U.S. and Canada, elected politicians are unlikely to go to bat for the rights of beleaguered minority groups, unless the minority group is territorially concentrated and able to exercise the franchise. African Americans and other minorities in the U.S. have enjoyed some political influence through the electoral system, at least in the post-Jim Crow era while, in Canada, francophones have exerted political influence in Canadian politics in part because of their influence as a territorially concentrated voting bloc in federal electoral politics. However, even territorially concentrated minorities with voting rights may find themselves captured by a particular political party, as has long been the case for African Americans and the Democratic Party (Frymer 1999). Judicial review and enforcement of constitutionally guaranteed rights is one means by which minorities may obtain protection, despite their political vulnerability in the electoral process. Although most knowledgeable observers argue that the U.S. Supreme Court has moved in a more conservative direction since 1980, the U.S. Supreme Court did rule in favor of lesbian and gay rights recognition in *Lawrence*. Furthermore, many state courts in the U.S. have recognized lesbian and gay rights in various forms, as we have seen throughout this volume and, in fact, the Hawai'i decision in *Baehr* in 1993 as well as the decision of the Massachusetts Supreme Judicial Court in *Goodridge* were very influential in shaping the debate in the U.S., in Canada, and, indeed, around the world in terms of their impact on the same-sex marriage debate. Therefore, U.S. courts cannot be dismissed as uniformly hostile to lesbian and gay rights or as irredeemably and uniformly "conservative," at least not over the period covered in this book.

Much of the scholarship on law and courts in political science is concerned principally with what courts do and why they do it, that is, with the types of decisions they produce (Spaeth, Segal and Benesh 2005; Baum 2006). This scholarship is based on the assumption that what courts say and the decisions they reach are important. Certainly, understanding why courts in Canada have so unabashedly embraced lesbian and gay rights is one part of the puzzle of explaining policy differences between Canada and the U.S. However, as we have seen, U.S. courts have also been willing to embrace same-sex marriage and other forms of lesbian and gay rights recognition. An analysis that centres solely on explaining differences in judicial behavior explains only part of the story of the development of policy variation. In order to explain policy variation, we must examine not only the decisions of courts, but also the effects of these decisions on the evolution of public policy. As has been demonstrated in other work on law and courts such as that of Gerald Rosenberg (1991) on the U.S. and Janet Hiebert (2002) on Canada, what courts say is rarely the end of the story on how policies are determined. Other political actors react to court decisions and the policy influence and impact of courts decisions rests on the reaction of the other political actors. Political parties and social movements operate with structured sets of political institutions, themselves encoded with the legacies of previous policies and governed by meta-institutional rules and norms that govern their interactions. Court decisions have a different meaning in a political system in which such decisions are limited to a territorially defined sub-state level, vulnerable to limitations or rollback through state constitutional amendment, appealed to other or higher courts, or circumvented or struck down through action of other levels of government. Measures of direct democracy such as ballot initiative, combined with the relative ease of constitutional amendment at the state level, create institutional levers for pushback against court decisions in the U.S. that do not exist in Canada. The checks and balances in U.S. political institutions limit the power of the courts, while Canadian courts, operating within a structure of political institutions, have fewer limits and constraints and are more easily able to rapidly reshape law and policy. While Canada is a federal system, it has become a unitary political space for the purpose of human rights policies, given the application of the Charter to provincial as well as federal action. Because the Charter covers provincial government action as well as federal government action, it sets limits on law and policy at the provincial level on human rights, including the operation of human rights commissions. In the U.S., judicial enforcement is limited with regard to private discrimination; federal enforcement faces many obstacles and its influence is often limited to cases in which private organizations have received federal funding or where interstate commerce is involved.

The impact of judicial federalism in the U.S. is also of prime importance. Judicial federalism creates complexities for litigation as there are two areas of jurisdiction that must be considered in bringing cases to courts. In the area of lesbian and gay rights, there are many key issues that fall into state jurisdiction and, thus, under the jurisdiction of state courts. In the U.S. civil rights experience, strong action in implementation and enforcement of civil rights has come from the federal government. While the role of progressive state courts in recognizing same-sex marriage has been important to the evolution of this policy issue, the unified jurisdiction of Canadian courts facilitated litigation *en masse* against the federal government in the three most populous provinces, where litigants were ready, willing and, indeed, eager to come forward. Courts in one province were bound to take into account the decisions of courts in other provinces and the federal government was easily pressured to create uniformity on the same-sex marriage issue because of its constitutional jurisdiction over the issue. The system of judicial federalism combined with the specific allocation of constitutional jurisdiction in the important areas of lesbian and gay rights policy such as criminal law and marriage greatly enhance the decentralized and fragmented process of policy-making in the U.S. In the end, the U.S. may arrive at the same destination as Canada, in the sense that policy changes such as sodomy law reform, anti-discrimination laws, and relationship recognition have proceeded across the states in the forty years since Stonewall. Change has occurred and, even in the case of criminal law reform and despite the decision in *Bowers*, many states eliminated sodomy laws (especially those against homosexuals) over the period between the 1986 decision and the *Lawrence* decision in 2003. However, the process in the U.S. is long and expensive for the lesbian and gay movement.

TIME AND TIMING: TRACING THE PROCESSES OF POLICY CHANGE

Time and timing are important elements in historical institutionalist analysis. In contrast to the statics of political culture arguments, which take nationally bounded political culture as given at a particular time, historical institutionalism emphasizes the dynamics of the interactions between institutions and political actors as they unfold in historical time. The lesbian and gay movements in the U.S. and Canada arose in the same historical period; however, they encountered very different structures of political institutions and the legacies of very different policies with respect to civil/human rights. In the U.S., the policy legacies of the 1960s created additional obstacles for the lesbian and gay rights movement while, in Canada, the policy legacies of the conflicts of this period had the very opposite effect. The partisan political environment was much more favorable for lesbian and gay rights claims in Canada while the partisan environment in the U.S. was very negative for the movement.

Some of this political context is captured by the notion of the "political opportunity structure," a concept used in social movement theory to capture the idea that social movements may be more or less successful in achieving their goals depending on opportunities and obstacles in the movement's external environment (see Kitschelt 1986; Tarrow 1998). However, the political process model treats the external environment as one undifferentiated category, without specifying the features of the external environment that may impede or facilitate movements. The analysis of this volume shows that specific institutional features of the political system such as the separation of powers, federalism, and constitutional rules play an important role in particular policy sectors and thus the analysis challenges political process theory to develop a more nuanced view of the specific role of political institutional factors in the external environment of social movement activism, an analysis that is especially pertinent in the context of institutionally stable democracies such as the U.S. and Canada. In addition, the analysis here suggests that social movement theory builds on historical institutionalism in considering the question of historical timing in the life of social movements. For the lesbian and gay movement in the U.S., the timing of its arrival relative to the backlash against the civil rights movement and the Great Society policies of the Johnson Administration disadvantaged the movement. For the lesbian and gay movement in Canada, the timing of it's arrival relative to the constitutional entrenchment of the Charter was incredibly fortuitous and advantaged the movement in making claims for legal recognition and equality. In contrast, the promotion of the rights frame in Canada is increasingly tied to national projects in both English-speaking Canada and Quebec. In English-speaking Canada, same-sex marriage is increasingly seen as a marker of Canadian tolerance when compared to the U.S., playing the same role that Medicare once played in contrasting the more communitarian Canada with the individualistic U. S. (Adams 2003). In the field of public discourse, it has become more difficult for same-sex marriage opponents to openly vaunt the superiority of heterosexuality. The popularity of the Charter of Rights and the rights frame it promotes have solidified a new legal regime for same-sex couples, which has become a source of national pride for a substantial majority and has undermined support for the Conservative Party and the Christian Right. In Quebec, tolerance of homosexuality has long been used to distinguish a progressive Quebec from a conservative English-speaking Canada, at least since the Quiet Revolution, although progressive nationalist discourse often elides the complexities of homophobia in Quebec society and history (Stychin 1998). The unanimous support for the passage of the same-sex civil union bill in 1999 and the passage of the bill on same-sex parenting rights in 2002 have been cited as evidence of the tolerance of Quebecers compared to English Canadians and Americans. In this sense, support for same-sex marriage and lesbian and gay rights is encoded in the otherwise dueling nationalisms of English-speaking Canada and Quebec. Although the rights frame suggests equality between heterosexuals and homosexuals, most of the debate in Canada has centered on the rights of same-sex couples compared to heterosexual couples, rather than the rights of the individuals (Cossman 2002).

In considering the role of time and timing, it is also important to consider the pacing of policy change. In a recent article, Ronald Kahn has argued that Supreme Court decision-making moves at a different pace from other political developments and has called attention to the time disjuncture between the glacial pace of change in law in relation to other political institutions such as the executive and legislatures (Kahn 2006). This observation recognizes the importance of pacing in relation to institutional structures.

The Canadian system produced steady policy change over the period under examination while, in the U.S. system, there is a swing from one policy to another in some areas, a sense in which gains made by the lesbian and gay movement may be reversed. In particular, sweeping policy changes at the national level are not likely to take hold; however, in the U.S. system, policy setbacks can be overcome through long-term incremental policy shift. In the area of sodomy laws, for example, the *Bowers* decision put a block on the Supreme Court as an avenue of policy change, at least in the short term; however, over time, the lesbian and gay movement was able to facilitate change incrementally on a state-by-state basis so that, by the time the Supreme Court overturned the *Bowers* ruling in the *Lawrence* decision in 2003, the lesbian and gay movement had made gains in the states as lower courts rejected the precedent of *Bowers*. The multiple veto points of the U.S. system also provide multiple points of access and the state-by-state battle, while expensive and time-consuming for the lesbian and gay movement, yielded incremental gains over a thirty-year time span. However, in contrast to Canada, multiple veto points mean that policy change can be blocked or slowed by opponents of change or defenders of the status quo while policy changes are often very slow-moving and incremental. Policy changes may occur over a long period—as the shift from criminalization of sodomy to its decriminalization over a thirty-five year period or the long scale of the debate over same-sex marriage. Social movements may face blockage or even reversal in the short term, although these blockages and reversals may be surmounted over the long term.

POLITICAL INSTITUTIONS, SOCIAL MOVEMENTS, AND PUBLIC OPINION

By far the most common argument for U.S. and Canadian differences in this policy area focuses on the role of religion and, specifically, the fact that there are more Christian evangelicals in the U.S. than in Canada. Arguments about evangelical influence neglect to consider the structural impact of political institutions in facilitating their policy impact in U.S. politics (e.g., Cox 2005; Rayside 2007; Rom 2007; Wilcox et al. 2007). Although there are more evangelicals in the U.S. than in Canada, Reimer's (2003) research found that these cultures were substantially similar with the exception of one area—politics. Evangelical political beliefs were similar, but the ways in which these beliefs were activated in the political arena were substantially different, according to Reimer's findings. Canadian evangelicals were much less likely to support the parties of the right than are American evangelicals. In both countries, the leadership of right-wing political movements is far to the right of the actual political beliefs of evangelicals (Reimer 2003: 125–126), a finding supported by Wilcox's research which found that, for example, while white evangelical leaders in the U.S.

support the ban on gays in the military, over 40% of evangelicals support an end to the ban (Wilcox 2006: 51). Yet, even taking into account the differences between leaders and followers in evangelical movements, Reimer found that Canadian evangelicals did not involve themselves in American-style right-wing politics and that American evangelicals were twice as likely to support political parties of the right (Reimer 2003: 127–128). In exploring this difference, Reimer found that American churches were much more politically involved than Canadian churches. As he comments, "the weight of social issues (abortion, gay rights, etc.) on political outcomes and the successful mobilization efforts of American groups like the Christian Coalition have pushed evangelical voters to align with the Republican party" (Reimer 2003: 130). Thus, while both countries have important Protestant evangelical subcultures, these have been mobilized into politics in different ways. Although the U.S. is largely considered to be more religious than Canada, the two countries are surprisingly similar with respect to the cultural and social role of evangelicals. Where they differ is in the role of evangelicals in politics.

Although it less often noted, Canada and the U.S. differ greatly not only in the mobilization of evangelicals in organized social movement and advocacy activity, but also in the extent of lesbian and gay political mobilization. As we have seen, in fact, the movement in Canada is very poorly organized and resourced compared to the professionalism, organizational variety, depth and skill of U.S. lesbian and gay organizations. Therefore, an explanation based solely on the resources or strength of the lesbian and gay movement not only fails to explain policy divergence between Canada and the U.S., in fact, it would lead us to predict that the American movement would be much more successful than the Canadian movement. The somewhat lower level of religiosity of Canadians compared to Americans cannot be treated as a static factor that explains policy outcomes. As we have seen, there have been important successes for lesbian and gay rights in the U.S., despite the strength and political influence of the Christian Right movement. In particular, despite the supposed religiosity and conservatism of Americans, as depicted in some of the political culture literature, we find that American public opinion has consistently moved in the direction of recognizing lesbian and gay rights over the course of the 1990s and 2000s, despite the dominant political conservatism of the Bush era. In addition, far from producing consistently negative outcomes for lesbian and gay rights policy recognition, U.S. courts have produced important victories for lesbian and gay rights over the course of the 2000s, especially the *Lawrence* decision, produced by a relatively conservative U.S. Supreme Court, and a large number of important decisions from state courts on same-sex marriage, many of which recognized the importance of lesbian and gay claims to conjugal equality and some of which went so far as to recognize the full right to civil marriage. The pattern of U.S. court decisions over the

1990s and 2000s does not support the view that the more conservative and religious political culture of Americans compared to Canadians explains the pattern of court decisions in any clear-cut fashion.

If we explore differences in public opinion between the U.S. and Canada, we discern the effects of social change in terms of changing attitudes towards sexuality and gender, but also some evidence of the effects of the political mobilization by political elites. At the time of the AIDS crisis, Ronald Reagan and other conservative political leaders in the U.S. ignored the crisis and the Supreme Court gave constitutional sanction to the stigmatization of lesbians and gay men in the form of the *Bowers* decision. During this period, public opinion in the U.S. became even more anti-gay. However, in the early 1990s, from the time of the *Baehr* decision in Hawai'i and through the *Romer*, *Lawrence* and *Goodridge* decisions in 2003, U.S. public opinion has become more positively inclined toward lesbian and gay rights (Wilcox et al. 2007: 227). Through the discussions on same-sex marriage in Massachusetts, public opinion in that state swung from minority to majority support for same-sex marriage. Similarly, in Canada, as Scott Matthews (2005) has shown, the decisions of the Canadian Supreme Court played a cueing role in shifting public opinion—which, as in Massachusetts, had been opposed to same-sex marriage—over the 50% mark in favor of it. This suggests that religiosity and public opinion must be mobilized by movement leaders. In this regard, institutional structures play a shaping role in social movement strategizing. Grassroots organizing for ballot initiatives cannot take place in political systems without the institutional mechanism of the ballot initiative. In this way, a historical institutionalist approach emphasizes that political institutions themselves produce different forms of politics. From this perspective, this book suggests that the decentralized and fragmented U.S. political structure, with its multiple entry points, its divided but powerful courts, and its institutional capacity for direct democracy facilitates a particular type of politics, providing political and institutional openings and incentives for well organized and well-resourced political actors such as the Christian Right. In turn, as Tina Fetner's (forthcoming) work shows, powerful movements such as the Christian Right have forced the U.S. lesbian and gay movement to defend itself with its own professionalized organizations.

I do not deny that there are cultural differences among regions of the U.S. and Canada, nor do I deny that evangelical Christians are more numerous, more politicized and more influential in American politics than in Canadian politics. However, I do argue that comparative policy analysis must read these political cultural factors as mediated and refracted through the lens of political institutional differences. The evolution of public policy on lesbian and gay rights in the U.S. cannot be evaluated solely with reference to advocacy organizations and changes in the political environment as the agenda-setting analyses suggest (Rom 2007). Politicians, judges and advocacy groups function in an institutional context and their behavior is fundamentally shaped by institutional rules. Without the institutional openings provided by the fragmented American system, Christian evangelicals in the U.S. might not be as interested in politics or as mobilized into politics as they are. A comparative analysis of U.S. politics highlights the importance of political institutional structures in producing the uniquely polarized swings and counterswings of movement and countermovement struggles as they play out in the policy process. By paying systematic attention to political institutions, we gain a much richer understanding of the causal mechanisms driving policy divergence as well as the process and timing of policy change.

POLITICAL IMPLICATIONS AND DIRECTIONS FOR FUTURE RESEARCH

Sweeping generalizations about political culture lead to political quietism. In the 1960s and 1970s, social scientists became suspicious of "culture" and, at least in political science, turned away from cultural analyses in favor of political economy, neo-Marxism, Weberianism (epitomized by the "return to the state") as well as rational choice theory and formal modeling. In recent years, there has been a turn back to political culture in particular because of the rise of constructivist and Foucauldian theory. Historical institutionalist analysis has also paid attention to the role of ideas in the policy process and to how institutions shape the preferences of societal actors. In turn, historical institutionalist approaches to the "role of ideas" have been criticized by Foucauldians as weak amendments that neglect the foundational role of culture and meaning in the construction of social and political reality (e.g., Murray 2007). While these are important debates for researchers, we often forget the enduring popularity of political culture as an everyday explanation of politics. National stereotypes provide a shortcut explanation for why things are the way they are for the popular audience. Commenting on Michael Moore's analysis of the U.S. health care system in the film *Sicko*, a *New Yorker* columnist wrote that Moore's film left the audience wondering why the U.S. did not adopt universal health care and why the U.S. persisted in apparent public policy stupidity with an expensive private health care system that was not serving its citizens. The columnist (Gawande 2007) opined that the real answer is "us," meaning that Americans are the problem and the obstacle in the way of universal public health care in the U.S. According to the writer, Americans mistrust big government and are not prepared to give over power to the government in an expensive new system that would mean higher taxes.

This is an example of how sweeping assertions about alleged political beliefs and values not only fail as explanations of public policy outcomes, but also how they fail to challenge political quiescence and quietism in popular political discussion. Such a view of political culture reproduces the dominant power structure of the U.S. by stating that political change is impossible because Americans just are what they are and they cannot or will not change. But, in fact, there is no "us." In democratic societies, people disagree. Even if Americans as a group did agree very substantially on a particular course of action, this is no guarantee that political leaders will follow suit. Americans have supported employment protections for lesbians and gays by a substantial majority since the early 1980s (Wilcox et al. 2007). Yet, the U.S. still does not have national rights protections for lesbians and gay men who are fired from their jobs because of their sexual orientation. The same is true of many other areas of public policy. Politicians and governments do not act or react because of "political culture" as a stand-alone factor. Neither do judges. If they did, all judges within a given political cultural space would agree with each other. The Lipset (1963, 1990) and Hartz ([1955] 1990) political cultural approach to understanding the divergent pathways of North America must not be popularized in a way that leads to stereotypes and generalizations about national character. Such generalizations are politically dangerous, especially when applied to the supposed national character of a global superpower. As Rogers Smith has reminded us, the U.S. is a country with multiple political traditions and not one single liberal tradition. Further, Smith's approach clearly anchors political culture within a broad range of laws, public policies, political institutions and social practices rather than defining political culture as a stand-alone factor that explains broad political outcomes (R. Smith 1993, 1999). In keeping with that approach, I emphasize that the U.S. and Canada differ in the ways in which they have politicized and mobilized racial, ethnic, national and linguistic diversity. These differences play a more important role in lesbian and gay rights policies than differences between individualist and collectivist strains of liberalism or the battle between liberalism and conservatism, as the dominant literatures on political culture would have it.

Rather than treating political culture as an inert factor that explains policy or judicial outcomes, historical institutionalist analyses explore specifically *how* political cultures are mobilized in politics and *how* political institutions form a cultural context for political mobilization. Political institutions provide the rules of the game for political actors and these rules are internalized by political actors and social movements. Historical institutionalism provides an analysis of the dynamic process through which religious and other social differences come to make a difference to policy outcomes. While most Canadians like to think of themselves as a secular and tolerant people, there *is* such a thing as a Canadian evangelical Christian who opposes same-sex marriage, believes that homosexuality is a sin and believes that society has gone too far in recognizing homosexual rights. However, institutional rules make it difficult for people with these opinions to exert political influence. The lesbian and gay movement in Canada is decentralized, fragmented, poorly resourced and weak by any measure compared to the professionalized U.S. NGOs such as the Task Force, the Human Rights Campaign, or Lambda Legal, which are among the most successful lesbian and gay organizations in the world in terms of their ability to secure policy change. This has occurred because of institutional openings, not because of social movement resources, money or organization.

Rather than setting up political culture as equivalent to public opinion or religiosity, this analysis suggests that it is more useful to explore how specific political values and beliefs are mobilized into politics and to define this "how" of the process as a dynamic that unfolds in historical terms. Public policies and political institutions suggest the range of possible strategic and policy choices and produce specific framings of issues. If it is meaningful at all to state that American and Canadian political cultures are different, then this difference becomes significant when we take account of the deeply confederal nature of the U.S. and the critically important role played by states and by "states' rights" in lesbian and gay rights policies (as in other civil rights issues in the U.S.) compared to the relatively centralized institutional framework of Canadian human rights policies. It is meaningful to discuss differences between the U.S. and Canada in terms of the relatively closed and centralized nature of the parliamentary system compared to the fragmentation and multiple access points of the U.S. system. It is meaningful to discuss differences in jurisprudential constructions of rights protections under the Fourteenth Amendment and section 15 of the Charter. It is meaningful to discuss differences in the rules governing political parties and how political parties mobilize partisan competition over civil rights in very different ways. It is meaningful to discuss American and Canadian differences in terms of the historical timing of the rise of social movements and the different policy and institutional legacies faced by these rising movements and how these differences produce different trajectories of political success and failure for rights claimants. But blanket generalizations regarding the religiosity or innate conservative beliefs and values of Americans neglect the role of political leadership and institutional structures in influencing the process by which beliefs and values are formed and the process by which they are mobilized to influence policy outcomes (e.g., Brewer 2003b).

Future research should build on the existing strengths in empirical political science in public opinion research in the lesbian and gay politics area and move beyond the prism in which judges and political leaders are seen as responding to public opinion (e.g., Rom 2007; Mezer 2007). There is no reason that lesbian and gay rights politics should be any more driven by waves of public opinion than is tax policy or social policy or why lesbian and gay rights should be any more uniquely driven by morality or religion than any other field of public policy. Morality framing is just that—a framing of a public policy problem in morality terms. As Manuel Castells ([1997] 2004:

7) has commented, "[i]t is easy to agree on the fact that, from a sociological perspective, all identities are constructed. The real issue is how, from what, by whom and for what." The same is true of policy framing. Policies may be framed this way or that way but the real is issue is how they have been framed, from what, by whom, and for what purpose. In order to understand the framing of lesbian and gay rights as a morality question in U.S. politics, rather than its framing as an equality question or a rights question, it is necessary to explore in full the dynamics of social movement politics in their institutional context, as presented here. To develop this analysis further, we need to explore the links between public opinion and political values and the process of political mobilization. Rather than assuming that public opinion is somehow given in political culture or given by religious beliefs, we need to explore the long-term historical evolution of political values in relation to political institutions and political leadership. How is public opinion shaped by political leadership—the political leadership of politicians and social movement leaders? To what extent is public opinion cued by court decisions and legal developments? Do U.S. political institutions reinforce the strength of political conservatism as well as the more radical politics of nativism and isolationism by permitting multiple openings for political mobilization? More generally, are the more closed and elite-driven political institutions of parliamentarism (especially with centralized rights protections and strong courts) better able to manage the challenges of diversity and to maintain the basic accountability that democratic political institutions are supposed to provide? Is it easier to provide strong human rights protections in democratic societies when such protections are enacted from the center and more difficult when sub-national units play a key role, institutionally and jurisdictionally, in the human rights arena?

Moreover, understanding the institutional context in which contending social movements and political actors are operating assists us in thinking about the ways in which we might work successfully within the realities of these institutions and even about how we might want to reform them. Rather than thinking about how political arguments fit in with a particular cultural context, it suggests that certain types of arguments will "fit" in the institutional context of each system. Social movement scholars in sociology have developed a rich literature on the cultural contexts of social movement claiming, and political scientists could usefully borrow from them in thinking about the ways in which social movement organizations fit with the political institutions of which they are part and the ways in which they institutionalize particular assumptions about social and political practice (Clemens 1997).

Despite the focus on deep structures in historical institutionalist analysis, there is also room for political leaders to make choices to mobilize one set of beliefs or another. In his book on race in U.S. politics, Paul Frymer (1999) argued that it was a political choice for leaders such as Bill Clinton to mobilize race in particular ways in the cause of winning elections. Similarly, as Kenneth McRoberts (1993) has argued, it was a political choice for the Trudeau Liberals to deal with the rise of Quebec nationalism by designing a constitutionally entrenched rights document. Each of these political choices was contested and other avenues of political choice were possible. As Canada swung to the political right with the election of 2006 and as the U.S. swung back toward the centre with the mid-term Democratic sweep of the same year, the picture of a tolerant Canada and an intolerant U.S. may begin to shift in part because of the specific choices made by political leaders in mobilizing race, ethnicity, gender, and sexuality for political gain. However, the choices made by political leaders will be exercised within specific nationally defined institutional contexts. For the lesbian and gay movement in the U.S., this context—the institutional barriers, policy legacies, and jurisdictional obstacles created by the specific configuration of U.S. political institutions—raises the bar for policy influence. Political institutions and legacies of previous policies have powerful structuring impacts in channeling political conflicts in particular directions. A macro-historical lens brings out the deep structural effects of institutions in explaining the *how* and *why* of diverging policy paths and processes. With such a longitudinal and comparative perspective, the unique features of U.S. political institutions are highlighted and their role in producing and retarding policy and political change can be best assessed. Scholars working in the field of American political development have focused attention on the development of the American state, citizenship, the welfare state, gender and race in American politics. This book has shown that the structural and institutional approach used in this study and, in particular, the structural and institutional focus to American political development and social policy can be fruitfully deployed in exploring the evolution of policies on lesbian and gay rights. By building on these approaches, we can bring the study of sexuality into the mainstream of the comparative study of American politics.

Notes

NOTES TO THE PREFACE

1. The terminology of "lesbian and gay" is highly contested and fluid in the field of sexuality studies. Many younger people reject the terms "lesbian" and "gay" and instead, identify under the umbrella of "queer"; others find the term "queer" to be offensive and, instead, identify as lesbian or gay. Many lesbians identify with the women's movement and have not felt that their interests were well represented in gay politics. The terms "trans," "transgender," and "transsexual" are used to refer to gender identity (which is not the same as sexual orientation). This book does not take up bisexual or trans issues in any systematic way and, therefore, I mainly use the terms "lesbian" and "gay" out of respect for the fact that bisexual and trans topics are not explicitly covered. The term "queer" is occasionally used throughout the book as an umbrella term. When I wish to refer to lesbian, gay, bisexual, and transgender, I deliberately use the term "lesbian, gay, bisexual, and transgender" (LGBT).

NOTES TO CHAPTER 1

1. When discussing Canada at the "national" level, I often use the term "pan-Canadian" in place of "national" to denote the multinational character of the Canadian state.
2. At the time, it was thought that same-sex marriage bans had affected turn-out; however, later studies of exit polls indicated that this was not the case and that same-sex marriage was not decisive in the campaign (Lewis 2005; Sherrill 2004).
3. Protection against gender identity discrimination is favoured by some trans people as a further layer of legal protection because it specifically protects people who may feel that they do not belong to the sex assigned to them at birth, people who feel they do not belong to either gender, or people who cross-dress. In the U.S., there has been substantial debate over including gender identity along with protection against sexual orientation discrimination in the proposed federal anti-discrimination legislation, ENDA (National Gay and Lesbian Task Force 2007a). Many lesbian, gay and bisexual people may also benefit from protection on the basis of gender identity or gender expression to the extent that failure to conform to gender stereotypes (e.g., failure to conform to gender roles in workplace dress) may place lesbians, gays, and bisexuals at risk of discrimination (Zalesne 2007). In Canada, some trans rights may be included under the rubrics of sex or sexual orientation and some provincial governments include gender identity under the rubric of these

other grounds, while some explicitly include gender identity as a specified category in human rights legislation (see, for example, Ontario 2000).

4. Defense of Marriage Act, Pub. L. No. 104–199, § 3(a), 110 Stat. 2419, codified as amended at 1 U.S.C. § 7 (2000).

5. Defense of Marriage Act, Pub. L. No. 104–199, § 2(a), codified as amended at 28 U.S.C. § 1738C (2000).

6. Civil Rights Act, Pub. L. No. 88–352, codified at 42 U.S.C. § 2000E (1964).

7. In the fall of 2007, a version of ENDA was passed in the House (H.R. 3685). That version did not include protection against discrimination on the grounds of gender identity. As of this writing, an amendment has been proposed that would include gender identity and its fate is uncertain. A large number of LGBT organizations supported the position of the National Gay and Lesbian Task Force: "One Community, One ENDA" (National Gay and Lesbian Task Force 2007c).

8. Canadian provinces might be deemed to have unwritten constitutions, comprised of statutes (for example, legislation that admitted a province to Confederation), Crown prerogatives, judicial precedents, and constitutional conventions (informal rules and norms) that govern the operation of political institutions within the province. Nonetheless, however these constitutions may be defined, they are not freestanding or written and, hence, they do not specify formula for amendment in the same way as U.S. state constitutions nor are they understood as constitutions or referred to as such in public political debate except on very rare occasions in a very few provinces. For example, the province of Manitoba has debated French language rights with reference to the 1870 Act that admitted Manitoba to Confederation (Roach 1993). Some provisions of the federal constitution also specify the way in which political institutions are to function in the provinces, including, for example, the constitutional right to denominational schools. These provisions of the federal constitution may be amended by the federal government at the request of and with the agreement of the province concerned. Specific statutes defined as constitutional law within a province may also be amended through the ordinary process of legislative change, federally or provincially, depending on jurisdiction.

9. Referenda and plebiscites have been used in Canada on issues such as conscription, prohibition, and Quebec sovereignty. These consultations are normally initiated by federal or provincial governments. There are a few very limited examples of citizen-initiated ballot measures and recall in Canada (e.g., in British Columbia) but these do not play an important role in Canadian politics. Further, more than half of popular consultations in Canada have been plebiscitary, that is, not binding on the governments that initiated them (for details, see Canada 2003).

10. The first version of this was passed in the House with this sweeping wording: "Marriage in the United States shall consist only of the union of a man and a woman. Neither this Constitution or the constitution of any State, nor state or federal law, shall be construed to require that marital status or the legal incidents thereof be conferred upon unmarried couples or groups" (H.J. Res. 56, 108th Congress, 1st Session, May 23, 2003).

NOTES TO CHAPTER 2

1. The Human Rights Campaign Fund dropped the word "fund" from its name in 1995 and became simply The Human Rights Campaign (Human Rights Campaign 2006).

2. The name was changed from National Gay Rights Coalition to Canadian Lesbian and Gay Rights Coalition over the course of the 1970s both to recognize the identity of lesbians in the movement and to remove the reference to "national" consistent with the movement's strong membership from Quebec and the links between the Quebec gay liberation movement and the Quebec nationalist movement (see Smith 1999: 63–66).
3. Canadian Human Rights Act, R.S., 1985, c. H-6, as amended.
4. The legislation in Quebec is entitled the *Charte des droits et libertés de la personne* (L.R.Q. c. C-12) and is often referred to in Quebec as *la Charte* (the Charter). In addition, Quebec has another Charter, the *Charte de la langue française* (L.R.Q. c. C-11) which sets out French language rights in the province. This is also sometimes referred to in shorthand as *la Charte*. Both of these are different and distinct from the Canadian Charter of Rights and Freedoms (the Charter), which comprises one section of the Constitution Act 1982 (Schedule B of Canada Act 1982 U.K.). In turn, this Act forms the most important part of the written constitution of Canada. In Quebec, in common parlance, the term "charter" has multiple meanings and its signification in a particular instance must be further specified or inferred from context. To make things even more complicated, the province of Quebec did not consent to the constitutional amendment of 1982 (Constitution Act 1982, including the Canadian Charter of Rights and Freedoms) and, as such, Quebec is often considered not to have "signed the constitution." However, provincial government consent—while politically important—has no legal or constitutional effect on Constitution Act 1982 (including the Charter), which applies in Quebec as it does in every other province and territory (Schneiderman 1992; Russell 2004).
5. Official Languages Act, S.C. 1969, c. O2, s. 2.
6. Prior to 1982, the core of Canada's written constitution, British North America Act 1867, U.K. as an Act of the British Parliament, could only be changed by the British Parliament. In 1982, the constitution was "patriated" by means of Canada Act 1982, U.K. so that it can be amended in Canada without recourse to Britain.

NOTES TO CHAPTER 3

1. Egale was originally named Equality for Gays and Lesbians Everywhere/ *Egalité pour les gais et les lesbiennes* or EGALE, for short. In 2001, it was renamed Egale Canada and it is commonly referred to as Egale. The name is easy to render in a bilingual English-French context and the word *égale* means "equal" in French. The 2001 name change was prompted by a debate on changing the name of the organization to reflect the identities and interests of bisexuals and transgendered people within the group.

NOTES TO CHAPTER 4

1. By this, I do not mean to suggest that the state was not interested in the regulation of sexuality, especially the sexuality of single mothers. Among others, see Little (1998).
2. *Hurley* deals with expressive rights under the First Amendment and, as such, it is of less interest in this analysis, which focuses more specifically on criminal law, employment discrimination and same-sex marriage.

3. The Western-based right-populist Reform Party was renamed the Canadian Alliance in 2000. Officially, the party's name was Canadian Reform Conservative Alliance, but in everyday practice, the party used the name Canadian Alliance. In 2003, the party merged with the Progressive Conservative Party to form the Conservative Party of Canada.

4. As stated in the *Shahar* decision: "We acknowledge that some reasonable persons may suspect that having a Staff Attorney who is part of a same-sex 'marriage' is the same thing as having a Staff Attorney who violates the State's law against homosexual sodomy" *Shahar v. Bowers*, 114 F.3d 1097, 1105 n.16 (11th Cir. 1997). Michael Bowers was the Attorney General of Georgia in Michael Hardwick's case as well as Robin Shahar's.

NOTES TO CHAPTER 5

1. Many states did not explicitly restrict marriage to opposite-sex couples but started to amend their statutes to this effect even prior to the Hawai'i decision (see Pasco 2000). On Canadian marriage provisions, see Hogg (2006).

2. There are a number of indicators of the emergence of same-sex couples and same-sex couples with children as a significant demographic. The growth of the lesbian and gay communities in urban areas and the growth and diversity of urban community institutions demonstrates that larger numbers of people are living in same-sex relationships. In both the U.S. and Canada, there has been a substantial growth in the institutions of the LGBT communities. Parenting groups and support groups for parents have existed in many cities since lesbian mothers first organized in defense of their custody rights in the 1970s and most major cities now boast organizations for same-sex couples who are parenting or for individual gays and lesbians who are parents or co-parenting (Smith 2005b). In the U.S., 2005 data shows that about 5% of the population identifies as lesbian, gay, or bisexual (Gates 2006). The 2001 census in Canada showed 6% of all couples in Canada were same-sex couples and, of those, 15% of female same-sex couples had children living with them while 3% of male couples had children living with them. It is likely that these numbers drastically underestimate the number of same-sex couples and the number of LGBT people who are parents because this was the first time the question was asked (Canada 2001). The advocacy and support group Children of Lesbians and Gays Everywhere (COLAGE), which operates in both the U.S. and Canada, estimates that there are 10 million children with an LGBT parent in the U.S. (COLAGE 2006). This estimate highlights the fact that LGBT people may have children from heterosexual relationships, that they may be divorced or separated (from same-sex or opposite-sex partners), and that they may not be living with their children.

3. It is very important to emphasize that this absence does not denote a lack of racism in Canada or a lack of white condemnation of interracial marriage in the 19th and early 20th centuries. In her important historical study, Constance Backhouse (1999: 145–155) provides evidence that such marriages were sometimes refused by the officiating clergy, despite the lack of explicit legal sanction against them.

4. The *Baehr* litigation began in 1991 and ended in 1999. Useful accounts of the litigation and the fascinating political battle over same-sex marriage in Hawai'i can be found in Goldberg-Hiller (2002); Wolfson (2004); Andersen (2005); Pinello (2006) and Hull (2006).

5. In the pivotal case of *Halpern v. Ontario* (2003), the plaintiffs engaged a linguistic philosopher who demonstrated that the argument that "marriage just is heterosexual" begs the question (Mercier 2001). In other words, the plaintiffs disputed the definitional argument against same-sex marriage by using a philosopher to show that the legal re-assertion of the traditional (male-female) definition of marriage failed to answer the legal question posed to the court by the same-sex couples as plantiffs in the case.
6. Although the use of the state ERA to find in favor of same-sex marriage worked in Hawai'i, an analysis of a very broad range of other cases shows that sex cannot be used as a way to ban discrimination based on sexual orientation in areas such as employment (Linton, 2002; see also Duncan, 2002). A similar result was reached in Canadian jurisprudence in *Canada v. Mossop* (1993). Nonetheless, the linkages between sex and sexual orientation have political consequences for feminist analyses of marriage, as Pascoe (2000) discusses.
7. The following groups and organizations intervened in *M v. H* (1999): The Foundation for Equal Families, the Women's Legal Education and Action Fund (LEAF), Equality for Gays and Lesbians Everywhere (EGALE), the Ontario Human Rights Commission, the United Church of Canada, the Evangelical Fellowship of Canada, the Ontario Council of Sikhs, the Islamic Society of North America, Focus on the Family and REAL Women of Canada. These represent two small lesbian and gay groups, women's groups, liberal and conservative religious groups, and one anti-feminist women's group (REAL Women).

NOTES TO CHAPTER 6

1. *An Act to Amend Certain Statutes Because of the Supreme Court of Canada Decision in M. v. H.* S.O. 1999, c. 6.
2. *Marriage Amendment Act* 2000 R.S.A. 2000 c. 3.
3. *Alberta Adult Interdependent Act* R.S.A. 2000, c. A-4.5.
4. *Modernization of Benefits and Obligations Act* S.C. 2000, c. 12.
5. A *Marriage Protection Act* was first introduced in the House of Representatives in October 2003. Representative Barney Frank also introduced a bill *State Regulation of Marriage is Appropriate Act*, in 2003 which would have repealed the federal DOMA.
6. barbara findlay spells her name without capitals.
7. The question of whether or not marriage commissioners in the provinces may refuse to perform same-sex marriages on religious grounds has been the subject of debate and litigation (MacDougall 2006).

NOTES TO CHAPTER 7

1. I put the term "biological" in quotation marks because the "biological" origins of children born to married couples have traditionally been defined in law, not in biology. Under common and civil law in the U.S. and Canada, paternity is legally assigned to the husband of the child's biological mother although it is possible that the legal husband is not the biological father of the child.

References

U.S. CASES

Alons v. Iowa District Court 698 N.W.2d 858 (Iowa 2005)
Baehr v. Lewin, 74 Haw. 645, 852 P.2d 44 (1993)
Baehr v. Miike, Civ. No. 91–1394 (Haw. Cir. Ct. Dec. 3, 1996)
Baehr v. Miike, 994 P.2d 566 (1999)
Baker v. State of Vermont, 744 A.2d 864 (1999)
Bowers v. Hardwick 478 U.S. 186 (1986)
Boy Scouts of America v. Dale, 530 U.S. 640 (2000)
Brause v. Bureau of Vital Statistics, No. 3AN-95–6562 CI, 1998 WL 88743 (1998)
Brown v. Board of Education, 347 U.S. 483 (1954)
Chicoine, 479 N.W.2d . 891, 894 (S.D. 1992)
Equality Foundation of Greater Cincinnati, Inc. v. City of Cincinnati, 128 F. 3d 189 (6th Cir. 1997)
Evans v. Romer, 882 P.2d 1335 (Colo. 1994)
Goodridge v. Dept. of Public Health, 798 N.E.2d 941 (2003)
Godfrey v. Spano, 15 Misc.3d 809, 836 N.Y.S.2d 813 (Sup. Ct. 2007)
Griswold v. Connecticut, 381 U.S. 479 (1965)
Hernandez v. Robles, 7 N.Y.3d 338 (2006)
Hurley v. Irish-American Gay, Lesbian & Bisexual Group, 515 U.S. 557, 571 (1995)
In re Kandu, 315 B.R. 123 (Bkrcy., W.D. Wash. 2004),
In re R.E.W., 472 S.E.2d 295, 296 (1996)
Lawrence v. Texas, 539 U.S. 558 (2003)
Lewis v. Harris, 188 N.J. 415, 433 (2006)
Loving v. Virginia, 388 U.S. 1 (1967)
Morrison v. Sadler, No. 49A02–0305-CV-447, slip op, (Ind. Ct. App. 2005)
Opinion of the Justices to the Senate, 802 N.E.2d 565, 572 (Mass. 2004)
Padula v. Webster, 822 F. 2d 97 (1987)
Perez v. Sharp, 32 C2d 711 (1948)
Planned Parenthood of Southeastern Pa. v. Casey, 505 U.S. 833, 850 (1992)
Plessy v. Ferguson, 163 U.S. 537 (1896)
Roe v. Wade, 410 U.S. 113 (1973)
Romer v. Evans, 517 U.S. 620 (1996)
Shahar v. Bowers, 70 F.3d 1218 (1995)
State v. Carswell, 114 Ohio St.3d 210 (2007)
Varnum v. Brien, No. CV5965 (Polk Cty., 30 August 2007)

CANADIAN CASES

Andrews v. Law Society of British Columbia [1989] 1 S.C.R. 143
Barbeau v. British Columbia (Attorney General) [2003] BCCA 251
Boutilier v. Nova Scotia (Attorney General) [2004] N.S.J. No. 357 (Q.L.), 24 September 2004 (N.S. Sup. Ct.)
Canada (A.G.) v. Mossop [1993] 1 S.C.R. 554
Douglas v. Canada (1992), [1993] 1 F.C. 264 (T.D.)
Egale Canada Inc. et al. v. Att. Gen. of Canada et al. [2001] BCSC 1365
Egan v. Canada [1995] 2 S.C.R. 513
Haig v. Canada (1991), 5 O.R. (3d) 245 (Gen. Div.), affirmed (1992), 9 O.R. (3d) 495 (C.A.)
Halpern v. Canada (Attorney General) (2002), 60 O.R. (3d) 321
Halpern v. Canada (Attorney General) (2003), 65 O.R. (3d) 161 (C.A)
Hendricks et al. v. Québec (Procureur général) [2002] R.J.Q. 2506 (Sup. Crt)
Layland v. Ontario (1993), 14 O.R. (3d) 658, 104 D.L.R. (4th) 214 (Ontario Court (General Division, Divisional Court)
Law v. Canada (Minister of Employment and Immigration), [1999] 1 S.C.R. 497
Ligue catholique pour les droits de l'homme c. Hendrick, [2004] J.Q. No. 2593 (Q.L.) (C.A.Q.)
M v. H [1999] S.C.J. No. 23
Morrissey & Coll v. The Queen (filed, settled out of court)
Reference re Same-Sex Marriage [2004] 3 S.C.R. 698
Rosenberg v. Canada (Attorney General) [1995] 25 O.R. (3d) 612
Rosenberg v. Canada (Attorney General) [1998] 38 O.R. (3d) 577
Veysey v. Correctional Services (Canada) [1990] 1 F.C. 321
Vriend v. Alberta [1998] 1 S.C.R. 493

U.K. CASES

Wilkinson v. Kitzinger and others [2006] EWHC 2022 (Fam)

OTHER SOURCES

Abrahamson, Shirley S. and Diane S. Gutmann. 1987. "The New Federalism: State Constitutions." *Judicature* 71: 2 (August–September): 88–99.
Abreu, Veronica C. 2002. "The Malleable Use of History in Substantive Due Process Jurisprudence: How the 'Deeply Rooted' Test Should Not Be a Barrier to Finding the Defense of Marriage Act Unconstitutional under the Fifth Amendment Due Process Clause." *Boston College Law Review* 44 (2002): 177–205.
Adam, Barry D. 1995. *The Rise of a Gay and Lesbian Movement.* Revised. New York: Twayne.
Adam, Barry D. 2003. "The 'Defense of Marriage Act' and American Exceptionalism." *Journal of the History of Sexuality* 12 (2): 259–276.
Adams, Michael. 2003. *Fire and Ice: The United States, Canada and the Myth of Converging Values.* Toronto: Penguin.
Alberta. Department of Justice. 1999, March 3. *Report of the Ministerial Task Force.* http://solgen.gov.ab.ca/publications/report_of_ministerial_task_force/index.html
Alexander, Sharon E. Debbage. 2002. "*Romer v. Evans* and the Amendment 2 Controversy: The Rhetoric and Reality of Sexual Orientation Discrimination in America." *Texas Forum on Civil Liberties & Civil Rights* 6: 2 (Winter): 261–302.

Altman, Dennis. ([1971] 1993). *Homosexual Oppression and Liberation*. New York and London: New York University Press.

Altman, Dennis. 1994. *Power and Community: Organizational and Cultural Politics of AIDS*. London: Taylor and Francis.

American Civil Liberties Union (ACLU). 2004, August 12. "California Supreme Court Invalidates Marriages from San Francisco, Without Resolving Whether Same-Sex Couples Have the Right to Marry." Press release. http://www.aclu. org/lgbt/relationships/12391prs20040812.html?s_src=RSS

Andersen, Ellen Ann. 2005. *Out of the Closets and Into the Courts: Legal Opportunity and Gay Rights Litigation*. Ann Arbor: University of Michigan Press.

Andriote, John-Manuel. 1999. *Victory Deferred: How AIDS Changed Gay Life in America*. Chicago: University of Chicago Press.

Archer, Bert. 2004. *The End of Gay and the Death of Heterosexuality*. New York: Thunder's Mouth Press.

Arnup, Katherine ed. 1995. *Lesbian Parenting: Living with Pride and Prejudice*. Charlottetown, P.E.I.: Gynergy Books.

Backhouse, Constance. 1999. *Colour-Coded: A Legal History of Racism in Canada, 1900–1950*. Toronto: University of Toronto Press.

Bailey, Martha. 2004a. "Regulation of Cohabitation and Marriage in Canada." *Law and Policy* 26: 1 (January): 153–175.

Bailey, Martha. 2004b. "Same-Sex Relationships Across Borders." *McGill Law Journal* 49: 4 (October): 1005–1033.

Bailey, Robert. 1999. *Urban Politics: Identity and Economics in the Urban Setting*. New York: Columbia University Press.

Bain, Alison and Catherine Jean Nash. 2007. "'Reclaiming Raunch': Spatializing Queer Identities at Toronto Women's Bathhouse Events." *Social and Cultural Geography* 8 (1): 16–42.

Bakvis, Herman and Steven Wolinetz. 2005. "Canada: Executive Dominance and Presidentialization." In Thomas Poguntke and Paul Webb (eds.) *The Presidentialization of Politics: A Comparative Study of Modern Democracies*. Oxford: Oxford University Press, 199–220.

Barclay, Scott and Thomas Birkland. 1998. "Law, Policymaking, and the Policy Process: Closing the Gaps." *Policy Studies Journal* 26 (2): 227–243.

Barlow, Anne and Rebecca Probert. 2004. "Regulating Marriage and Cohabitation: Changing Family Values and Policies in Europe and North America—An Introductory Critique." *Law & Policy* 26 (1): 1–11.

Barnes, Jeb. 2007. "Bringing the Courts Back In: Interbranch Perspectives on the Role of Courts in American Politics and Policy-Making." *Annual Review of Political Science* 10: 25–43.

Barron, Chris. 2004. "A Big Question for Gay Republicans." *The Gay and Lesbian Review* (September–October): 27–29.

Bashevkin, Sylvia. 1996. "Rethinking Retrenchment: North American Social Policy During the Early Clinton and Chrétien Years." *Canadian Journal of Political Science* 33 (1): 7–36.

Bashevkin, Sylvia. 2002. *Welfare Hot Buttons: Women, Work and Social Policy Reform*. Toronto: University of Toronto Press.

Baum, Lawrence. 2006. *Judges and Their Audiences: A Perspective on Judicial Behavior*. Princeton: Princeton University Press.

BBC News Online. 2006. "Lesbians Lose Legal Marriage Bid." July 31. http://news.bbc.co.uk/2/hi/uk_news/england/north_yorkshire/5230708.stm

Belluck, Pam. 2007. "Massachusetts Gay Marriages Remain Legal." *New York Times* (June 14). http://www.nytimes.com/2007/06/15/us/15gay.html?_r=1&n =Top%2FReference%2FTimes%20Topics%2FSubjects%2FM%2FMarriages &oref=slogin

Bercuson, David, J.L. Granatstein and W.L. Young. 1986. *Sacred Trust? Brian Mulroney and the Conservative Party in Power.* Toronto: Doubleday Canada.

Bernstein, Mary. 2003. "Nothing Ventured, Nothing Gained? Conceptualizing Social Movement 'Success' in the Lesbian and Gay Movement." *Sociological Perspectives* 46 (3): 353–379.

Beyond Marriage. 2006. *Beyond Same-Sex Marriage: A New Strategic Vision for All Our Families and Relationships.* (July 28) http://www.beyondmarriage.org/about.html

Bibby, Reginald. 1987. *Fragmented Gods: The Poverty and Potential of Religion in Canada.* Toronto: Irwin.

Bibby, Reginald. 1993. *Unknown Gods: The Ongoing Story of Religion in Canada.* Toronto: Stoddart.

Bibby, Reginald. 2002. *Restless Gods: The Renaissance of Religion in Canada.* Toronto: Stoddart.

Blandin, Randall. 1999/2000. "Case Note: *Baker v. Vermont*: The Vermont State Supreme Court Held that Denying Same-Sex Couples the Benefits and Privileges of Marriage is Unconstitutional." *Law & Sexuality: A Review of Lesbian, Gay, Bisexual, and Transgender Legal Issues* 9: 1 (Spring): 349–374.

Bodi, Robert F. 1999. "Democracy at Work: The Sixth Circuit Upholds the Right of the People of Cincinnati to Choose Their Own Morality in *Equality Foundation of Greater Cincinnati, Inc. v. City of Cincinnati*, 128 F. 3d 189 (6th Cir. 1997)." *Akron Law Review* 32 (4): 667–698.

Bonauto, Mary. 2001. "Memorandum in Support of Plaintiffs' Motion for Summary Judgment, *Goodridge v. Department of Public Health, Massachusetts.*" Superior Court County of Suffolk No. 01–1647-A (August 20).

Bonauto, Mary et al. 2002. "Brief of Plaintiffs-Appellants', Commonwealth of Massachusetts." Supreme Judicial Court, Suffolk County, Suffolk County, No. SJC-08860 (November 8).

Bonauto, Mary, Susan M. Murray and Beth Robinson. 1999. "The Freedom to Marry for Same-Sex Couples: The Reply Brief of Plaintiffs Stan Baker et al. in *Baker et al. v. State of Vermont.*" *Michigan Journal of Gender & Law* 6 (1): 1–46.

Bossin, Phyllis G. 2005. "The Legislative Backlash to Advances in Rights for Same-Sex Couples." *Tulsa Law Review* 40 (Spring): 381–424.

Bourassa, Joe and Kevin Varnell. 2002. *Just Married: Gay Marriage and the Expansion of Human Rights in Canada.* Toronto: Doubleday Canada.

Boyd, Susan and Claire F. L. Young. 2003. "From Same-Sex to No Sex? Trends towards Recognition of Same-Sex Relationships in Canada." *Seattle Journal of Social Justice* 3: 757–793.

Brandenburg, Nathan M. 2005. "Preachers, Politicians, and Same-Sex Couples: Challenging Same-Sex Civil Unions and Implications on Interstate Recognition." *Iowa Law Review* 91 (1): 319–348.

Brewer, Paul D. 2003a. "The Shifting Foundations of Public Opinion about Gay Rights." *Journal of Politics* 65 (4): 1208–1220.

Brewer, Paul D. 2003b. "Values, Political Knowledge, and Public Opinion About Gay Rights: A Framing-Based Account." *Public Opinion Quarterly* 67: 173–201.

Brewer, Sarah E., David Kaib and Karen O'Connor. 2000. "Sex and the Supreme Court: Gays, Lesbians, and Justice." In Craig A. Rimmerman, Kenneth D. Wald and Clyde Wilcox (eds.) *The Politics of Gay Rights.* Chicago and London: University of Chicago Press, 377–408.

Brodie, Janine and Jane Jenson. 1988. *Crisis, Challenge and Change: Party and Class in Canada Revisited.* Rev. Ed. Ottawa: Carleton University Press.

Brodie, Janine, Jane Jenson and Shelley Gavigan. 1992. *The Politics of Abortion.* Toronto: Oxford University Press.

Brown, Eleanor. 2001. "The Arrogance of Egale." *Xtra* [Toronto] (September) http://archives.xtra.ca/story.aspx?s=1440915

Brown, Wendy. 2006. *Regulating Aversion: Tolerance in the Age of Identity and Empire.* Princeton: Princeton University Press.

Burgess, Susan R. 1992. *Contest for Constitutional Authority: The Abortion and War Powers Debates.* Lawrence: University Press of Kansas.

Buseck, Gary. 2004. "Symposium Transcription: Keynote Address: Civil Marriage for Same-Sex Couples." *New England Law Review* 38 (3): 495–504.

Butler, Judith. 1990. *Gender Trouble: Feminism and the Subversion of Identity.* New York: Routledge.

Button, James W., Barbara A. Rienzo and Kenneth D. Wald. 1997. *Private Lives, Public Conflicts: Battles over Gay Rights in American Communities.* Washington, DC: CQ Press.

Button, James W., Barbara A. Rienzo and Kenneth D. Wald. 2000. "The Politics of Gay Rights at the Local and State Levels." In Craig A. Rimmerman, Kenneth D. Wald and Clyde Wilcox (eds.) *The Politics of Gay Rights.* Chicago and London: University of Chicago Press, 269–289.

Cabell, Brian. 1999. "Alabama Considers Lifting Interracial Marriage Ban." CNN (March 12) http://www.cnn.com/US/9903/12/interracial.marriage/

Cahill, Sean. 2004. *Same-Sex Marriage in the United States: A Focus on the Facts.* Lanham, MD: Lexington Books.

Cahill, Sean, Ellen Mitra and Sarah Tobias. 2002. *Family Policy: Issues Affecting Gay, Lesbian, Bisexual and Transgender Families.* New York: The National Gay and Lesbian Task Force Policy Institute.

Cahill, Sean and Sarah Tobias. 2007. *Policy Issues Affecting Lesbian, Gay, Bisexual and Transgender Families.* Ann Arbor: University of Michigan Press.

Cain, Patricia A. 1993. "Litigating for Lesbian and Gay Rights: A Legal History." *Virginia Law Review* 79: 7 (October): 1551–1641.

Cain, Patricia A. 2000. *Rainbow Rights: The Role of Lawyers and Courts in the Lesbian and Gay Civil Rights Movement.* Boulder: Westview.

Cairns, Alan C. 1992. *Charter versus Federalism: The Dilemmas of Constitutional Reform.* Montreal & Kingston: McGill-Queen's University Press.

Cairns, Alan C. 1995. *Reconfigurations: Canadian Citizenship and Constitutional Change.* Toronto: McClelland & Stewart.

Campbell, Andrea Louise. 2007. "Parties, Electoral Participation and Shifting Voting Blocs." In Paul Pierson and Theda Skocpol (eds.) *The Transformation of American Politics: Activist Government and the Rise of Conservatism.* Princeton: Princeton University Press, 68–102.

Campbell, Colton C., and Roger H. Davidson. 2000. "Gay and Lesbian Issues in the Congressional Arena." In Craig A. Rimmerman, Kenneth D. Wald, and Clyde Wilcox (eds.) *The Politics of Gay Rights.* Chicago and London: University of Chicago Press, 347-376.

Canada. 1981. Special Joint Committee on the Constitution of Canada. *Minutes of Proceedings and Evidence*, 2980-81. Ottawa: Queen's Printer.

Canada. 1982. Special Joint Committee of the Senate and the House of Commons on the Constitution of Canada. *Minutes of Proceedings and Evidence.*

Canada. 1985. Minister of Justice and Attorney General of Canada. *Equality Issues in Federal Law: A Discussion Paper.* Ottawa: Queen's Printer.

Canada. 1986. Department of Justice. *Toward Equality: The Response to the Report of the Parliamentary Committee on Equality Rights.* Ottawa: Queen's Printer.

Canada. 2001. Statistics Canada. *Same-sex common-law couples* http://www12
.statcan.ca/english/census01/products/analytic/companion/fam/canada.cfm
#same_sex_common_law

Canada. 2003. Elections Canada. *Compendium of Election Administration in
Canada.* Ottawa: Supply and Services Canada.

Canada. 2005. House of Commons. *Edited Hansard* (058) 38th Parliament, 1st Session (February 16): 1520–1739.

Canada. 2007. Heritage Canada. *Canada's Commitment to Cultural Diversity.*
http://www.pch.gc.ca/progs/ai-ia/rir-iro/global/divers/index_e.cfm

Canaday, Margot. 2003. "Building a Straight State: Sexuality and Social Citizenship under the 1944 G.I. Bill." *Journal of American History* 90: 3 (December):
935–957.

Canadian Press. 2007. "Chretien Surprised by Gay Marriage Rulings." CTV News
(April 15). http://www.ctv.ca/servlet/ArticleNews/story/CTVNews/20070415/
chretien_charter_070415?s_name=&no_ads=

Carpenter, Dale. 2004. "HRC and the End of ENDA." *Independent Gay Forum.*
http://www.indegayforum.org/news/show/26676.html

Carty, R. Kenneth, William Cross and Lisa Young. 2000. *Rebuilding Canadian
Party Politics.* Vancouver: University of British Columbia Press.

Castells, Manuel. 2004. *The Power of Identity.* 2nd ed. Oxford: Blackwell.

Caswell, Donald G. 2001. "Any Two Persons in Canada's Lotusland, British
Columbia." In Robert Wintemute and Mads Andenaes (eds.) *Legal Recognition of Same Sex Partnerships.* Oxford and Portland Oregon: Hart Publishing,
215–236

Chaffey, Douglas Camp. 1993. "The Right to Privacy in Canada." *Political Science Quarterly* 108:1 (Spring): 117-132.

Chauncey, George. 2004. *Why Marriage? The History Shaping Today's Debate
Over Gay Equality.* New York: Basic Books.

Children of Gays and Lesbians Everywhere (COLAGE). 2006. *People and Place.*
http://www.colage.org/index.htm

Chrisman, Sue. 1994–1995. "*Evans v. Romer*: An 'Old' Right Comes Out." *Denver University Law Review* 72 (3): 519–548.

Clarkson, Stephen. 2005. *The Big Red Machine: How the Liberal Party Dominates Canadian Politics.* Vancouver: University of British Columbia Press.

Clarkson, Stephen and Christina McCall. 1990. *Trudeau and Our Times: The
Magnificent Obsession.* Toronto: McClelland and Stewart.

Clemens, Elisabeth S. 1997. *The People's Lobby: Organizational Innovation and
the Rise of Interest Group Politics in the United States, 1890–1925.* Chicago:
University of Chicago Press.

Coalition for Lesbian and Gay Rights in Ontario (CLGRO). 2000. *Relationships
Recognition Issue Sheet.* http://www.web.net/~clgro/frames.htm

Cohen, Cathy. 1999. *The Boundaries of Blackness: AIDS and the Breakdown of
Black Politics.* Chicago: University of Chicago Press.

Compas. 2005. *Same-Sex: Public Embraces Gay Rights, Opposes Gay Marriage,
Advocates National Referendum.* Compas Polling. http://www.queensu.ca/
cora/polls/February2-same_sex.pdf

Coolidge, David Orgon. 2000. "The Hawai'i Marriage Amendment: Its Origins,
Meaning and Fate." *Hawai'i Law Review* 22: 1 (Spring): 19–188.

Cossman, Brenda. 2002. "Sexing Citizenship, Privatizing Sex." *Citizenship Studies* 67: 4 (December): 483–506.

Cox, Cece. 2005. "To Have and to Hold—Or Not: The Influence of the Christian Right on Gay Marriage Laws in the Netherlands, Canada, and the United
States." *Law and Sexuality* 14: 1–50.

Craig, Stephen C., Michael D. Martinez, James G. Kane and Jason Gainous. 2005. "Core Values, Value Conflict, and Citizens' Ambivalence About Gay Rights." *Political Research Quarterly* 58: 1 (March): 5017.

Cruz, David B. 2001. "'Just Don't Call It Marriage': The First Amendment and Marriage as an Expressive Resource." *Southern California Law Review* 74: 4 (May): 925–1026.

Cruz, David B. 2002. "The New 'Marital Property': Civil Marriage and the Right to Exclude?" *Capital University Law Review* 30 (2): 279–313.

CTV News. 2004. "Harper Lacks Courage on Same-Sex Bill: PM" December 17 http://www.ctv.ca/servlet/ArticleNews/story/CTVNews/1103206680591_18/

Davey, Monica. 2006. "Liberals Find Rays of Hope on Ballot Measures." *New York Times* (November 9) http://www.nytimes.com/2006/11/09/us/politics/09ballots .html?_r=1&oref=slogin

Davies, Alysia. 2006. "Invading the Mind: The Right to Privacy and the Definition of Terrorism in Canada." *University of Ottawa Law and Technology Journal.* 3(1): 249-296.

DeCew, Judith Wagner. 1997. *In Pursuit of Privacy: Law, Ethics and the Rise of Technology.* Ithaca: Cornell University Press.

Deitcher, David. 1995. "Law and Desire." In David Deitcher (ed.) *The Question of Equality: Lesbian and Gay Politics in America since Stonewall.* New York: Scribner, 136–181.

D'Emilio, John. [1983] 1998. *Sexual Politics, Sexual Communities: The Making of a Homosexual Minority in the United States, 1940–1970.* 2nd ed. Chicago and London: University of Chicago Press.

D'Emilio, John. 2007. "Will the Courts Set Us Free?: Reflections on the Campaign for Same-Sex Marriage." In Craig A. Rimmerman and Clyde Wilcox (eds.) *The Politics of Same-Sex Marriage.* Chicago and London: University of Chicago Press, 39–64.

Dinan, John J. 2006. *The American State Constitutional Tradition.* Lawrence: University Press of Kansas.

Docherty, David. 2004. "Parliament: Making the Case for Relevance." In James Bickerton and Alain-G. Gagnon (eds.) *Canadian Politics.* 4th ed. Peterborough: Broadview Press, 163–183.

Donovan, Todd and Shaun Bowler. 1998. "Direct Democracy and Minority Rights: An Extension." *American Journal of Political Science* 42 (3): 1020–1024.

Donovan, Todd, Jim Wenzel and Shaun Bowler. 2000. "Direct Democracy and Gay Rights Initiatives After Romer." In Craig A. Rimmerman, Kenneth D. Wald, and Clyde Wilcox (eds.) *The Politics of Gay Rights.* Chicago and London: University of Chicago Press, 161–190.

Duberman, Martin. 1993. *Stonewall.* New York: Dutton.

Duchschere, Kevin. 2004. "Is Gay Marriage a Civil-Rights Issue?" *Star Tribune* [Minneapolis] (March 26): 1B.

Duncan William C. 2002. "'The Mere Allusion to Gender': Answering the Charge That Marriage is Sex Discrimination." *St. Louis University Law Journal* 46: 4 (Fall): 963–971.

Dupuis, Martin. 2002. *Same Sex Marriage, Legal Mobilization, and the Politics of Rights.* New York: Peter Lang.

Earl, Jennifer. 2003. "The Gay 90s? Models of Legal Decision-Making, Change and History." *Journal of Historical Sociology* 16 (1): 111–134.

Egale. 1998. *Annual Report.* Ottawa: Egale, 1–2.

Egan, Patrick J. and Kenneth Sherrill. 2005. "Marriage and the Shifting Priorities of a New Generation of Lesbians and Gay Men." *PS: Political Science and Politics* (April): 229–232.

Elliott, Douglas [counsel for MCCT] 2002. *Personal Interview with Miriam Smith*. Toronto.

Engel, Stephen M. 2007. "Organizational Identity as a Constraint on Strategic Action: A Comparative Analysis of Gay and Lesbian Interest Groups." *Studies in American Political Development* 21 (Spring): 66–91.

English, John. 2006. *Citizen of the World: The Life of Pierre Elliott Trudeau*. Toronto: Albert A. Knopf Canada.

Epp, Charles. 1998. *The Rights Revolution: Lawyers, Activists, and Supreme Courts in Comparative Perspective*. Chicago: University of Chicago Press.

Epstein, David and Sharyn O'Halloran. 1999. "A Social Science Approach to Race, Redistricting, and Representation." *American Political Science Review* 93: 1 (March): 187–191.

Epstein, Lee and Jack Knight. 1998. *The Choices Justices Make*. Washington, DC: CQ Press.

Epstein, Steven. 1987. "Gay Politics, Ethnic Identity: The Limits of Social Constructionism." *Socialist Review* 17 (May–August): 9–54.

Epstein, Steven. 1996. *Impure Science: AIDS, Activism, and the Politics of Knowledge*. Berkeley: University of California Press.

Eskridge, William N. Jr. 1999. "Mutlivocal Prejudices and Homo Equality: Addison C. Harris Lecture." *Indiana Law Journal* 74: 4 (October): 1085–1128.

Eskridge, William N. Jr. 2000. "No Promo Homo: The Sedimentation of Antigay Discourse and the Channeling Effect of Judicial Review." *New York University Law Review* 75: 5 (November): 1327–1411.

Eskridge, William N. Jr. 2001. "Channeling Identity-Based Social Movements and Public Law." *University of Pennsylvania Law Review* 150: 1 (November): 419–525.

Eskridge William N. Jr. 2004. "Lawrence's Jurisprudence of Tolerance: Judicial Review to Lower the Stakes of Identity Politics." *Minnesota Law Review* 88: 5 (May): 1021–1102.

Eskridge, William N. Jr. and Nan Hunter. 2006. *Sexuality, Gender and Law*. Abridged. New York: Foundation Press and Thomson West.

Esping-Andersen, Gøsta. 1990. *The Three Worlds of Welfare Capitalism*. Princeton: Princeton University Press.

Evangelical Fellowship of Canada. [1996] 2000. *Marriage and Family Status in Canada: A Position Paper of the Evangelical Fellowship of Canada*. Ottawa.

Faderman, Lillian. 1991. *Odd Girls and Twilight Lovers: A History of Lesbian Life in Twentieth Century America*. New York: Columbia University Press.

Feldblum, Chai R. 2000. "The Federal Gay Rights Bill: From Bella to Enda." In John D'Emilio, William B. Turner and Urvashi Vaid (eds.) *Creating Change: Sexuality, Public Policy and Civil Rights*. New York: St. Martin's, 149–187.

Feldblum, Chai. 2002. "Gay Rights." In Herman Schwartz (ed.) *The Rehnquist Court: Judicial Activism on the Right*. New York: Hill and Wang.

Fetner, Tina. 2001. "Working Anita Bryant: The Impact of Christian Anti-Gay Activism on Lesbian and Gay Movement Claims." *Social Problems* 48 (3): 411–428.

Fetner, Tina. Forthcoming. *Fighting the Right: How the Religious Right Changed Lesbian and Gay Activism*. Minneapolis: University of Minnesota Press.

Fischer, Frank. 2003. *Reframing Public Policy: Discursive Politics and Deliberative Practices*. Oxford: Oxford University Press.

Fisher, John [Executive Director, Egale]. 2001. *Personal Interview with Miriam Smith*. Ottawa.

Fitzgerald, Mary and Alan Cooperman. 2004. "Marriage Protection Act Passes: House Bill Strips Federal Courts of Power Over Same-Sex Cases." *Washing-

ton Post (July 23) http://www.washingtonpost.com/wp-dyn/articles/A6217–2004Jul22.html

Forbes, H.D. 1987. "Hartz-Horowitz at Twenty: Nationalism, Toryism and Socialism in Canada and the United States." *Canadian Journal of Political Science* 20 (2): 287–315.

Foreman, Sean [lawyer and member of Nova Scotia Rainbow Action Project]. 2006. *Personal Interview with Miriam Smith*. Halifax.

Fournier, Patrick, André Blais, Joanna Everitt, Elisabeth Gidengil and Neil Nevitte. 2004. "How the Liberals Lost Quebec." *Globe & Mail* (July 21): A15.

Frank, David John and Elizabeth H. McEneaney. 1999. "The Individualization of Society and the Liberalization of State Policies on Same-Sex Sexual Relations, 1984–1995." *Social Forces* 77: 3 (March): 911–944.

Friedman, Lawrence. 2006. "Ordinary and Enhanced Rational Basis Review in the Massachusetts Supreme Judicial Court: A Preliminary Investigation." *Albany Law Review* 69: 2 (Spring): 414–448.

Frymer, Paul. 1999. *Uneasy Alliances: Race and Party Competition in America.* Princeton: Princeton University Press.

Gagnon, Alain-G. and Raffaele Iacovino. 2007. *Federalism, Citizenship, and Quebec: Debating Multinationalism.* Toronto: University of Toronto Press.

Galie, Peter J. 1987. "State Supreme Courts, Judicial Federalism and the Other Constitutions." *Judicature* 71: 2 (August-September): 100–110.

Gamble, Barbara S. 1997. "Putting Civil Rights to Popular Vote." *American Journal of Political Science* 41: 1 (January): 245–269.

Garner, Christopher and Natalie Letki. 2005. "Party Structure and Backbench Dissent in the Canadian and British Parliaments." *Canadian Journal of Political Science* 38: 2 (June): 463–482.

Gates, Gary J. 2006. *Same-Sex Couples and the Gay, Lesbian, Bisexual Population: New Estimates from the American Community Survey.* Los Angeles: The Williams Institute on Sexual Orientation Law and Public Policy, UCLA School of Law.

Gawande, Atul. 2007. "Sick and Twisted." *New Yorker* (July 23). http://www.newyorker.com/talk/comment/2007/07/23/070723taco_talk_gawande/?printable=true

Gerstmann, Evan. 1999. *The Constitutional Underclass: Gays, Lesbians and the Failure of Class-Based Equal Protection.* Chicago and London: University of Chicago Press.

Gillman Howard and Cornell Clayton eds. *The Supreme Court in American Politics: New Institutionalist Interpretations.* Lawrence: University of Kansas Press.

Go, Avvy and John Fisher. 1998. *Working Together Across Our Differences: A Discussion Paper on Coalition-Building, Participatory Litigation and Strategic Litigation.* Ottawa: Court Challenges Program.

Goldberg-Hiller, Jonathan. 1999. "The Limits to Union: Labor, Gays, and Lesbians, and Marriage in Hawai'i." In Gerald Hunt (ed.) *Laboring for Rights: Unions and Sexual Diversity Across Nations.* Philadelphia: Temple University Press, 121–139.

Goldberg-Hiller, Jonathan. 2002. *The Limits to Union: Same-Sex Marriage and the Politics of Civil Rights.* Ann Arbor: The University of Michigan Press.

Goldstein, Amy. 2006. "Same Sex Unions Ruled Out in New York, Georgia." *New York Times* (July 7): A6.

Gotell, Lise. 2002. "Queering Law—Not by Vriend." *Canadian Journal of Law and Society* 17: 1–34.

Gould, Deborah. 2001. "Rock the Boat, Don't Rock the Boat, Baby: Ambivalence and the Emergence of Militant AIDS Activism." In Jeff Goodwin, James M.

Jasper and Francesca Polletta (eds.) *Passionate Politics: Emotions and Social Movements.* Chicago and London: University of Chicago Press, 135–157.

Grabb, Edward and James Curtis. 2005. *Regions Apart: The Four Societies of Canada and the United States.* Don Mills: Oxford University Press.

Graefe, Peter. 2007. "Political Economy and Canadian Public Policy." In Michael Orsini and Miriam Smith (eds.) *Critical Policy Studies.* Vancouver: University of British Columbia Press, 19–40.

Green, John C. 2000. "Antigay: Varieties of Opposition to Gay Rights." In Craig A. Rimmerman, Kenneth D. Wald, and Clyde Wilcox (eds.) *The Politics of Gay Rights.* Chicago and London: University of Chicago Press, 121–138.

Greene, Ian. 2006. *The Courts.* Vancouver: University of British Columbia Press.

Grodzins, Morton. 1982. *The American System: A New View of Government in the United States.* Edited by Daniel Elazar. Boston: Transaction.

Grossman, Cathy Lynn. 2003. "Public Opinion Divided on Same Sex Marriage." *US News & World Report.* (October 10) http://www.usatoday.com/news/nation/2003-10-06-marry-inside-usat_x.htm

Gulliver, Tanya. 2004. "Smart Supreme Decision Unleashes Political Firestorm." *Xtra* [Toronto]. December 23. http://archives.xtra.ca/Story.aspx?s=15261907

Hacker, Jacob S. 2004. "Dismantling the Health Care State? Political Institutions, Public Policies and the Comparative Politics of Health Reform." *British Journal of Political Science* 34: 693–724.

Hacker, Jacob S. and Paul Pierson. 2005. *Off Center: The Republican Revolution and the Erosion of American Democracy.* New Haven: Yale University Press.

Haider-Markel, Donald P. 2003. "Gay Rights." In Robert Singh (ed.) *Governing America: The Politics of a Divided Democracy.* New York: Oxford University Press, 428–448.

Haider-Markel, Donald P. and Kenneth J. Meier. 2003. "Legislative Victory, Electoral Uncertainty: Explaining Outcomes in the Battles Over Lesbian and Gay Civil Rights." *Review of Policy Research* 20 (4): 671–690.

Hall, Peter A. and Rosemary Taylor. 1996. "Political Science and the Three New Institutionalisms." *Political Studies* 44 (4): 936–957.

Halley, Janet. 1999. *Don't: A Reader's Guide to the Military Anti-Gay Policy.* Durham: Duke University Press.

Hamilton, Vivian. 2004. "Mistaking Marriage for Social Policy." *Virginia Journal of Social Policy & the Law* 11: 3 (Spring): 307–371.

Harder, Lois. 2007. "Rights of Love: the State and Intimate Relationships in Canada and the United States." *Social Politics* 14: 2 (Summer): 155–181.

Harlow, Ruth E. et al. 2002. *In the Supreme Court of the United States, Petition for Writ of Certiorari, John Geddes Lawrence and Tyron Garner v. State of Texas* (July 16).

Harlow, Ruth E. et al. 2003. *John Geddes Lawrence and Tyron Garner v. State of Texas.* Reply Brief. No. 02–102 (March 10).

Harrison, Trevor. 1995. *Of Passionate Intensity: Right-Wing Populism and the Reform Party of Canada.* Toronto: University of Toronto Press.

Hartz, Louis. ([1955] 1991). *The Liberal Tradition in America.* 2nd ed. New York: Harcourt.

Harvard Law Review. 2004. "Litigating the Defense of Marriage Act: The Next Battleground for Same Sex Marriage." 117: 8 (June): 2684–2707.

Hassel, Diana. 2001. "Use of Criminal Sodomy Laws in Civil Litigation." *Texas Law Review* 79: 4 (March): 813–848.

Hassel, Diana. 2004. "National Interest: *Lawrence v. Texas*: Evolution of Constitutional Doctrine." *Roger Williams University Law Review* 9: 2 (Spring): 565–577.

Herman, Didi. 1989. "Are We Family?: Lesbian Rights and Women's Liberation." *Osgoode Hall Law Journal* 28 (4): 789–815.

Herman, Didi. 1997. *The Antigay Agenda: Orthodox Vision and the Christian Right.* Chicago: University of Chicago Press.

Hickey, Gemma. [Egale President]. 2006. *Personal Telephone Interview with Miriam Smith.*

Hiebert, Janet. 1995. "Debating Policy: The Effect of Rights Talk." In F. Leslie Seidle (ed.) *Equity and Community: The Charter, Interest Advocacy, and Representation.* Montreal: Institute for Research on Public Policy, 34–41.

Hiebert, Janet. 2002. *Charter Conflicts: What Is Parliament's Role?* Montreal and Kingston: McGill-Queen's University Press.

Hiebert, Janet. 2007. "Compromise and the Notwithstanding Clause: Why the Dominant Narrative Distorts our Understanding." Paper presented at the Annual Meeting of the Canadian Political Science Association, Saskatoon, Saskatchewan, May 30–June 1.

Hogg, Peter W. 2006. "Canada: The Constitution and Same-Sex Marriage." *International Journal of Constitutional Law* 4 (3): 712–721.

Horowitz, Gad. 1968. *Canadian Labour in Politics.* Toronto: University of Toronto Press.

Howe, R. Brian and David Johnson. 2000. *Restraining Equality: Human Rights Commissions in Canada.* Toronto: University of Toronto Press.

Hubins, Jeffery. 2001. "Proposition 22: Veiled Discrimination or Sound Constitutional Law?" *Whittier Law Review* 23: 1 (Fall): 239–266.

Hull, Kathleeen E. 2006. *Same-Sex Marriage: The Cultural Politics of Love and Law.* Cambridge: Cambridge University Press.

Human Rights Campaign. 2004. "The Human Rights Campaign: A Historical Snapshot." http://www.hrc.org/Content/NavigationMenu/About_HRC/HistoricalSnapshot.htm

Human Rights Campaign. 2006. "Who We Are." http://www.hrc.org/about_us/2514.htm

Human Rights Campaign. 2007a. Statewide Marriage Prohibitions (September 19). http://www.hrc.org/documents/marriage_prohibit_20070919.pdf

Human Rights Campaign. 2007b. *Employment Nondiscrimination Act.* http://www.hrc.org/laws_and_elections/enda.asp

Human Rights Campaign. 2007c. *Federal Marriage Amendment.* Online at http://hrc.org/Template.cfm?Section=Federal_Marriage_Amendment1&Template=/TaggedPage/TaggedPageDisplay.cfm&TPLID=23&ContentID=14688

Human Rights Campaign. 2007d. *Corporate Equality Index* (September). http://www.hrc.org/documents/HRC_Corporate_Equality_Index_2008.pdf

Hurley, Mary C. 2005. *Sexual Orientation and Legal Rights: A Chronological Overview.* Ottawa: Parliamentary Information and Research Service, Library of Parliament.

Hurley, Mary C. 2007. *Sexual Orientation and Legal Rights.* Ottawa: Parliamentary Information and Research Service, Library of Parliament.

Ipsos Reid. 2003. "Slim Majority (54%) Support Same Sex Marriage" www.ipsos-reid.com (June 13).

Iyer, Nitya. 1993. "Categorical Denials: Equality Rights and the Shaping of Social Identity," *Queen's Law Journal* 19 (1): 179–207.

Jackson, Ed and Stan Persky. 1982. *Flaunting It! A Decade of Journalism from the Body Politic.* Vancouver and Toronto: New Star Books and Pink Triangle Press.

Jacobs, Andrew M. 1996. "Romer Wasn't Built in a Day: The Subtle Transformation in Judicial Argument Over Gay Rights." *Wisconsin Law Review* 893–940.

James, Matt. 2006. *Misrecognized Materialists: Social Movements in Canadian Constitutional Politics.* Vancouver and Toronto: University of British Columbia Press.

Jefferson, James E. 1985. "Gay Rights and the Charter." *University of Toronto Faculty of Law Review* 43: 70–89.

Johnson, Kirk. 2006. "Gay Marriage Losing Punch as Ballot Issue." *New York Times* (October 14) http://www.nytimes.com/2006/10/14/us/politics/14marriage.html ?hp&ex=1160884800&en=882b3ae02a33e0bb&ei=5094&partner=homepage

Joslin, Courtney J. 1997. "Recent Development: Equal Protection and Anti-Gay Legislation: Dismantling the Legacy of *Bowers v. Hardwick.*" *Harvard Civil Rights-Civil Liberties Law Review* 32: 1 (Winter): 225–247.

Kahn, Ronald. 2006. "Social Constructions, Supreme Court Reversals, and American Political Development: *Lochner, Plessy, Bowers,* but Not *Roe.*" In Ronald Kahn and Ken I. Kersch (eds.) *The Supreme Court & American Political Development.* Lawrence: University of Kansas Press, 67–113.

Kane, Melinda. 2003. "Social Movement Policy Success: Decriminalizing State Sodomy Laws." *Mobilization* 8 (3): 313–34.

Kane, Melinda. 2007. "Timing Matters: Shifts in the Causal Determinants of Sodomy Law Decriminalization, 1961–1998." *Social Problems* 54 (2): 211–239.

Kaplan, Esther. 2004. *With God on Their Side: How Christian Fundamentalists Trampled Science, Policy, and Democracy in George W. Bush's White House.* New York and London: The New Press.

Karlan, Pamela. 1997. "Just Politics? Five Not So Easy Pieces of the 1995 Term." *Houston Law Review* 34: 2 (Summer): 289–313

Karlin, Rick. 2007. "One I Do for Gay Marriage." *TimesUnion.Com* [Albany]. June 20. http://timesunion.com/AspStories/story.asp?storyID=599353&category=STATE&BCCode=&newsdate=6/21/2007

Kelly, James B. 2005. *Governing With the Charter: Legislative and Judicial Activism and Framers' Intent.* Vancouver: University of British Columbia Press.

Kelly, Jon-Peter. 1997. "Act of Infidelity: Why the Defense of Marriage Act Is Unfaithful to the Constitution." *Cornell Journal of Law and Public Policy* 39 (Fall): 203–253.

Kelly, Scott. 2002. "Scouts' (Dis)Honor: The Supreme Court Allows the Boy Scouts of America to Discriminate against Homosexuals in *Boy Scouts of America v. Dale.*" *Houston Law Review* 39 (1): 243–274.

Kimpel, Jason D. 1999. "Distinctions Without a Difference": How the Sixth Circuit Misread *Romer v. Evans.*" *Indiana Law Journal* 74 (Summer 1999): 991–1017.

Kinsman, Gary. 1996a. *The Regulation of Desire: Homo and Hetero Sexualities.* 2nd ed. Montreal and New York: Black Rose Rooks.

Kinsman, Gary. 1996b. "Responsibility as a Strategy of Governance: Regulating People Living with AIDS and Lesbians and Gay Men in Ontario." *Economy and Society* 213 (3): 393–409.

Kinsman, Gary. 2000. "Constructing Gay Men and Lesbians as National Security Risks, 1950–1970." In Dieter K. Buse, Gary Kinsman and Mercedes Steedman (eds.) *Whose National Security?: Canadian State Surveillance and the Creation of Enemies.* Toronto: Between the Lines, 143–153.

Kinsman, Gary. 2003. "Sex Police Are Still With Us." *Xtra* [Toronto] (June 12) http://www.sodomylaws.org/world/canada/caeditorial007.htm

Kirkpatrick, David D. 2007. "The Evangelical Crackup." *New York Times* (October 28) http://www.nytimes.com/2007/10/28/magazine/28Evangelicals-t.html ?ref=magazine

Kitschelt, Herbert P. 1986. "Political Opportunity Structures and Political Protest: Anti-Nuclear Movements in Four Democracies." *British Journal of Political Science.* 16 (1): 57–86.

Klinkner, Philip A. and Rogers M. Smith. 1999. *The Unsteady March: The Rise and Decline of Racial Equality in America.* Chicago and London: University of Chicago Press.

Knauer, Nancy. 2004. "When 'Profound and Deep Convictions' Collide with Liberty Interests." *Cardozo Women's Law Journal* 10 (2): 325–336.

Kome, Penney. 1983. *The Taking of Twenty-Eight.* Toronto: Women's Press.

Koppelman, Andrew. 2006. *Same Sex, Different States: When Same-Sex Marriages Cross State Lines.* New Haven and London: Yale University Press.

Korinek, Valerie J. 2003. "'The Most Openly Gay Person for at Least a Thousand Miles': Doug Wilson and the Politicization of a Province, 1975–1983." *Canadian Historical Review* 84: 4 (December): 517–550.

Krane, Dale. 2007. "The Middle Tier in American Federalism: State Government Policy Activism During the Bush Year." *Publius* 37 (3): 454–477.

Kristen, Elizabeth. 1999. "Recent Developments: The Struggle for Same-Sex Marriage Continues." *Berkeley Women's Law Journal* 14: 104–146.

Lambda Legal. 1997. "Lambda Responds to 'Disturbing' Anti-Gay Federal Court Decision." June 1. http://www.lambdalegal.org/cgi-bin/iowa/news/press.html?record=36

Lambda Legal. 2003. *Get the Facts About Sodomy Laws.* http://www.lambdalegal.org/cgi-bin/iowa/news/fact.html?record=1231

Lambda Legal. 2006. *Legal Recognition of Same-Sex Relationships by State.* http://www.lambdalegal.org/cgi-bin/iowa/news/fact.html?record=1490

Lambda Legal. 2007. *Marriage, Relationships and Family.* http://www.lambdalegal.org/our-work/issues/marriage-relationships-family/

Lambertson, Ross. 2005. *Repression and Resistance: Canadian Human Rights Activists, 1930–1960.* Toronto: University of Toronto Press.

Larocque, Sylvain. 2006. *Gay Marriage: The Story of a Canadian Social Revolution.* Toronto: James Lorimer.

Larsen, Matt. 2004. "Lawrence v. Texas and Family Law: Gay Parents' Constitutional Rights in Child Custody Proceedings." *New York University Annual Survey of American Law.* 60: 53-96.

Lauren, Paul Gordon. 1998. *The Evolution of International Human Rights: Visions Seen.* Philadelphia: University of Pennsylvania Press.

LaVaque-Manty, Mika. 2006. "Bentley, Truman, and the Study of Groups." *Annual Review of Political Science* 9: 1–18.

Law Commission of Canada. 2001. *Beyond Conjugality.* Ottawa: Supply and Services Canada.

Laycock, David. 2001. *The New Right and Democracy in Canada: Understanding Reform and Canadian Alliance.* Don Mills: Oxford University Press.

Leeson, Howard. 2000. *Section 33—The Notwithstanding Clause: A Paper Tiger?* Ottawa: Institute for Research on Public Policy.

Leman, Christopher. 1977. "Patterns of Policy Development: Social Security in the United States and Canada." *Public Policy* 25 (Spring): 261–291.

Leslie, Christopher R. 2000. "Creating Criminals: The Injuries Inflicted by 'Unenforced' Sodomy Laws." *Harvard Civil Rights-Civil Liberties Law Review* 35: 103–156.

LeVay, Simon and Elisabeth Nonas. 1995. *City of Friends: A Portrait of the Gay and Lesbian Community in America.* Boston: MIT Press.

Levinson, Sanford. 2006. *Our Undemocratic Constitution: Where the Constitution Goes Wrong.* Oxford: Oxford University Press.

Lewis, Kevin H. 1997. "Equal Protection After *Romer v. Evans*: Implications for the Defense of Marriage Act and Other Laws." *Hastings Law Journal* 49 (November): 175–224.

Lewis, Gregory B. 2005. "Same-Sex Marriage and the 2004 Presidential Election." *PS: Political Science and Politics* XXXVIII: 2 (April): 195–199.

Lewis, Gregory B. and Marc A. Rogers. 1999. "Does the Public Support Equal Employment Rights for Gays and Lesbians?" In Ellen D. B. Riggle and Barry L. Tadlock (eds.) *Gays and Lesbians in the Democratic Process: Public Policy, Public Opinion, and Political Representation*. New York: Columbia University Press, 118–119.

Lieberman, Robert C. 2005. *Shaping Race Policy: The United States in Comparative Perspective*. Princeton: Princeton University Press.

Lim, Karen. 2003. "Freedom to Exclude after *Boy Scouts of America v. Dale*: Do Private Schools Have a Right to Discriminate Against Homosexual Teachers?" *Fordham Law Review* 71: 6 (May): 2599–2642.

Linton, Paul Benjamin. 2002. "Same-Sex 'Marriage' Under State Equal Rights Amendments." *Saint Louis University Law Journal* 46: 4 (Fall): 909–962.

Lipset, Seymour Martin. 1963. *The First New Nation*. New York: Basic Books.

Lipset, Seymour Martin. 1990. *Continental Divide: The Values and Institutions of the United States and Canada*. New York: Routledge.

Little, Margaret H. 1998. *No Car, No Radio, No Liquor Permit: The Moral Regulation of Single Mothers in Ontario, 1920–1997*. Toronto: Oxford University Press.

Loewy, Karen M. 2004. "Symposium Transcription: The Unconstitutionality of Excluding Same-Sex Couples from Marriage." *New England Law Review* 38: 3 (2004): 555–561.

Lofton, Katie and Donald P. Haider-Markel. 2007. "The Politics of Same-Sex Marriage Versus the Politics of Gay Civil Rights." In Craig Rimmerman and Clyde Wilcox (eds.) *The Politics of Same-Sex Marriage*. Chicago: University of Chicago Press, 313–340.

Lowndes, Joseph, Julie Novkov, and Dorian Warren. 2007. "Race and American Political Development." Paper presented at the Annual Meeting of the American Political Science Association, Chicago, August 29–September 1, 2007.

MacDougall, Bruce. 2006. "Refusing to Officiate at Same-Sex Civil Marriages." *Saskatchewan Law Review* 69: 351

MacLennan, Christopher. 2003. *Toward the Charter: Canadians and the Demand for a National Bill of Rights, 1920–1960*. Montreal and Kinston: McGill-Queen's University Press.

Maioni, Antonia. 1998. *Parting at the Crossroads: The Emergence of Health Insurance in the United States and Canada*. Princeton: Princeton University Press.

Mandel, Michael. 1994. *The Charter of Rights and the Legalization of Politics in Canada*. Rev. ed. Toronto: Thompson Educational Publishing.

Marchildon, Gilles [Executive Director, Egale]. 2005. *Personal Interview with Miriam Smith*. Ottawa.

Matthews, J. Scott. 2005. "The Political Foundations of Support for Same-Sex Marriage in Canada." *Canadian Journal of Political Science* 38 (4): 841–866.

Mayhew, David. 2005. *Divided We Govern: Party Control, Lawmaking and Investigations, 1946–2002*. New Haven: Yale University Press.

McAdam, Doug. 1995. "'Initiator' and 'Spin-off' Movements: Diffusion Processes in Protest Cycles." In Mark Traugott (ed.) *Repertoires & Cycles of Collective Action*. Durham and London: Duke University Press, 217–239.

McCammon, Holly J., Karen E. Campbell, Ellen M. Granberg and Christine Mowery. 2001. "How Movements Win." *American Sociological Review* 66 (1): 49–70.

McCann, Michael W. 1993. *Rights at Work: Pay Equity Reform and the Politics of Legal Mobilization.* Chicago: University of Chicago Press.

McFeeley, Tim. 2002. "Getting It Straight: A Review of the 'Gays in the Military' Debate." In John D'Emilio, William B. Turner and Urvashi Vaid (eds.) *Creating Change: Sexuality, Public Policy and Civil Rights.* New York: St. Martin's, 236–250.

McGhee Derek. 2000. "Wolfenden and the Fear of 'Homosexual Spread': Permeable Boundaries and Legal Defences." *Studies in Law, Politics, and Society* 2: 65–100.

McGowan, David. 2001. "Making Sense of Dale." *Constitutional Commentary* 18: 1 (Spring): 121–176.

McGowan, Miranda Oshige. 2004. "From Outlaws to Ingroup: Romer, Lawrence, and the Inevitable Normativity of Group Recognition." *Minnesota Law Review* 88: 5 (May): 1312–1345.

McIntosh, Deborah. 1999. "Court Cases in Which Sexual Orientation Arguments Under Section 15 of the Charter Were Raised." In Miriam Smith, *Lesbian and Gay Rights in Canada: Social Movements and Equality-Seeking, 1971–1995.* Toronto: University of Toronto Press, 157–163.

McKenzie, Chris. 2005. *Pro-Family Politics and Fringe Parties in Canada.* Vancouver: University of British Columbia Press.

McRoberts, Kenneth. 1993. *Quebec: Social Change and Political Crisis.* 3rd ed. Toronto: McClelland & Stewart.

McRoberts, Kenneth. 1997. *Misconceiving Canada: The Struggle for National Unity.* Toronto: Oxford University Press.

Mercier, Adèle. 2001. *Affidavit of Dr. Adèle Mercier in Halpern v. Canada.* (July 11).

Merin, Yuval. 2002. *Equality for Same-Sex Couples: The Legal Recognition of Gay Partnerships in Europe and the United States.* Chicago: University of Chicago Press.

Mettler, Suzanne. 1998. *Dividing Citizens: Gender and Federalism in New Deal Public Policy.* Ithaca: Cornell University Press.

Mezey, Susan Gluck. 2007. *Queers in Court: Gay Rights Law and Public Policy.* Lanham, MD: Rowman and Littlefield.

Michaelson, Jay. 2000. "On Listening to the Kulturkampf, or, How America Overruled *Bowers v. Hardwick.*" *Duke Law Journal* (April): 1559–1618.

Millett, Kate. 1972. "Sexual Politics: A Manifesto for Revolution." Reprinted in *The Body Politic* 3 (March–April): 1

Minkoff, Debra C. 1997. "The Sequencing of Social Movements." *American Sociological Review* 62: 5 (October): 779–799.

Moats, David. 2004. *Civil Wars: A Battle for Gay Marriage.* Orlando: Harcourt.

Mohr, Richard D. 2005. *The Long Arc of Justice: Lesbian and Gay Marriage, Equality, and Rights.* New York: Columbia University Press.

Morton, Ted. 2000. "Presentation on Bill C-23" [Verbal presentation on Bill C-23, Modernization of Benefits and Obligations Act] House of Commons (Canada), *Standing Committee on Justice and Human Rights—Evidence* (March 15): 1640–1655.

Munter, Alex [Co-Chair, Canadians for Equal Marriage]. 2005. *Personal Interview with Miriam Smith.* Ottawa.

Murray, Karen B. 2007. "Governmentality and the Shifting Winds of Policy Analysis." In Michael Orsini and Miriam Smith (eds.) *Critical Policy Studies.* Vancouver: University of British Columbia Press, 161–184.

Nash, Catherine Jean. 2005. "Contesting Identity: Politics of Gays and Lesbians in Toronto in the 1970s." *Gender, Plac,e & Culture* 12 (1): 113–135.

National Gay and Lesbian Task Force. 2006. *Anti-Gay Marriage Measures in the U.S. as of November 2006.* http://www.thetaskforce.org/downloads/reports/issue_maps/Marriage_Map_06_Nov.pdf

National Gay and Lesbian Task Force. 2007a. "One Community, One ENDA." http://www.thetaskforce.org/enda07/enda07.html

National Gay and Lesbian Task Force. 2007b. *State Nondiscrimination Laws in the U.S. as of January 2007.* http://www.thetaskforce.org/downloads/reports/issue_maps/nondiscrimination_01_07.pdf

National Gay and Lesbian Task Force. 2007c. *One Community, One ENDA* (October) http://www.thetaskforce.org/enda07/enda07.html

National Organization of Women (NOW). 2004. "Phyllis Lyon and Del Martin Make History Again." (February 13). http://www.now.org/issues/lgbi/021304lyon-martin.html

Neckerman, Kathryn M., Robert Aponte and William Julius Wilson. 1988. "Family Structure, Black Unemployment, and American Social Policy." In Margaret Weir, Ann Shola Orloff and Theda Skocpol (eds.) *Politics and Social Policy in the United States.* Princeton: Princeton University Press, 397–419.

Nevitte, Neil. 1996. *The Decline of Deference.* Peterborough: Broadview Press.

Nicol, Nancy (director and producer). 2005. *Politics of the Heart* [film]. Vtape: Toronto, Canada.

Nicol, Nancy (director and producer). 2006. *The End of Second Class* [film]. Vtape: Toronto, Canada.

Nicol, Nancy and Miriam Smith. 2009 in press. "Legal Struggles and Political Resistance: Same-Sex Marriage in Canada and the U.S." *Sexualities.*

O'Malley, Martin. 2003. "Same-Sex Marriage: Yes or No." *CBC News Viewpoint* (August 22) http://www.cbc.ca/news/viewpoint/vp_omalley/20030822.html

Ontario. 2000. Ontario Human Rights Commission. *Policy on Discrimination and Harassment Because of Gender Identity.* http://www.ohrc.on.ca/en/resources/Policies/PolicyGenderIdent

Orloff, Ann Shola. 2005. "Social Provision and Regulation: Theories of States, Social Policies, and Modernity." In Julia Adams, Elisabeth S. Clemens, and Ann Shola Orloff (eds.) *Remaking Modernity: Politics, History, and Sociology.* Durham and London: Duke University Press.

Orren, Karen. 1992. *Belated Feudalism: Labor, the Law, and Liberal Development in the United States.* Cambridge: Cambridge University Press.

Orren, Karen and Stephen Skowronek. 2004. *The Search for American Political Development.* New York: Cambridge University Press.

Ota, Nancy K. 2001. "'Family' and the Political Landscape for Lesbian, Gay, Bisexual and Transgender People." *Albany Law Review* 64: 889–904.

Pal, Leslie A. and R. Kent Weaver. 2003. "The Politics of Pain" In Leslie A. Pal and R. Kent Weaver (eds.) *The Government Taketh Away: The Politics of Pain in the United States and Canada.* Washington, DC: Georgetown University Press, 1–41.

Pascoe, Peggy. 2000. "Sex, Gender, and Same-Sex Marriage." In Social Justice Group (eds.) *Is Academic Feminism Dead? Theory in Practice.* New York and London: New York University Press, 86–129.

Patrias, Carmela and Ruth A. Frager. 2001. "'This Is Our Country, These Are Our Rights': Minorities and the Origins of Ontario's Human Rights Campaigns." *Canadian Historical Review* 82 (1): 1–35.

Payne, Jacqueline. 2003. "Transcript: The Michigan Journal of Gender & Law Presents a Symposium: Marriage Law: Obsolete or Cutting Edge?" *Michigan Journal of Gender & Law* 10 (1): 21–142.

Pedriana, Nicolas and Robin Stryker. 2004. "The Strength of a Weak Agency: Enforcement of Title VII of the 1964 Civil Rights Act and the Expansion of State Capacity, 1965 1971." *American Journal of Sociology* 110: 709–760.

Peterson, Kevin. 2004. "50-state rundown on gay marriage laws." *Stateline* (November 3) http://www.stateline.org/live/ViewPage.action?siteNodeId=136 &languageId=1&contentId=15576

Petry, François. 1999. "The Opinion–Policy Relationship in Canada." *Journal of Politics* 61: 2 (May): 540–550.

Phelan, Shane. 2000. "Queer Liberalism?" *American Political Science Review* 94: 2 (June): 431–442.

Phelan, Shane. 2001. *Sexual Strangers: Gays, Lesbians, and Dilemmas of Citizenship*. Philadelphia: Temple University Press.

Pierceson, Jason. 2005. *Courts, Liberalism, and Rights: Gay Law and Politics in the United States and Canada*. Philadelphia: Temple University Press.

Pierson, Paul. 1994. *Dismantling the Welfare State? Reagan, Thatcher and the Politics of Retrenchment*. Cambridge: Cambridge University Press.

Pierson, Paul. 2004. *Politics in Time: History, Institutions, and Social Analysis*. Princeton: Princeton University Press.

Pierson, Paul. 2006. "Public Policies as Institutions." In Ian Shapiro et al. (eds.) *Rethinking Political Institutions: The Art of the State*. New York: New York University Press, 114–131.

Pierson, Paul. 2007. "The Rise and Reconfiguration of Activist Government." In Paul Pierson and Theda Skocpol (eds.) *The Transformation of American Politics: Activist Government and the Rise of Conservatism*. Princeton: Princeton University Press, 19–38.

Pierson, Paul and Theda Skocpol. 2002. "Historical Institutionalism in Contemporary Political Science." In Ira Katznelson and Helen Milner (eds.) *The State of the Discipline*. New York: Norton, 693–721.

Pierson, Paul and Theda Skocpol eds. 2007. *The Transformation of American Politics: Activist Government and the Rise of Conservatism*. Princeton: Princeton University Press.

Pinello, Daniel R. 2003. *Gay Rights and American Law*. Cambridge: Cambridge University Press.

Pinello, Daniel R. 2006. *America's Struggle for Same-Sex Marriage*. Cambridge: Cambridge University Press.

Quadagno, Jill. 2000. "Another Face of Inequality: Racial and Ethnic Exclusion in the Welfare State." *Social Politics* 7: 227–237.

Rayside, David. 1998. *On the Fringe: Gays and Lesbians in Politics*. Ithaca and London: Cornell University Press.

Rayside, David. 2007. "The United States in Comparative Context." In Craig A. Rimmerman and Clyde Wilcox (eds.) *The Politics of Same-Sex Marriage*. Chicago and London: University of Chicago Press, 341–364.

Rayside, David, and Evert Lindquist. 1992. "AIDS Activism and the State in Canada." *Studies in Political Economy* 39 (Autumn): 37–76.

Reese, Ellen. 2001. "The Politics of Motherhood: The Restriction of Poor Mothers' Welfare Rights in the United States, 1949–1960." *Social Politics* 8: 65–112.

Reimer, Sam. 2003. *Evangelicals and the Continental Divide: The Conservative Protestant Subculture in Canada and the United States*. Montreal and Kingston: McGill-Queen's University Press.

Richards, David A.J. 2005. *The Case for Gay Rights: From Bowers to Lawrence and Beyond*. Lawrence: University Press of Kansas.

Richardson, Diane. 2000. "Constructing Sexual Citizenship: Theorizing Sexual Rights." *Critical Social Policy* 20 (1): 105–135.

Richardson, Diane. 2005. "Desiring Sameness? The Rise of a Neoliberal Politics of Normalisation." *Antipode* 37 (3): 515–535.

Rimmerman, Craig A. 2002. *From Identity to Politics: The Lesbian and Gay Movement in the United States*. Philadelphia: Temple University Press.

Rimmerman, Craig A. and Clyde Wilcox eds. 2007. *The Politics of Same-Sex Marriage*. Chicago: University of Chicago Press.

Roach, Kent. 1993. "The Role of Litigation and the Charter in Interest Advocacy." In F. Leslie Seidle (ed.) *Equity and Community: The Charter, Interest Advocacy and Representation*. Montreal: Institute for Research on Public Policy, 159–188.

Robb, Barbara A. 1997. "The Constitutionality of the Defense of Marriage Act in the Wake of *Romer v. Evans*." *New England Law Review* 32 (Fall): 263–342.

Robson, Ruthann 2004. "Privacy Rights in a Post-Lawrence World: Responses to *Lawrence v. Texas*: The Missing Word in *Lawrence v. Texas*." *Cardozo Women's Law Journal* 10 (Winter): 397–409.

Rocher, François and Miriam Smith. 2003. "The Four Dimensions of the Canadian Constitutional Debate." In François Rocher and Miriam Smith (eds.) *New Trends in Canadian Federalism*. 2nd ed. Peterborough: Broadview Press, 21–44.

Rom, Mark Carl. 2007. "Introduction: The Politics of Same-Sex Marriage." In Craig A. Rimmerman and Clyde Wilcox (eds.) *The Politics of Same-Sex Marriage*. Chicago and London: University of Chicago Press, 1–38.

Rose-Ackerman, Susan. 1980. "Risk Taking and Re-election: Does Federalism Promote Innovation?" *Journal of Legal Studies* 9: 3 (June): 593–616.

Rosenberg, Gerald A. 1991. *The Hollow Hope: Can Courts Bring About Social Change?* Chicago: University of Chicago Press.

Rosenthal, Charles A. Jr., William J. Delmore III and Scoot A. Durfee. 2001. "Respondent's Brief in Opposition—*Lawrence v. Texas*." (October 21).

Rosenthal, Charles A. Jr. William J. Delmore III and Scoot A. Durfee. 2003. "Respondent's Brief—*Lawrence v. Texas*." U.S. Briefs 102 (February 17).

Rudacille, Deborah. 2006. *The Riddle of Gender*. New York: Anchor Books.

Russell, Peter H. 1983. "The Political Purposes of the Canadian Charter of Rights and Freedoms." Canadian Bar Review 16: 1 (March): 30–54.

Russel, Peter H. 1987. *The Judiciary in Canada: The Third Branch of Government*. Toronto: McGraw-Hill Ryerson.

Russell, Peter H. 2004. *Constitutional Odyssey: Can Canadians Become a Sovereign People?* 3rd ed. Toronto: University of Toronto Press.

Ryan, Brett P. 2000. "Love and Let Love: Same-Sex Marriage, Past, Present, and Future, and the Constitutionality of DOMA." *University of Hawai'i Law Review* 22: 1 (Spring): 185–235.

Ryder, Bruce. 1990. "Equality Rights and Sexual Orientation." *Canadian Journal of Family Law* 9: 1 (Fall): 39–97.

San Francisco. Office of the Mayor. 2004. Press release. *San Francisco to Continue Issuing Marriage Licenses* (February 17) http://www.sfgov.org/site/mayor_-page.asp?id=22918

Sanders, Douglas. 1994. "Constructing Lesbian and Gay Rights," *Canadian Journal of Law and Society* 9: 2 (Fall): 350–379.

Savoie, Donald J. 1999. *Governing from the Centre: The Concentration of Power in Canadian Politics*. Toronto: University of Toronto Press.

Scheingold, Stuart A. 1974. *The Politics of Rights: Lawyers, Public Policy, and Political Change*. New Haven and London: Yale University Press.

Scherpe, Jens M. 2007. "Equal But Different?" *Cambridge Law Journal* 66 (1): 32–35.

Schneiderman, David. 1992. "Dual (ling) Charters: The Harmonics of Rights in Canada and Quebec" 24 *Ottawa Law Review* 24 (1): 235–263.

Segal, Jeffrey A., Harold J. Spaeth and Sarah Benesh. 2005. *The Supreme Court in the American Legal System.* Cambridge: Cambridge University Press.

Shepard, Benjamin H. 2001. "The Queer/Gay Assimilationist Split: The Suits vs. the Sluts." *Monthly Review* 53: 1 (May): 41–62.

Sherrill, Kenneth R. 2004. *Same-Sex Marriage, Civil Unions and the 2004 Presidential Election.* New York: National Gay and Lesbian Task Force.

Shilts, Randy. 1988. *And the Band Played On: People, Politics and the AIDS Epidemic.* New York: St. Martin's Press.

Siplon, Patricia D. 2002. *AIDS and the Policy Struggle in the United States.* Washington: Georgetown University Press.

Skocpol, Theda. 1985. "Bringing the State Back In: Strategies of Analysis in Current Research." In Peter B. Evans, Dietrich Rueschemeyer, and Theda Skocpol (eds.) *Bringing the State Back In.* Cambridge: Cambridge University Press, 3–37.

Skocpol, Theda. 1988. "The Limits of the New Deal System and the Roots of Contemporary Welfare Dilemmas." In Margaret Weir, Ann Shola Orloff and Theda Skocpol (eds.) *Politics and Social Policy in the United States.* Princeton: Princeton University Press, 293–312.

Skocpol, Theda. 1992. *Protecting Soldiers and Mothers.* Cambridge, MA: Harvard University Press.

Skowronek, Stephen. 1982. *Building a New American State: The Expansion of National Administrative Capacities.* Cambridge: Cambridge University Press.

Skrentny, John. 1996. *The Ironies of Affirmative Action: Politics, Culture, and Justice in America.* Chicago: University of Chicago Press.

Smith, Anna Marie. 1994. *New Right Discourse on Race and Sexuality: Britain 1968–1990.* Cambridge: Cambridge University Press.

Smith, Anna Marie. 2001. "The Politicization of Marriage in Contemporary American Public Policy: The Defense of Marriage Act and the Personal Responsibility Act." *Citizenship Studies* 5 (3): 303–320.

Smith, Anna Marie. 2007. *Welfare Reform and Sexual Regulation.* New York: Cambridge University Press.

Smith, Daniel A. and Caroline J. Tolbert. 2004. *Educated by Initiative: The Effects of Direct Democracy on Citizens and Political Organizations.* Ann Arbor: University of Michigan Press.

Smith, Miriam. 1998. "Reluctant Recognition: The Liberal Government and Lesbian and Gay Rights." In Leslie A. Pal (ed.) *How Ottawa Spends, 1998–1999: The Post-Deficit Mandate* (Toronto: Oxford University Press, 1998) 293–314.

Smith, Miriam. 1999. *Lesbian and Gay Rights in Canada: Social Movements and Equality-Seeking, 1971–1995.* Toronto: University of Toronto Press.

Smith, Miriam. 2002. "Recognizing Same Sex Relationships: The Evolution of Recent Federal and Provincial Policies." *Canadian Public Administration* 45: 1 (Spring): 1–23.

Smith, Miriam. 2004. "Questioning Heteronormativity: Lesbian and Gay Challenges to Educational Practice in British Columbia, Canada." *Social Movement Studies* 3: 2 (October): 131–145.

Smith, Miriam. 2005a. "Social Movements and Judicial Empowerment: Courts, Public Policy and Lesbian and Gay Organizing in Canada." *Politics & Society* 33: 2 (June): 327–353.

Smith, Miriam. 2005b. "Diversity and Identity in the Nonprofit Sector: Lessons from LGBT Organizing in Toronto, Canada." *Social Policy & Administration* 39: 5 (October): 463–480.

Smith, Miriam. 2007. "Framing Same-Sex Marriage in Canada and the United States: *Goodridge, Halpern* and the National Boundaries of Political Discourse." *Social and Legal Studies* 16: 1 (March): 5–26.

Smith, Rogers M. 1993. "Beyond Tocqueville, Myrdal, and Hartz: The Multiple Traditions in America." *American Political Science Review* 87: 3 (September): 549–566.

Smith, Rogers M. 1999. *Civic Ideals: Conflicting Visions of Citizenship in U.S. History.* New Ed. New Haven: Yale University Press.

Solokar, Rebecca Mae. 2001. "Beyond Gay Rights Litigation: Using a Systematic Strategy to Effect Political Change in the United States." In Mark Blasius (ed.) *Sexual Identities, Queer Politics.* Princeton: Princeton University Press, 256–285.

Soss, Joe and Sanford F. Schram. 2007. "A Public Transformed? Welfare Reform as Policy Feedback." *American Political Science Review* 101: 111–127.

Soss, Joe, Sanford F. Schram and Richard C. Fording. 2003a. "Introduction." In Sanford F. Schram, Joe Soss and Richard C. Fording (eds.) *Race and the Politics of Welfare Reform.* Ann Arbor: University of Michigan Press, 1–20.

Soss, Joe, Sanford F. Schram, Thomas P. Vartanian and Erin O'Brian. 2003b. "The Hard Line and the Color Line: Race, Welfare, and the Roots of Get-Tough Reform." In Sanford F. Schram, Joe Soss and Richard C. Fording (eds.) *Race and the Politics of Welfare Reform.* Ann Arbor: University of Michigan Press, 225–253.

Soule, Sarah A. 2004. "Going to the Chapel?: Same-Sex Marriage Bans in the United States, 1973–2000." *Social Problems* 51 (4): 453–477.

Sparks, Holloway. 2003. "Queens, Teens, and Model Mothers: Race, Gender, and the Discourse of Welfare Reform." In Sanford F. Schram, Joe Soss and Richard C. Fording (eds.) *Race and the Politics of Welfare Reform.* Ann Arbor: University of Michigan Press, 171–195.

Stein, Edward R. 2004. "Introducing *Lawrence V. Texas:* Some Background and a Glimpse of the Future." *Cardozo Women's Law Journal* 10: 2 (Winter): 263–288.

Stevenson, Garth. 1993. *Ex Uno Plures: Federal-Provincial Relations in Canada 1867–1896.* Montreal and Kingston: McGill-Queen's University Press.

Strasser, Mark. 1997. *Legally Wed: Same-Sex Marriage and the Constitution.* Ithaca: Cornell University Press.

Strasser, Mark. 2004. "Lawrence, Same-Sex Marriage and the Constitution: What is Protected and Why?" *New England Law Review* 38 (3): 667–681.

Stychin, Carl F. 1998. *A Nation By Rights: National Cultures, Sexual Identity Politics, and the Discourse of Rights.* Philadelphia: Temple University Press.

Suk, Julie Chi-hye. 2006. "Antidiscrimination Law in the Administrative State." *University of Illinois Law Review* 2: 405–474.

Tarr, G. Alan. 1998. *Understanding State Constitutions.* Princeton: Princeton University Press.

Tarrow, Sidney. 1998. *Power in Movement: Social Movements and Contentious Politics.* 2nd edition. Cambridge: Cambridge University Press.

Teixeira, Ruy and Joel Rogers. 2001. *Why the White Working Class Still Matters.* New York: Basic Books.

Thelen, Kathleen. 1999. "Historical Institutionalism in Comparative Politics." *Annual Review of Political Science* 2: 369–404.

Tribe, Laurence H. 2004. "*Lawrence v. Texas:* The "Fundamental Right" That Dare Not Speak Its Name." *Harvard Law Review* 117: 6 (April): 1893–1955.

Trudeau, Pierre Elliott. 1968. "The Practice and Theory of Federalism." In *Federalism and the French Canadians.* New York: St. Martin's Press, 124–150.

U.K. Wolfenden Report. 1957. *Report of the Committee on Homosexual Offences and Prostitution.* London: HMSO.

U.S. Census Bureau. 2006. "Americans Marrying Older, Living Alone More." *U.S. Census Bureau News.* Washington (May 26).

U.S. Senate. 2004. *Senate Joint Resolution* 30. 108th Congress (March 22).

Vaid, Urvashi. 1995. *Virtual Equality: The Mainstreaming of Gay and Lesbian Liberation.* New York: Anchor.

Valocchi, Steve. 2001. "Individual Identities, Collective Identities, and Organizational Structure: The Relationship of the Political Left and Gay Liberation in the United States." *Sociological Perspectives* 44 (4): 445–467.

Waite, Brian and Cheri DeNovo. 1971. "We Demand." *The Body Politic* 1 (November-December): 4–7.

Wald, Kenneth, James Button, and Barbara Rienzo. 1996. "The Politics of Gay Rights in American Communities: Explaining Anti-discrimination Ordinances and Policies." *American Journal of Political Science* 40 (November): 1152–1178.

Walker, James. 1997. *Race Rights and the Law in the Supreme Court of Canada: Historical Case Studies.* Toronto and Waterloo: Osgoode Society and Wilfrid Laurier University Press.

Warner, Tom. 2002. *Never Looking Back: A History of Queer Activism in Canada.* Toronto: University of Toronto Press.

Watts, Ronald. 1987. "The American Constitution in Comparative Perspective: A Comparison of Federalism in the United States and Canada." *Journal of American History* 74: 3 (December): 769–792.

Weaver, R. Kent and Bert A. Rockman. 1993. "Assessing the Effects of Institutions." In R. Kent Weaver and Bert A. Rockman (eds.) *Do Institutions Matter? Government Capabilities in the United States and Abroad.* Washington, DC: The Brookings Institution, 1–41.

Weir, Margaret. 1988. "The Federal Government and Unemployment: The Foundation of Policy Innovation from the New Deal to the Great Society." In Margaret Weir, Ann Shola Orloff and Theda Skocpol (eds.) *Politics and Social Policy in the United States.* Princeton: Princeton University Press, 149–190.

Weir, Margaret, Ann Shola Orloff and Theda Skocpol (eds.) 1988. *Politics and Social Policy in the United States.* Princeton: Princeton University Press.

Werum, Regina and Bill Winders. 2001. "Who's 'In' and Who's 'Out': State Fragmentation and the Struggle Over Gay Rights, 1974–1999." *Social Problems* 48 (3): 386–410.

Whittington, Keith E. 2000. "Once More Unto the Breach: Post-Behavioralist Approaches to Judicial Politics." *Law and Social Inquiry* 25: 2 (Spring): 601–634.

Whittington, Keith E. 2007. *Political Foundations of Judicial Supremacy: The Presidency, the Supreme Court, and Constitutional Leadership in U.S. History.* Princeton: Princeton University Press.

Wilcox, Clyde. 2006. *Onward Christian Soldiers? The Religious Right in American Politics.* 3rd ed. Boulder: Westview.

Wilcox, Clyde, Paul R. Brewer, Shauna Shames, and Celinda Lake. 2007. "If I Bend This Far I Will Break?: Public Opinion About Same-Sex Marriage." In Craig Rimmerman and Clyde Wilcox (eds.) *The Politics of Same-Sex Marriage.* Chicago: University of Chicago Press, 215–242.

Wildenthal, Bryan H. 1998. "To Say 'I Do': *Shahar v. Bowers,* Same-Sex Marriage, and Public Employee Free Speech Rights." *Georgia State University Law Review* 15 (Winter): 381–458.

Wolfson, Evan. 2004. *Why Marriage Matters: America, Equality, and Gay People's Right to Marry.* New York: Simon and Schuster.

Wolfson, Evan. 2006. *Personal Interview with Mike Graydon.* New York City (June 16).

Yalda, Christine A. 1999. "Walking the Straight and Narrow: Performative Sexuality and the First Amendment After *Hurley.*" *Social and Legal Studies* 8 (1): 25–45.

Yang, Alan S. 1997. "The Polls—Trends: Attitudes Toward Homosexuality." *Public Opinion Quarterly* 61: 477–507.

Yoaz, Yuval. 2006. "In precedent-setting ruling court says state must recognize gay marriage." *Haaretz.com* (November 22) http://haaretz.com/hasen/spages/790724.html

Young, Jim. 1983. "Human Rights in Canada: A Gay Perspective." *Goinfo* [Ottawa] 10: 8 (October).

Zalesne, Deborah. 2007. "Lessons from Equal Opportunity Harasser Doctrine: Challenging Sex-Specific Appearance and Dress Codes." *Duke Journal of Gender Law and Policy* 14: 535–560.

Index

political institutions 3; practices 54–57;
    structures 83–87
political parties 15–16, 184; *see also
    specific parties*
privacy rights 37, 39–40, 60–61, 63,
    65, 66–67, 70; same-sex mar-
    riage 117, 119, 147
Progressive Conservative Party (govern-
    ment), Canada 74–75, 81–82,
    92, 95, 96, 98, 105, 130
public opinion 25, 26–27, 170,
    190–191

Q

Quebec 25, 42; Bloc Québécois 105,
    159; *Hendricks v. Quebec*
    152–153, 154–156; human
    rights legislation and commis-
    sion 49; nationalism 16, 23, 40,
    50, 53–54, 72–73, 83, 135
Queer Nation 34, 78

R

race issues 23, 26, 32–33; backlash poli-
    tics 51, 52, 59; Canadian minor-
    ity groups 42–43; co-habitation
    114–115; "ethnic model" of gay
    rights 91; Fourteenth Amendment
    21, 44–45, 65–66, 67, 70, 175,
    176, 177; immigration/naturaliza-
    tion 71, 115; interracial marriage
    111–113, 147–148; protection
    rights 84–85, 89; "special treat-
    ment" 80–81, 83; *see also* civil
    rights; Civil Rights Act (1964)
Reagan, R. (administration) 58, 59, 80,
    98, 190
reciprocal benefits bill 122, 123–124
    Reference re Same-Sex Marriage
    (2004), Canada 157
Reform Party (Canadian Alliance Party)
    83, 98, 105, 130
Reimer, S. 27, 63, 189
relationship recognition 5, 6–7; Cana-
    dian cases 96–97, 116, 125–129
religion: Metropolitan Community
    Church Toronto (MCCT) 1–2,
    46, 79, 131, 154; US vs Canada
    111; *see also* Christian Right
religious minorities, Canada 42–43
Republican Party, US 51, 52, 80; *see
    also specific administrations*
Rimmerman, C.A. 38, 47, 86; and
    Wilcox, C. 11–12

Roe v. Wade, US 52, 59, 60–61, 66, 67,
    105–106, 139–140
Romer v. Evans 38, 62, 80, 83–92,
    128–129, 136–137
Rosenberg, G.A. 9, 10, 12, 19, 186
Rosenberg v. Canada 116, 126–127,
    131, 152, 153
Rosenthal, C.A. et al. 137–138
Russell, P.H. 16, 18, 19–20, 72–73, 83

S

same-sex marriage 1–3, 4, 11–12;
    approaches to 168–172; Can-
    ada 1–2, 129–132, 152–159;
    comparative responses to court
    decisions 159–162; countermo-
    bilization 121–125, 129–132;
    cross-national differences 4–7,
    17–18, 19, 25, 26–27; emergence
    of (1991–99) 109–133; legal cases
    100–101, 116–120, 146–149; as
    "moral" issue 168–170; origins of
    litigation 115–116; policy legacies
    110–115; and relationship rec-
    ognition, Canada 125–129; and
    sodomy laws 140–141, 146–147;
    US 116–120, 121–125, 147–152
Scheingold, S. 9
separation of powers 40, 41–42, 92–95,
    182–184, 187; and federal pro-
    tection 92–95; vs. parliamentary
    (Westminster) system 14–16,
    37–38, 55, 145–146, 149–150,
    182–185
Shahar v. Bowers 100–101
Dale and *Vriend* case comparisons
    98–104
Skocpol, T. 7, 51; Pierson, P. and 7, 8,
    12
Skrentny, J. 50, 52
Smith, A.M. 36–37, 52–53, 81, 114,
    170
Smith, M. 5, 8, 19, 23, 33, 48–49, 75,
    79, 96, 104, 130, 131
social movements 12–13, 22, 31, 159–
    160, 187, 188; *see also* Christian
    Right (evangelical movement);
    civil rights; feminist movement;
    gay and lesbian movement;
    human rights
sodomy laws 5–6, 7, 17, 54, 55, 58,
    173–174; decriminalization issues
    6, 7, 36–40, 46–48, 60, 61; and
    same-sex marriage 140–141,